A Short Walk Down Fleet Street

A Short Walk Down Fleet Street

from Beaverbrook to Boycott

Alan Watkins

Duckworth

First published in 2000 by
Gerald Duckworth & Co. Ltd.
61 Frith Street, London W1D 3JL
Tel: 020 7434 4242
Fax: 020 7434 4420
Email: enquiries@duckworth-publishers.co.uk
www.ducknet.co.uk

A catalogue record for this book is available
from the British Library

ISBN 0 7156 2910 7

Typeset by Ray Davies
Printed in Great Britain by
Redwood Books Ltd, Trowbridge

For
my grandsons
Roy and Harry

Contents

Acknowledgments   ix

Introduction   1

1. Heredity   5
2. Environment   23
3. Only Poofs Drink Rosé   39
4. The Weekly World   61
5. Great Turnstile   85
6. Forward with the People   115
7. In London Last Night   131
8. St Andrew's Hill   155
9. Living with Lonrho   183
10. This Sporting Life   213
11. Boycott and Beyond   235

Index   257

(Plates between pages 150 and 151)

Acknowledgments

My principal debt is to Julia Mount, who put my hand-written ms
on to a word-processor speedily and accurately. Without her help
and encouragement the book would not have been written. I should
also like to thank Vanessa Tyrrell-Kenyon, librarian of the *Spectator*, for rapidly retrieving several articles which had appeared in
that paper, and Christine Woodland, chief archivist of the Modern
Records Centre, University of Warwick, for guiding me through the
unpublished parts of R.H.S. Crossman's diaries. Having mislaid or
lent my own copy of Lord Radcliffe's report on the D Notice affair,
I was able to consult it again through the efficiency of the staff of
Lincoln's Inn library. Robert Low provided me with details of the
letter which he took to R.W. ('Tiny') Rowland and which persuaded
him to sell the *Observer* to the *Guardian* rather than to the *Independent* group. Donald Trelford provided a copy of the poster that
is the epigraph to Chapter 8 and answered several questions.
Anthony Howard answered even more and was particularly helpful
on matters of chronology. Ian Jack and Kim Fletcher gave permission to quote their communications to me which are in Chapter 11.
I am solely responsible for what follows.

12 July 2000   Alan Watkins

Introduction

You have to marvel that anyone still wants to publish loving accounts
of Fleet Street's alcoholic triumphs and expenses fiddles.

Ian Hargreaves, Independent,
16 October 1999

In 1980, at Robertsbridge in Sussex, Malcolm Muggeridge said to
me that in 20 years' time 'you will be as dead as the *dodo*, dear boy'.

He pronounced the name of the extinct bird with the first syllable
prolonged and heavily accented, as if enjoying the whole performance, as, indeed, he must have been.

'I, on the other hand,' he went on, 'shall have proceeded to
another destination, an event to which I am looking forward de-
voutly' (he was to die in 1990 at 87).

Muggeridge, Anthony Powell and Colin Welch (all of whom appear in the pages that follow) talked in an exaggerated but pleasing
accent, with much of 'dear ...' or 'my dear boy'. Was this the way
people spoke in the 1920s? They had all worked in one capacity or
another for the *Daily Telegraph* after the war. Was there, perhaps,
an old *Telegraph* man, revered in his day, forgotten now, whose
speech they had imitated, half in jest?

After Muggeridge had pottered off to do something or other, his
wife Kitty advised me not to 'take any notice of Malcolm'. He was
always saying that people would shortly stop reading. But there
would always, she thought, be people who would want to buy
newspapers and read books. So I was not to be depressed by
anything Malcolm said. I assured her that I was not in the least
depressed and was enjoying the performance as much as he evidently was himself.

In those days Muggeridge, perhaps still the brightest star of
postwar television in this country, was expecting print on paper to

be supplanted by pictures on television rather than by words – and pictures too – on a grey screen. Nor did he realise fully that newspapers would be printed differently from the way they had been printed in his own days in journalism. It would, incidentally, be inconceivable today for a journalist with the known drinking (and, indeed, heterosexual) habits of the 50-year-old Muggeridge to become deputy editor of the *Daily Telegraph* and, later, editor of *Punch*, or to be seriously considered, as he also was, for the editorship of both the *Sunday Times* and the *Daily Mail*. It is part of the purpose of this book to describe those days, which lasted roughly from the end of paper rationing in the 1950s to the Fleet Street diaspora of the 1980s. I lived and worked through 30 years of the period, from joining the *Sunday Express* in 1959 to leaving Fleet Street (in reality St Andrew's Hill, Blackfriars) to go to Battersea with the rest of the *Observer* in 1988. The period has already been commemorated by, among others, Keith Waterhouse in *Streets Ahead* (1995). To my friend Geoffrey Wheatcroft, it is as remote as the Byzantine empire.

Surely such self-consciously modernist persons as Ian Hargreaves should at least be interested in it? He does, after all, profess the subject of journalism at Cardiff University. It was a period which existed and in which things happened. Some people, admittedly, find the history of the 18th century tedious. Sometimes they are even professors of history. Mr Hargreaves clearly belongs to this category.

In 1988, just after the *Observer* had left St Andrew's Hill for Battersea, I returned to Fleet Street. In postal terms I returned to the Strand, to the Royal Courts of Justice, as a defendant (in the end successful) in the case of *Meacher* v. *Trelford and Others*, in which I was one of the others. But I have always thought of Fleet Street as beginning at St Clement Dane's church rather than at Temple Bar to the east. I tried to describe the return:

> Some of the establishments I had continued to use: Louis Simmonds's excellent bookshop [by 2000 defunct], and El Vino's, opposite the junction of Fleet Street with Fetter Lane ('El Vino's public house', as Lord Beaverbrook used to call it dismissively). Other places I had grown out of the habit of using, such as the Wig and Pen Club opposite the Law Courts, where neither wigs nor pens were greatly in evidence, rather, large men in public relations and red braces with trains from Waterloo to miss, and where, in the early days when I

was not a member, I would sign myself in as 'Alastair Hetherington'. Other establishments had gone out of business or been pulled down, such as the Red Lion in Poppins Court by the *Express* building, known as Poppins and victim of the vandalism and greed of the new Express Newspapers. Also no more was a pleasant luncheon club, the Temple Bar Club, consisting of a high-ceilinged bar with early-19th-century mouldings and a similar dining-room, above a coffee-shop, whose respectability was attested by the patronage of John Beavan (later Lord Ardwick) and Samuel (later Sir Samuel) Brittan. The Law Courts were still where they used to be. They will still be where they are in the next [the 21st] century, as will Lincoln's Inn, Gray's Inn and the Temple. So will Harley Street, and Broadcasting House too. Doctors, lawyers, even broadcasters are treated – or treat themselves – with a measure of respect. It is only writing journalists who allow themselves to be pushed into inhospitable and often uninhabited regions of London by insensitive and grasping owners and managers.[1]

This is not an autobiography. There is very little in it about my personal life. I have had much happiness and some unhappiness. There is hardly anything here about either. But Chapters 1 and 2 give some particulars of who I am and where I come from. It is intended as a book about journalism; specifically, about political journalism.

I think I have probably worked for more politician-editors than anybody else – in chronological order, Iain Macleod, Nigel Lawson, Richard Crossman and Conor Cruise O'Brien – and two politician-proprietors in Lord Beaverbrook and Ian Gilmour. And John Junor would have become a Liberal MP if he had won Aberdeen West in 1945, Edinburgh East in 1948 or Dundee West in 1951.

Lawson and Gilmour went on to politics after a career in journalism (though both continued to write extensively). Crossman ended his career as editor of the *New Statesman*, having been a Labour cabinet minister for six years and, before that, an active journalist. Macleod regarded his editorship of the *Spectator* as an interlude in his political career. O'Brien became editor-in-chief of the *Observer* almost by accident, having, equally fortuitously, been Minister for Posts and Telegraphs in the Irish Republic. Beaverbrook was first a financier, then a Conservative MP, then a journalist and proprietor, then a minister in Winston Churchill's wartime coalition.

[1] Alan Watkins, *A Slight Case of Libel* (1990), 69-70.

I knew Beaverbrook less well than the rest. I was fortunate in being on reasonably good terms with all of them. But if this book has a hero, it is Fleet Street in its silver age, from about 1955 to about 1985, the only place where I have ever felt entirely at home. It is a book less about politicians than about journalists.

The sections on my father, on Lord Beaverbrook and on Iain Macleod are substantially as they appeared in my *Brief Lives* (1982), which is now out of print.

1

Heredity

The most conservative of all religions – ancestor worship.
Aneurin Bevan, *In Place of Fear*, 1952

I

'*Juden, Juden*,' the German prisoners-of-war muttered excitedly to one another, pointing to my father, who was standing outside our house in Penygarn Road, Tycroes ('House on the crossroads'), as they were marching raggedly towards a day's forced labour on one of the neighbouring farms.

'*Nein, nein*,' he said, with great good humour, 'I am a Welshman.'

He could understand what they were saying because, with some other local teachers, he was learning German from a refugee at a night class in Ammanford. He could say *nein* but not, at that stage, if he ever reached it: 'I am a Welshman.' Not long afterwards, in April 1945, when the news of the liberation of Buchenwald and Belsen came through, he broke down and cried.

David John Watkins was, in his later years, of reclusive habits but great influence within a restricted circle. He was born in 1894 at a small stone house, no more than a cottage, called Lighthouse, in Penygarn Road and was accordingly sometimes known as 'Dai Lighthouse'. His family shortly acquired a slightly larger house, Bryntirion, almost directly opposite. On his marriage to my mother he rented an even larger house, Proskairon – the name, devised by a Nonconformist minister who had been a previous tenant, was of Persian rather than Welsh origin – about a hundred yards distant on the same road. In 1937 he had built for him, for £600, another house, Tregarn, directly opposite Proskairon. There was no need for him to do this. He could have bought Proskairon for less money; with a balcony and angled (rather than curved) bay windows, it was

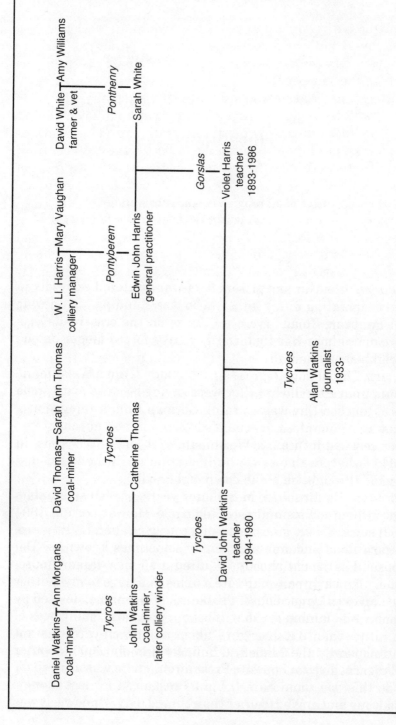

Note: The villages of Tycroes, Gorslas, Pontyberem and Ponthenry are in East Carmarthenshire.

a more attractive building. But he was, for whatever reason, determined to 'build my own house'. Even so, his periods of teacher training, war service and teaching in London apart, he spent his entire life in the same spot.

His father, John Watkins, was the winder – the man responsible for raising and lowering the cage of miners up and down the pit shaft – of the Rhôs colliery, Tycroes. John Watkins and his relations possessed some local fame as pit-sinkers, for, in the 19th century, quite small pits were dug in that part of the world as a form of private enterprise. His wife, Catherine Thomas, came originally from Penybanc, a small village outside Llandeilo; her maternal grandfather, William Thomas, who is outside the family tree on page 6, had been a forester on Lord Dynevor's estate. John and Catherine Watkins were illiterate in both Welsh and English, though John possessed considerable ability in practical engineering. Their children, in addition to David John, were Sarah Ann (known as 'Saran') and Daniel. Sarah suffered from epilepsy, was none too bright and married a Londoner from an orphanage who, with his two brothers, had come to the district after the First World War, in which they had all served, to work in the mines. Dan was a miner and a local rugby player of, by all accounts, a simple and affectionate nature. Old photographs show him looking almost exactly like my son David (born 1959). Dan was killed in the Battle of Jutland.

My father was educated, to begin with, at the Tycroes Church of England School, though his own father was a Calvinistic Methodist and his mother a Baptist. (In Wales the Methodists came in at least three varieties: the Primitive Methodists, the Wesleyan, also called the English, Methodists and the Calvinistic Methodists. The last were the preponderant group not only among the Nonconformists – the other main Communions being the Independents and the Baptists – but in the entire country, where they were known in the 19th and for the early part of the 20th century as *Yr Hen Gorff*, 'The Old Body'.) He could not read English until he was 12. However, he passed 'the scholarship' – the then equivalent of the 11-plus, though taken somewhat later – to the Llanelli County School for Boys, subsequently the Llanelli Grammar School, some 12 miles away. He travelled to Llanelli by train from Pantyffynnon, an important railway junction in the years immediately before and after the First World War, owing to its function of channelling the anthracite coal of the Amman Valley and the villages around Ammanford, including Tycroes, down the Loughor Valley towards the coastal towns of Swansea and Llanelli. He would, in the late 1940s, recall the great days of coal, when he could hear the trains clanking down the valley throughout the night.

He was frightened of his father, who was neither scholarly nor gentle and had a disposition to resort to fisticuffs, as much with his contemporaries as with his children. 'My father had a hell of a punch,' he would say. He felt affection for his mother, who was small and timid, but pitied or even despised her for her ignorance, foolishness and superstition. Though he too retained many of the characteristics of the peasant throughout his life – he possessed a strong sense of the importance of property, was close with money and regarded any attempt to deprive him of either as the equivalent of a physical assault – he was not one to romanticise the characteristics and habits of rural Wales, as was the convention among patriotic Welshmen.

However, his recollections of rural Wales before 1914 (or of the area of Wales that was partly rural, partly industrial, but neither urban nor suburban) differed markedly from those of Welsh Socialists. People worked hard, he said, but there was always enough to eat: virtually every household kept chickens and a pig. Above all, people were happy. Happiness, he said, disappeared in 1914.

Though he was comfortable with his past, he was not a countryman; nor did he possess his father's skill in practical matters. He was reluctant to undertake the simplest household tasks, such as inserting a screw or replacing a tap-washer. He did not attempt to do any cooking, which would, admittedly, have been considered eccentric in a man of his generation living in his part of the world. He even considered it shaming to be seen carrying a shopping bag. Though he ate meat, he could well have been a vegetarian. Like most Welshmen, he did not care for underdone meat, but he pushed this disposition to extremes, saying, if a touch of blood was in evidence: 'This tastes of the farmyard.' Throughout his life, indeed, he felt uneasy about the exploitation of animals, saying: 'What have the poor cows and pigs ever done to us?' He hated to visit a market-place such as Carmarthen's because the cattle and sheep were so abused physically by the farmers. Yet he continued to eat meat, in small quantities, and over-cooked.

II

At Llanelli my father determined to be a schoolmaster. He could possibly have gone on to a university – though in those days it was more difficult than it became later – but he was always unambitious and settled for becoming a 'certificated teacher'. Having left school with the School Certificate, he worked for some time in the Wernos colliery, Tycroes (until 1944 the village boasted two mines), though as a labourer rather than as a miner, to raise the money to take him to the teachers' training department of Bristol University.

His local *reclame* as a boxing-booth practitioner derived from this period. These booths were a favourite form of entertainment in the fairgrounds of South Wales. There would be a manager, or entrepreneur, and 'the pro', a professional fighter down on his luck, old or obscure, but nevertheless formidable to a layman. You paid money for fighting the pro, which was returnable if certain conditions were fulfilled, among them, I think, survival for four rounds. Naturally the young miners of that age queued up to accept the challenge. My father not only survived these encounters: on one occasion, I was told by elderly male neighbours shortly after his death, he knocked out the pro, to consternation on the part of the management, for this was not supposed to happen in a well-regulated boxing booth. But he never made the claim himself, not to me at any rate, though he did remark on his boxing-booth days and how easy it was to survive given a little skill and common sense; so the story of his knocking out the pro may be legend.

He made most of his lifelong friends in this Bristol period, the majority of them Englishmen; visited the music-hall; and, having previously played rugby, appeared as a notably unsuccessful goalkeeper (or so he said) for the soccer team. Physically he was an arresting man, a half-inch or so under six feet, something under 12 stones, though he later put on weight, with a large head and powerful back, shoulders and upper arms. His legs, however, were too thin and led to the nickname in Tycroes, in addition to 'Dai Lighthouse', of 'Dai *coesau-rhubarb*' or 'Dai rhubarb-legs'. He was sensitive about this sobriquet and became angry whenever it was mentioned, even when it was referred to as something that had belonged to the distant past. Even when he was not angry, his eyes appeared to change colour disconcertingly from hazel through green to grey. His hair was black and curly and grew in a peak. He had thick lips which did not create any impression of coarseness. His general cast of feature was Spanish, or Jewish. In his later years he resembled the conductor Otto Klemperer or one of the more obscure prophets of the Old Testament.

III

Apart from fire-watching at Parcyrhun School, Ammanford, my father played no part in the 1939-45 war: at its outbreak he was 45. He took the view, about which he was perfectly open, that he had done quite enough for King and Country in 1914-18. He was proud that he had joined up from the Bristol teachers' training department and had not been conscripted. In all other respects he was unmilitary, neither wearing nor otherwise displaying his two campaign medals. He served as a naval chemist in Dover, London and France, where he remained for some months, though he would emphasise in conversation that he had never been 'in the trenches' or 'in the front line'. His task was to install in tanks devices for creating smoke screens. Quite why the Army was unable to perform this function on its own, without calling on the Navy for assistance, remained mysterious, but there it was. The one photograph I have from this period shows industrial-chemical tanks and suchlike in the background, a group of young men, smartly uniformed in peaked caps, white shirts, black ties and double-breasted jackets with black buttons, with a solitary, elderly, putteed Army officer in the middle of the front row.

My father's experiences of the First World War left him with not only a detestation of war in general but a dislike of what he would variously call 'swank', 'pretence' and 'nonsense': words which to him comprehended the virtues of the parade ground, officer qualities, pageantry, the royal family, law courts, High Court judges and Winston Churchill (though not R.A. Butler, whom he admired). This dislike of the ceremonial aspects of English life did not, however, lead him to celebrate the homelier traditions of his native land. 'Lot of talk' was one of his favourite dismissive phrases. Or: 'Jim Griffiths' – the Member for Llanelli and a Minister in the Labour Governments of 1945, 1950 and 1964 – 'has the gift of the gab all right, but what does he know about anything when you come down to it?' This was an over-severe criticism, though not without an element of justice, of a politician who recreated the national insurance scheme and was an outstanding Colonial Secretary. But for reasons that will appear, my father was suspicious of politicians.

The other aspect of his war service was to make him liable to nightmares, which ceased only when he became old. Though he had not himself been gassed, he would imagine he could not breathe, that something or somebody was at his throat. These nightmares were distressing to his family and dangerous to himself, for he would get out of bed still asleep. He had a particular penchant for attacking wardrobes, the more so if they were equipped with a looking-glass on the outside of the door. Seeing his own reflection dimly, he would imagine he was about to be attacked by an intruder – perhaps a German soldier – and would accordingly engage the wardrobe in combat. Despite numerous such assaults over the years, he luckily remained unharmed himself, whereas the wardrobes were less fortunate.

IV

After the 1914-18 war he taught at an elementary school in Stratford, East London. He held no high opinion of the London teachers who were his colleagues, finding them (or so he claimed later) lacking in conscientiousness. He was even more shocked by their frequent resort to the cane, for quite severe corporal punishment was then as common in State as in private schools. He never used the cane, though he had no objection in principle to slapping an obstreperous child on the leg. As a disciplinarian he relied on the menace of his size – he was remarkably large for a South-West Walian of his generation – and on his resonant baritone voice. As a singer, however, he was shy and inept. As a speaker he never attempted to modify his Carmarthenshire accent, with every R pronounced and short As, to the extent that 'plaice', as in plaice-and-chips, would be rendered as 'plăce'.

He also played rugby as a forward for the London Welsh's first XV. He said later that he would 'never have got into the team if it hadn't been for the war'. He added that he had been 'knocked about terribly'. Certainly the middle finger of his left hand was permanently crooked as a result of being broken in the match against Llanelli at Stradey Park. This was also one of the great eras of English forward play. He was proud of having appeared against such figures as A.F. Blakiston, C.H. Pillman, A.T. Voyce and W.W. Wakefield, even though 'they gave me a terrible time, *fel ceffylau* ("like horses")'. In truth he exaggerated the size of these undoubtedly formidable players, transforming them in his mind into the 16-stone monsters of the 1970s, who were to become more monstrous still in the decades after his death. The records show that the England forwards of the early 1920s were about the same height as he was, though a stone to a stone-and-a-half heavier.

V

My father left London because, he said, he could not afford to live there any longer. He was then a normal social beer-drinker, though he was careful to add that he was 'never a real boozer'. 'Boozer' was one of his favourite words of disapproval, together with 'waster'. In his later years he was virtually a complete abstainer. He returned from London to teach at Blaenau School, not far from Ammanford, where he met and married another teacher, Violet Harris, my mother, who will be described more fully later in this chapter. From Blaenau he went on to become headmaster of Llanedi, a small country school three miles from Tycroes on the main road to Swansea. There was an adverse inspector's report. In the year of my birth, 1933, he was deprived of his headmastership and given the choice of becoming headmaster of another small school in Pembrokeshire or joining the staff of Parcyrhun School in Ammanford as an ordinary teacher. He chose the latter and remained embittered for the rest of his life, often falling into rages, though these became less frequent as he grew older.

It is difficult to say whether his deprivation or dismissal was unjust. Certainly it was rare for a headmaster to be so treated, as it remains rare today. He claimed that the standards of the school were acceptable, given the material he had to work on – almost entirely the children of small farmers or of farm labourers. The episode left him with a permanent dislike of county councillors and of the Welsh Labour establishment generally, though he continued reluctantly to vote Labour.

But he did not participate in local activities. Instead he read, virtually continuously, for about 40 years. He was neither a browser nor a book-collector. He subscribed to the *Hibbert Journal*; his basic diet was the Everyman's Library; he belonged to the pre-Penguin generation. He also read Balzac, Dumas, Maupassant and Victor Hugo in French. He tried to teach himself classical Greek, though without much success. With German, in which he had a teacher, he was more successful.

His pattern of reading is or, perhaps, was familiar enough. But his lack of knowledge of fashionable opinion, combined with a paucity of acquaintances with similar interests to his own, led him to form quite independent views. Nor were these views provincial or eccentric. He perceived the merits of Thomas Hardy as a novelist (Hardy's poetry he had not read) well before his reputation reached its present size. In the 1950s, when J.M. Keynes's economic views were virtually unquestioned, he nevertheless had his doubts:

'Keynes [which he pronounced Keenz rather than Keynes] took his ideas from Alfred Marshall, but Marshall was the sounder economist. I would read Marshall if I were you. What Keynes is telling us to do is to live beyond our means. Any fool in the pub can say that.'

Another of his maxims was:

'Go to church or chapel, because there you will make real friends. You may think that the people you meet in the pub are your friends, but they are not. At the slightest sign of trouble they will be off.'

Though he did not have an elegant mind, he possessed an instinct for detecting exaggeration, falsity and fraud, as much in writers as in the people he met. After his retirement he became happier, partly because, with no more teaching to do, the memory of his Llanedi disgrace was receding; partly because he had grandchildren by now; partly because he saw more people, who would drop in for a chat and a cup of tea. Though he smoked 15 or, often, 20 cigarettes a day, he drank, moderately, only at Christmas time, or on his occasional trips to the seaside, after rugby internationals on his annual visit to St Helen's ground, Swansea, to see Glamorgan play the visiting touring team at cricket. It was a game to which he was attached but which, like many equally enthusiastic Welshmen, he never properly understood as he instinctively understood rugby.

VI

Like many people of pacific instincts, he became angry at contradiction and had a quick temper. His sense of humour was partly of the custard-pie variety, partly ironical. For instance, he had been at school with Dr Jeffrey Samuel, who later married Dr Edith Summerskill and was a vice-president of the London Welsh club. One Saturday after his retirement he was about to accompany me – casually dressed and tieless – to a match at Old Deer Park.

'Put a tie on, boy,' he said. 'Who knows? We might meet Dr Jeff Samuel.'

It was impossible to tell whether he was being serious or making a Carmarthenshire joke directed at swank, pretence and nonsense. He died at his home on Boxing Day 1980 at the age of 86. His death certificate stated that he had died of arteriosclerosis, chronic bronchitis and – pretty obviously, I should have thought – cardiac failure. He had been in some discomfort but no pain; his faculties were intact. His last words to me were 'Never buy Japanese bonds', a reference to a recent financial scandal, and 'I could never manage gin-and-tonic', a reference to his inability in old age to unscrew the metal cap of the solitary bottle of Gordon's gin which he would purchase at Christmas. There were numerous callers at the house. One of them asked:

'Tell me, Mr Watkins ...'

'Call me Alan, please, Mrs Davies.'

'Tell me, Alan, did he suffer at all?'

'No, not at all. He went like a baby.'

'But there must have been *some* suffering.'

'No, none at all, really.'

'They were saying that he was screaming in agony.'

'Who were saying, exactly?'

'You know, down the road.'

'Well, you can tell them they're wrong. Thank you for calling, Mrs Davies. Much appreciated.'

Another caller was a cleanly but roughly dressed man I had never seen before. He looked like a small farmer rather than a former miner and was, I supposed, in his late sixties. He came from outside the village. It turned out that my father had cured him of stammering as a boy by advising him always to carry loose change in his trouser pocket and to jangle the coins when he found difficulty with a word. The cure had worked: he was accordingly calling at the house to pay tribute to the young teacher who had effected it. I found this a moving moment.

D.J. Watkins was buried at St Edmund's Church, Tycroes, in which he had been confirmed after his marriage to my mother, so that he could accompany her to the Anglican church with a clear conscience, with, as he would say, 'everything above board'.

VII

My mother, Violet, was born on 7 September 1893, the youngest daughter of Dr Edwin Harris, general practitioner, of Gorslas ('Green bog'). Her elder sisters were Lily, the oldest, and Rose; the youngest in the family was William, always called Will. The family joke was that, as all three girls had been named after flowers, so likewise had he, after Sweet William. All four became teachers. Violet was her father's favourite and used to accompany him on his rounds, often assisting in sanguinary operations on kitchen tables. These early experiences left her with no horror of blood and with an aptitude for first-aid from which I was to benefit. But her work as her father's young assistant did not make her hard or cynical. She remained sensitive to the pain and injuries of others. Later on, indeed, she fussed too much about my health.

She passed out at or near the top of the list for the whole of Carmarthenshire in the 'scholarship examination' and went on to the Llandeilo County (later Grammar) School, one of those mixed establishments which had been set up following the Intermediate Education Act 1889 and have produced individuals of such varying talents as Roy Jenkins (Abersychan), Barry John (Gwendraeth) and Donald Peers (Amman Valley). She distinguished herself at school, excelling at Mathematics, English and Latin, and won numerous prizes for being top of the class. I have them still on my shelves: handsome, leather editions of Shakespeare's works, Macaulay's essays, and the poetry of Milton, Keats and J.R. Lowell, who presumably enjoyed a higher reputation at the beginning of the 20th century than he does today.

She was also a fine sprinter and long jumper, but had to confine these activities to school hours. The reason was that to get to Llandeilo from Gorslas entailed a walk of four miles from Gorslas to the railway station; to get to Gorslas from Llandeilo meant another four miles. So my mother, accompanied at different times by both her sisters, her elder sister or her brother, would walk eight miles a day.

When she was 17 her father died unexpectedly at 57 of bronchitis. He left little money because he would not have earned much:

the coal-miners and farmworkers who made up the bulk of his practice were in no position to pay generously or, often, at all. He also had the reputation of being 'a bit of a boozer'. At all events, Violet Harris had to leave Llandeilo County School to become an uncertificated teacher.

VIII

My mother's principal interests at this time were music, dancing and dressmaking, at which she remained adept throughout her life, until her sight began to go in her eighties. Dancing she loved as an activity: she could not understand why the chapels denounced it for immorality; while even her own Anglican church (in Wales still established during her youth) regarded it as a form of exercise liable to bring about temptations best avoided. She regarded dancing as simply something she enjoyed doing and was good at. There was no piano at the house, Glaspant ('Green hollow'), until later. She and her sister Rose sent away to London for sheet music and played it on a piano keyboard which they had drawn on paper and used as a basis for singing. The result was that I was brought up on music-hall songs of an earlier period such as 'Hello, hello, who's your lady friend?' and Lionel Monckton compositions such as 'A bachelor gay am I', a particular favourite of my mother's.

When she did acquire a piano, she discovered a gift for playing by ear. You could whistle or hum a tune and she would reproduce it on the piano without the slightest trouble. Whether this facility was the result of her earlier exertions with sheet music, a gift from the gods or both, I do not know. What was unquestionable was that she possessed it. Though she could read music as well, she preferred to thump away like a pub pianist. As far as I know, she never set foot in a pub in her life. She was certainly a non-smoker and a complete abstainer, not because of any puritanical or other religious convictions, but because she did not like the taste of alcohol in any form.

My parents' original intention had been to have four children; as, indeed, in a sense they did, but there was a miscarriage and two deaths in early infancy. It was a time when, she told me later, 'I couldn't look at anyone else's baby.' Her sanity was perhaps saved – I was certainly born – through the good offices of the family doctor, Dr Jenkins of Ammanford, a small, sandy, foxy man who had raced cars at Brooklands. 'You and I can do this together,' he said to her. On 3 April 1933, at the St Helen's Nursing Home, Swansea, just up the road from the rugby-and-cricket ground, she gave birth to me by Caesarean section, then a rarer and more hazardous operation than it is today.

She loved me extravagantly, as did my father, though it was considered unmanly for men of his generation to show affection towards other males, sons included, in too physical a fashion. My mother felt no such inhibitions. She was, in her forties (she was 39 when I was born), five feet six inches in height and slimly but strongly built, though she put on weight steadily for the rest of her life. She had blue eyes and thick brown hair which did not start to go grey till her eighties. My father had a rolling, sailor's gait, which was not explained by his period of service in the Navy, most of it spent on dry land; my mother, by contrast, walked as if she had been taught deportment, which I do not think she ever had been. Mothers, sometimes fathers too, would commend her example to their daughters. She was, in the word of the area, 'smart', which did not mean clever or fashionable but well turned out. Alas, she failed to pass on any of her characteristics in this area to me.

IX

She was an Anglican, a Conservative, a pacifist and a feminist in the sense in which Bernard Shaw or H.G. Wells would have understood the word. She never wanted to live in Tycroes and would have preferred my father to acquire a house somewhere between Ammanford and Llandybie, on the Llandeilo road. She always looked towards Llandeilo, where she had been to school and Lord Dynevor had his seat (to which she had been invited to tea as a young girl). Tycroes people, she used to say, had 'long faces', which was I think true. When my father replied that most of them had endured hard lives, she replied that so too had the inhabitants of other mining villages in East Carmarthenshire, including her own native Gorslas, but that did not mean they looked miserable all day long.

Her indictment of her adopted village as lacking in *joie de vivre* was not flaunted before its natives. On the contrary: she was a popular local figure. Though my father was respected, he was also feared, even disliked, on account of his bad temper and his habit of ignoring people's greetings because he was preoccupied with other matters or simply did not notice them. My mother had perfect manners and a kind or friendly word for everyone. Sometimes, however, she could be sharp. She was once organising a whist drive (as these occasions were called) in the church hall. One of her fellow members of the church was not only puritanical but rich, with a car, an Opel, I seem to remember, which – irrespective of whether it was an Opel or some other make – was rare in those days.

'There'll be no cards in Heaven,' she said.

'There'll be no cars there either,' my mother replied.

On another occasion she was crossing Tycroes Square to go shopping, accompanied by me, then about 10, and the family dog Nap, a combination of chow, alsatian and golden spaniel. It caused me much unhappiness when he had to be put down a year or so later for attacking people. I could always control him, as could my mother (my father was more hesitant), together with a boy, slightly older than I was, who now lived opposite us in Proskairon and was called Russell James. There was a group of three or four miners leaning or squatting beside the telephone kiosk outside Gladstone Thomas's hardware store. There was another dog in the vicinity. They tried to set him and Nap at each other's throats by hissing.

'Huss-er,' they whispered.

'Stop that at once,' my mother said.

They stopped, looked both surly and surprised, but made no reply. The three of us, woman, child and dog, proceeded on our way to the Co-op. Though personally shy, my mother possessed complete social self-assurance, for in the Carmarthenshire of the pre-1914 period and, indeed, for long afterwards, there had been no intermediate class between local doctor (who, in esteem, ranked above vicar, Nonconformist minister, solicitor or schoolmaster) and Lord Dynevor himself. Her natural language was English.

In addition, though she could speak perfectly good demotic Welsh – my father could speak proper literary Welsh – she possessed an antipathy both to the language and to what might be described as Welsh ways. It would be tempting to explain this hostility, which sometimes verged on contempt, by saying that it was natural in a doctor's daughter born in 1893, long before Welshness became *chic*. However, her feelings were not shared by her brother or two elder sisters, who did not possess either her dictionary-vocabulary or her collection of Edwardian phrases, of which I give a selection:

Honour bright ('I'm telling the truth' or interrog. 'Are you telling the truth?'); couldn't knock the skin off a rice pudding; buck up; pull your socks up; togs (clothes, esp. new); coat (never 'jacket', unless of the cut-away sort); like greased lightning; in double-quick time; double dose; tummy (rarely 'stomach', never 'belly'); looking-glass; gyp (pain); four feet above contradiction (of any preacher, Anglican or Nonconformist); cross as two sticks; thin as a rake; ass; silly ass; silly billy; juggins; silly juggins; 'I prefer God's time to Lloyd George's' (originally used by her own mother of British Summer Time, but quoted with approval).

As a child I naturally reproduced these phrases in conversation; equally naturally, in a Welsh-speaking mining village, my usage did not enhance my popularity either with contemporaries or with seniors. I soon learnt to desist and to reserve my mother's English idioms for the family circle. There was, however, no social pressure outside the home to speak English that was incorrect. On the contrary: good English was admired. Here my mother was supreme: more knowledgeable, more accurate, better at explaining grammar, syntax and – trickiest of all – idiom than any teacher I ever had outside the house. She knew about sequence of mood and sequence of tenses, the relative pronoun as subject in its own clause, and the difference between a straight and a subjunctive conditional: all matters which were largely mysteries in Fleet Street when I arrived there, as they remain to this day, if anything, indeed, more mysterious still.

And yet she was also highly practical, capable of making a shirt or reupholstering a sofa. She did not have her husband's literary or philosophical interests or his powers of memory, particularly for the ramifications of family relationships. But she was by far the more competent of the two. She did not put things off, find excuses for not acting, as my father was constantly doing. Every letter was answered by return of post, in pen and ink (she went through life without once possessing either a fountain-pen or a watch). If the letter was a business letter, she would make an exact copy and file it.

X

In 1973, when he was 79, my father had an operation for prostate trouble. It was not cancer; the operation was successful; but it took the stuffing out of him and afterwards he treated himself as an invalid. My mother urged him to go out more, to take a short but regular walk, but her advice was repulsed. Despite his early success as a rugby player, he had always been disinclined to physical effort, a characteristic I have inherited. Now he would sit by the fire in flannel trousers and an old cardigan, smoking cigarettes, drinking cups of tea and reminiscing about the great days of coal and the London of the 1920s. Every Friday night my mother would bathe him, wash and sometimes cut his hair, and cut his toenails. He would shave himself with a safety razor, having soon discarded the battery-operated electric razor which I had bought for him on his admission to Morriston hospital for the prostate operation.

My mother's Friday-night exertions on his behalf were taxing not only because she was as old as he was, six months older in fact, but also because she was starting to go blind. She knew this, as I did, but my father did not realise how bad her condition was until much later. Like Kingsley Amis, he was afraid of being left alone in the house at night (though he did not share Amis's terror of public transport). For this reason, my mother refused to leave him for the night or nights which the operation then required. After he had died, it was too late for anything to be done to restore her sight.

She was able to carry on living at Tregarn, Tycroes, because of the kindness of two neighbours, Stuart and Lorraine (Lorrie) Smith, Stuart a former colliery worker. He was never allowed to work at the coalface because, like the husband of my father's sister – to whom the same restriction was applied – he had come originally from London: a piece of hardly known racism perpetrated by what would then have been the South Wales Miners' Federation.

One winter the tank and pipes froze. On their unfreezing, in the middle of the night, a cascade destroyed part of a ceiling and a wall on the ground floor. Somehow my mother roused the Smiths, who did what they could to comfort her and to repair the damage. But it was obvious that she could not go on living alone, blind, dependent on Mr and Mrs Smith and on the nurse who would visit her daily to dress the skin cancer which she had acquired on her breast. Accordingly she was removed to an old people's home run by what was then, in the mid-1980s, the Dyfed County Council, in Tirydail ('Land of the leaves') just outside Ammanford, on the way to Llandybie.

It was clean, efficient and humane but nevertheless depressing, old people in armchairs looking eternally into the middle distance, a veritable departure lounge for the afterlife. I now visited my mother monthly, whereas previously I had visited her three or four times a year. If I was going to put in an appearance on a radio programme (rarer then than 20 years previously), I would try to let her know beforehand.

'That's my son, that's my son,' she had said to her aged companions, so she told me on my next visit.

They had shown no interest whatever – had continued to gaze into the middle distance. There was no reason for them to do anything else. Even so, the episode depressed her. She was unhappy also because the principal language was Welsh. As I have said, she spoke perfectly adequate colloquial Welsh but did not enjoy doing so and much preferred to speak English.

By this time I was living with my daughter Jane, then 21, in a three-bedroomed house in Islington. She said we ought to have her grandmother to live with us. I demurred, saying that she hated London as my father had not, which was true, and that the house was on four floors including basement, which was also true. But I realised I was making excuses, finding reasons for inaction, as my father would have done. True, I could not have afforded full-time nursing care, but I could have afforded some. And the social services department of the Islington Borough Council would, I am sure, have provided some help. We should have managed somehow. In retrospect, I am ashamed I did not make the attempt.

In August 1986 I was told she had broken a hip in falling over while seeking the lavatory during the night, and had been taken to the main county hospital outside Carmarthen. I knew that when very old people were taken into hospital they generally died there. I hurried to Carmarthen, to be told that the operation had been successful. She was sitting up in bed, looking remarkably cheerful in the circumstances. 'Thank you for coming,' she said. Returned to London, I received a message that she had died peacefully in her sleep of a stroke, a blood-clot on that formidable brain of hers. She was a week short of her 93rd birthday. She was buried at St Edmund's Church, Tycroes, in the same grave as my father's.

Unlike him, she enjoyed an argument. 'Argument' is now used, as much in the broadsheets as in the tabloid press, as a synonym for 'row'. 'They were having a bit of an argument, like,' means they were screaming and shouting and saucepans were flying all over the place. To my mother, an argument was the occasion of a reasonable dispute conducted in civilised language. This was an admirable preparation for having to deal with C.A.R. Crosland and R.H.S. Crossman. Throughout her life also she was my censor not only of grammar and syntax but also of taste. 'Would Mama approve of that?' I would ask myself with a hesitant pen in my left hand. Almost 15 years after her death, I ask it still.

2

Environment

Parched pob byw ei orchwyl ('Let every living being respect his or her occupation')
Motto of the Amman Valley Grammar
School, Ammanford

It was summer 1999 when, to my surprise (and, I must confess, gratification), I had just been made an Honorary Fellow of the University of Wales, Lampeter. I was being driven by a woman friend through the Carmarthenshire lanes between Carreg Cennen castle and Llandeilo. Fifty years previously I had travelled on my bike over these same hilly little roads, thinking chiefly tortured thoughts about girls but also thoughts about becoming a writer. Even then I had no delusions about being a great novelist. What I was interested in at that stage was journalism of the polemical, pamphleteering sort. Such notions had been put into my mind by reading the prefaces to Bernard Shaw's plays, which rested in a long line in their original pale brown paper covers (published by Constable) in my father's somewhat daunting bookcase. Indeed, after the volumes in their Everyman art nouveau bindings of Hobbes, Locke, Berkeley and Hume, with the addition of Spinoza and Descartes to demonstrate a denial of any native empiricist bias, Shaw was, with *Moby Dick* and *Tristram Shandy*, something of a light relief.

We took the *News Chronicle* at home. Most families in the village of Tycroes took the *Daily Mirror*, the *Daily Herald* or the *Daily Worker*. In the 1940s, Communism was both a powerful and a legitimate force in the miners' union, producing such excellent leaders as Arthur Horner and Will Paynter. It was the companionable practice of the area to drop in on a neighbour of a morning (or, sometimes, an afternoon) and ask to read the paper. The request would almost always be granted, with a complimentary cup of tea.

The journalist and former rugby player Gerald Davies tells me that the practice was equally common in Kidwelly, on the coast and some miles to the west. I never went in for it myself, but others would come occasionally to our house, to have a look at the *News Chronicle*.

On Sundays we took the *Observer*. With one of the village's three chapel ministers, we made up the total sale of two. Thirty years later, over 20 *Observer*s were being sold in a village which had changed from a mining community into a commuting centre for Swansea and even faraway Cardiff. On Saturday, or, if we were lucky, on Friday we had the *Listener* delivered. When I was in the second year of the sixth form of the Amman Valley Grammar School, Ammanford – it would have been some time in 1949-51 – I persuaded my parents to order the *New Statesman* as well.

Of the four papers we took regularly, it was the one with which I felt least at ease. The *News Chronicle* was not exactly homely but it was certainly comprehensible. In Robert Lynd you knew you were reading one of the last – perhaps the last – of the great English essayists or, rather, of the essayists who wrote in English, for Lynd was an Irishman from the North. When he died in 1949, the *Chronicle* telephoned Max Beerbohm in exile in Rapallo to ask for a short tribute. Beerbohm duly obliged, describing Lynd as, among other things, 'very noble'. This appeared as 'very able', to which Beerbohm rightly took exception. Even then 'able' was becoming an adjective of official approval, early Whitehallese that has persisted to this day. Lynd was replaced by Ian Mackay, who was not such a good essayist but more of a man-about-Fleet Street, though naturally I did not know this at the time.

The *Observer* – likewise I was not to know this – was at the beginning of its golden age, roughly the 1950s. The film critic was the redoubtable C.A. Lejeune, who with Dilys Powell of the *Sunday Times* dominated their branch of the trade. The theatre critic was not yet Kenneth Tynan, who did not arrive till 1954, but Ivor Brown, who had edited the paper before David Astor asserted his proprietary rights in 1948. Brown, one of the last professional men of letters, greatly preferred going to the theatre to editing a newspaper. He also disliked political writing as a *genre* and could not understand why anyone should take the slightest interest in what went on in Westminster.

And yet the *Observer* of that time possessed one of the finest political columnists of the postwar period: Hugh Massingham. He wrote as 'Our Political Correspondent', for bylines were then rare and scarce, while unflattering pictures of columnists or reporters were displayed, if at all, only in the comparatively staid tabloid press of the time. Massingham's column was set out in the top left-hand corner of the page facing the leader-page. It was straplined 'A London Diary'. Until Henry Fairlie turned up in the *Spectator* in the mid-1950s, Massingham's column was my favourite reading in any newspaper.

The *Listener* did not have a political luminary. As a BBC publication, it could scarcely have had one, certainly not at that time, when – it seems hardly believable today – discussion was prohibited of any topic which was due to be debated in Parliament within the next fortnight. It was known as 'the 14-day rule'. But the paper was strong on the literary and arts side. It had Wyndham Lewis himself on art and the young Simon Raven on novels. Its chief function, however, was to reprint talks from the then relatively new Third Programme. I am convinced that it was reading the series 'Ideas and Beliefs of the Victorians' which, more than anything else, got me into Cambridge.

II

In December 1950 I sat the scholarship for the group of colleges which included my first choice, Queens'. Shortly before Christmas I received a telegram saying I had been placed in the exhibition class but that, owing to a shortage of awards, no exhibition was available. Perhaps understandably at the age of 17, I was in some doubt about what this communication meant. Was I in? Or was I out? My father had no doubt about its meaning. I was indisputably in. Why, otherwise, would the authorities have gone to the trouble and expense of sending a telegram? That was his reasoning, which proved to be correct. He was even more excited than I was, and would have opened a bottle if there had been any drink in the house.

Shortly after I had gone up to Queens' in autumn 1951, my tutor told me that, as I had already been awarded a county major scholarship – the Carmarthenshire County Council was particularly generous with its awards in the mid-1950s – the college saw no point in awarding me an additional exhibition which I did not need. I, by contrast, saw every point: not so much the financial point (for there was, I believe, a kind of equalisation procedure, whereby the cash disbursed was evened out) as, rather, the point of honour and prestige. If I had been placed in the exhibition class, lower than the scholarship class but a distinction nevertheless, I deserved to be an exhibitioner of the college. That I already possessed the award from the local authority was, or ought to have been, neither here nor there. This may have been petty of me, but there it was. It was what I thought at the time.

The *New Statesman* appeared to be a journal of intimidating metropolitan omniscience. G.D.H. Cole, R.H.S. Crossman and Harold J. Laski, as they styled themselves, treated the second Attlee administration with the utmost contempt. Politics, they seemed to say, was a simple matter. You did A and produced X. Alternatively, if you wanted to produce Y, you did B. This was the spirit in which most socialist journalism was conducted until Harold Wilson's July measures of 1966. These destroyed the foundations of socialist literature since 1919 and some of its edifices as well – including Anthony Crosland's *Future of Socialism*.

It is interesting that the circulation of the paper reached its peak of 93,000 in the previous year under the editorship of Paul Johnson and declined fairly steadily afterwards. The *NS*, however, did not have a regular political columnist until the arrival of Anthony Howard in 1961. Previously it had made do with short parliamentary sketches by J.P.W. Mallalieu and by Maurice Edelman. They were both Labour MPs and both good journalists. But their weekly contributions (Edelman succeeded Mallalieu) were poor hack stuff compared to what was to appear in the *Spectator* under the byline 'Taper' (Bernard Levin) or, earlier, by Henry Fairlie.

The arts and books pages I found more intimidating still. It was not that I was completely unaware of modern literature. I had read most of George Orwell in books supplied by the Ammanford Public Library (my mother had considered *Down and Out in Paris and London* unsuitable reading) and put in a special pre-publication order for *Nineteen Eighty-Four*, which duly arrived on time. From the same source I obtained most of Anthony Powell's pre-war novels and put in a similar order for *A Question of Upbringing*, buying its successors in the 'Music of Time' series as they came out.

I also read the novels of C.P. Snow. He was then considered by the *NS*, one of the arbiters of literary fashion – the principal reason

why I found it intimidating – an ornament of 20th-century literature. His critical fall came later. I adhere to the middle way. He was
the first novelist to take seriously a whole class of state-educated
intellectuals who had previously been either treated as comic char-
acters or ignored completely. In this respect he anticipated Kingsley Amis and other novelists of the 1950s.

But I preferred reading the novels of Evelyn Waugh, as I have
done ever since. I enjoyed the 'William' books by Richmal Crompton
almost as much, as I do still. My other favourite authors were A.J.
Ayer, A. Conan Doyle, Bertrand Russell, A.J.P. Taylor and P.G.
Wodehouse. Ayer and Taylor proved to be grievous disappoint-
ments – thoroughly nasty pieces of work, in my opinion – when I
came to meet them later on. Malcolm Muggeridge, by contrast,
whom my friends at Cambridge and I had turned into a demon in
the early 1950s on account of his zeal in the cold war, was completely charming.

People now tend to forget how dominated the early post-war
world was by the fear of nuclear incineration. It is wrong to think
that the cause of unilateral nuclear disarmament (or 'ban-the-
bomb', as most newspapers termed it) was inaugurated by the
formation of CND in 1958. It split the Labour movement before
then. It even split the Bevanite section of the party. Why otherwise
should Aneurin Bevan's speech at the Brighton conference of 1957
(the naked-into-the-conference-chamber speech) have brought
about the consternation it did? In foreign policy I was a Bevanite,
in the days before the great man had made his views on the nuclear
deterrent wholly clear.

In domestic policy, by contrast, I was even then a devoted follower of Anthony Crosland, who always accepted the invitations of
the Cambridge University Labour Club to address its Sunday
afternoon meetings in the Gramophone Room of the Union. He
would turn up in a dashing light brown suit and have a large gin
(paid for out of club funds) before lunch. With Richard Crossman
and the now maligned Robert Boothby, who often came to Cambridge as a respectively anti- and pro-European double-act,
Crosland was good with young people precisely because he was
prepared to be harsh with them ('Now exactly what evidence do you
have for believing that?').

I knew enough about politics, even at that stage, to realise that
you could not go about the business in this tolerant and ecumenical

fashion. Either you were a Bevanite; or you were not. If you were a Croslandite revisionist (though the term had not been invented then), you could not at the same time be a Bevanite. Despite this difficulty, which was neither intellectual nor dialectical but practical, I intended to become a Labour MP, having first practised as a barrister.

Our generation produced few politicians of pomp and power. John Morris became Secretary of State for Wales and Attorney-General. Douglas Hurd, whose voice barked even more fiercely in those days, was both Foreign and Home Secretary. He came relatively late to politics, certainly by the standards of the present day, after a 14-year spell as a diplomat. He would have been a better Prime Minister than John Major but was held back because the Tories considered him too exalted socially. In the election to succeed Margaret Thatcher, he did not help his cause by playing the game of lowlier-than-thou, asserting that his father (a Tory MP, Sir Anthony Hurd, later a life peer) was a tenant-farmer in Wiltshire and that he would not have been able to go to Eton if he had not won a scholarship.

Someone else who was to play a part in the politics of the Thatcher era was John Biffen. He was something of an elder statesman even then. However, he was more dandyish than he was later. When speaking at the Union he wore a maroon bow-tie with his dinner jacket, and maroon socks. Though he became perhaps the most highly regarded Leader of the House of the post-war period, he is better known for having been sacked by Margaret Thatcher and for describing her press secretary, Sir Bernard Ingham, as the sewer rather than the sewage. In his last period in the House, Biffen was the most respected of backbenchers.

His only rival in this field of endeavour was another Cambridge contemporary, Tam Dalyell. In those days, Dalyell was a Conservative. He learnt his socialism sitting literally at the feet of Richard Crossman at a Fabian summer school shortly after leaving the university. Dalyell became chairman of the Conservative Association but had no available partner for the association's annual ball, something of an event in the Cambridge social calendar. There was nothing odd or aberrant in this lack. In the Cambridge of the early 1950s, girls were in short supply. It was something of a triumph to persuade one of them even to come to tea ('I'm sorry,' – this would have been at about six – 'but I must get back to my college now').

The officials of the association managed to procure a suitable partner for the occasion from Girton. Slightly dishevelled on account of her three-mile bicycle ride from the women's college, she called on Dalyell in his rooms in King's.

'I believe it's conventional to give ladies flowers at times like this,' Dalyell said brusquely.

He then marched to a table, removed some daffodils from a vase and presented the dripping bunch to his surprised guest. History does not record what happened during the rest of the evening.

There was another undergraduate who became a professional backbencher: Nigel Spearing, who was Labour member for Newham South from 1974 to 1997. Though he was a physically impressive man, tall, dark, both broad and raw-boned, he was never a remotely glamorous character, either then or subsequently. He spent 18 years as a teacher before entering the House in 1974. He specialised in the European Community or the Common Market, as it was then called, and was a Eurosceptic before that misleading term was coined, for Eurosceptics are commonly opposed to the whole enterprise rather than rationally sceptical about it.

I think I was probably the sole journalist or politician who entered the House instead of making a swift departure when Spearing was speaking. I did so not only because I had known him when he was a young man but because he was usually worth listening to. He also personally supplied me with interesting information about the Community on such matters as comparative rates of VAT in the various member-countries, and the goods and services on which the tax was levied. Most people, certainly most journalists, consider such information far from interesting; rather as tedious beyond belief. I was not of that number. Neither was Spearing, though he made no concessions to popular appeal in his learned disquisitions.

But if the political haul of the early 1950s at Cambridge was sparse, as it was – in contrast both with the late 1940s and with the early 1960s – the journalistic catch was bigger. Geoffrey Wheatcroft believes that the 1950-5 period at Cambridge marked a crucial development in post-war Britain. It was a time when there was a decisive shift in the terms of trade between politics and journalism. Here is a short list of the Cambridge figures of that era who turned to newspapers or magazines as a means of making a living: Neal

Ascherson, Mark Boxer ('Marc'), Samuel Brittan, Michael Frayn, Peter Jenkins, Karl Miller, Brian Redhead, Claire Tomalin, Nicholas Tomalin and Richard West. It does not include George Gale, T.E. ('Peter') Utley, Colin Welch and Peregrine Worsthorne, who were of the 1940s. Nor does it include Peter Hall, Jonathan Miller and Hugh Thomas, who, though they later did occasional journalism, were better known for other activities.

Even without them, it is undoubtedly an impressive list. But of its members, only Nick Tomalin was clearly determined to use – even to exploit – the university as a staging post on his way to Fleet Street. He was the first man I saw wearing a dark green shirt and navy-blue tie. He had a habit of standing with his legs crossed, his hands clasped in front of him and his head to one side. This posture made him look both like a ballet dancer and like a bird.

Almost immediately after leaving the university, Tomalin joined the *Daily Express*, then beginning its silver age, and wrote both the anonymous 'William Hickey' column and a signed column from New York. This latter post was less impressive than it sounded. It entailed scanning American papers and news agencies for stories of the 'cor-fancy-that' variety which would subsequently be incorporated as seven or eight short items in a well-presented column in the top right-hand corner of page two (the foreign page). He later became one of the best 'Atticus' columnists of the *Sunday Times*. After some years, he persuaded his masters to allow him to roam more widely. Despite Tomalin's store of journalistic worldly wisdom, which he appeared to have possessed from his youth, he never seemed to realise that being cast early as a gossip columnist made it difficult to be recast as something else later on in life. This conveniently brings me to one of my Moral Maxims for Modern Journalists: Do not become a gossip columnist unless you are happy, as you may well be, to spend the rest of your career as one.

Having, in his case, escaped from the treadmill, Tomalin did some of the best journalism of his life – some of the best, indeed, since the war. He was most famous for one sentence, contained in a piece often anthologised and sometimes heard at Fleet Street memorial services:

'The only qualities essential for real success in journalism are ratlike cunning, a plausible manner, and a little literary ability.'[1]

---

[1] *Sunday Times Magazine*, 27 March 1966, reprinted as 'Stop the Press, I Want to Get On', in *Nicholas Tomalin Reporting* (1975), 77.

He also played the principal part in exposing the great British burgundy swindle. He was the first British journalist to reveal the callousness of the United States military in Vietnam.[2] And then, in 1973, he was killed covering the Arab-Israeli war when a rocket penetrated the roof of the car in which he was travelling.

Mark Boxer also died young, of a brain tumour. He developed his elegant drawing style early, in the magazine *Granta*, in those days the name of an undergraduate paper rather than of a publishing concern. He changed little in succeeding years. He was on the tall side but looked taller than he was on account of his slenderness and grace. He played cricket (a useful left-arm slow bowler) with his trousers supported by a tie, as if he were an Edwardian gentleman. He had abundant black curly hair and the beautiful manners which he retained throughout his life. Owing to this latter quality, and to his presence at King's, people assumed he was an Etonian. In fact his origins were not at all grand and he had been educated at Berkhamsted.[3]

People also tended to assume that he was homosexual or at least bisexual. His widow, Anna Ford, became angry at both assumptions. She declared that neither was correct. Her late husband, she said, was often seen in the company of older men in his younger days because he did not have any money. He went out with them because they would take him to expensive restaurants and places of that kind.

Boxer was rusticated (rather than sent down) from the university for publishing a blasphemous poem in *Granta*, which he was then editing. There was an impressive mock funeral, with a draped coffin and numerous orations. The poem was by an eccentric heir to a baronetcy, Anthony de Hoghton, a name that sounded as if it had been made up in Wormwood Scrubs but was genuine enough. Contrary to the mythology which has grown up around it, it did not begin:

---

[2] 'The Art of Cooking Bogus Burgundy', *Sunday Times*, 22 May 1966; 'The General Goes Zapping Charlie Cong', *Sunday Times*, 5 June 1966; both reprinted in *Nicholas Tomalin Reporting*, 101, 192.

[3] In a school which also produced Graham Greene, Hugh Greene, Peter Quennell and my future adversary in the Law Courts, Michael Meacher. There is an invaluable account of Boxer's early life by his sister Rosemary Sayigh in *The Collected and Recollected Marc*, ed. Mark Amory (1993), 5. See also Geoffrey Wheatcroft, 'Mark Boxer' in *Absent Friends* (1989), 249.

God, God, you silly old sod.

The beginning was altogether more decorous:

> Let God get up: he snores in bed
> With a dirty old stocking wrapped round his head.
> The household's all at sixes and sevens
> And the dust lies thick on his seven heavens.

Another went:

> Incognito you'd like to live,
> You parasite, you greasy spiv,
> In South America or Australia,
> You vindictive bloodstained failure.

Unlike the poem which the Labour Minister John Strachey submitted to C.R. Attlee for approval before sending it to a literary magazine, and which the Prime Minister rejected on the grounds that it did not rhyme and did not scan, de Hoghton's effort more or less passed both tests. It seemed to me a lively production. It went with a certain swing. Such, however, was not the opinion of literary Cambridge. At a meeting at the Union, Hugh Thomas – something of a figure both in literary and in political Cambridge – denounced both the poem and the university authorities in equally censorious terms. I thought this was carrying Voltaire's principle too far. This, however, was the official liberal line: the poem was rotten and should never have been published, but the university was repressive in acting as it had.

Later on, Boxer said that all his generation had invented was the colour magazine. As the first editor of the *Sunday Times Magazine*, this was true of him. He had done much more besides. So had others of his Cambridge generation, including Peter Jenkins. While Tomalin was set on a career in journalism, and Boxer looked likely to end up in something of the same kind (though he might equally well have owned an art gallery), Jenkins showed no interest in undergraduate journalism as a means of self-advancement. He might have done anything: gone into academic life or the law, for though he was reading History, he was at a college famous for its legal studies, Trinity Hall. His steps had been directed there by the judge Cyril (later Lord) Salmon, who had spotted him as a young man in Bury St Edmunds and encouraged him to think about a legal future.

At about the same stage Jenkins himself had contemplated making a career for himself as a professional jockey. It was fortunate that he desisted, for he would always have experienced trouble in making the weight. As it was, he maintained an interest in the Turf and in gambling generally. At Cambridge he was usually accompanied by a pretty girl. One of them was Judy Innes, later companion of Joseph, Lord Kagan and wife of Michael Astor. He subsequently married, first, Charlotte Strachey, who was reported to speak in the authentic tones of old Bloomsbury ('really' pronounced with exaggeration) and who died young. He married, secondly, Polly Toynbee, who, as the boxing posters of my youth used to put it, needs no introduction. While following his career as an industrial correspondent on the *Financial Times* and later the *Guardian* – his flowering as a commentator on both the *Guardian* and the *Independent* came later – he was also pursuing the life of pleasure at racecourses, afternoon drinking clubs and restaurants such as Wheeler's in Old Compton Street, where in the late 1950s and 1960s it was possible to feel both bohemian and smart. He cultivated the reputation of being raffish, even louche.

In the early 1970s he experienced a conversion. He decided he had been spending much of his time on worthless activities. He began to visit art galleries on Saturday mornings; started going to the fringe theatre (Howard Barker, Howard Brenton and David Hare then much to the fore); became theatre critic of the *Spectator* for a while.

He even wrote a play himself, *Illuminations*, which was put on at the Lyric Theatre, Hammersmith, with Paul Eddington (the star of the successful television series *Yes, Minister*) in the leading role because the producer hoped he would bring in the crowds. This part was almost entirely based on Anthony Crosland, who had died at 58 in 1977, before the play was put on. It was set at the party conference in Blackpool. It was an amusing and instructive play, except that it had no conclusion apart from an exploding bomb. This was a fashion set for sketches by the lamentable, uncraftsmanlike *Monty Python* programmes in the late 1960s. Now it had spread to plays as well. But it deserved to transfer to the West End and would have done had it not been for some spiteful reviews.

I met Jenkins on the District Line in the late 1950s, he on his way to his paper's office in the City, I to the Temple underground station. I was not at all surprised to learn he was a journalist on the *Financial Times* (then at Coleman Street). He was in the right job, I thought, even though he had done little or no writing at the university. But I was astonished to find that Sam Brittan had ended up at the same destination. Brittan and I used to talk about philosophy, especially about political theory. Academically, he was the outstanding economist of his Cambridge generation. He remains the cleverest person I have ever known, apart possibly from G.E. Moore. He is also one of the kindest, except for a tendency to fuss unnecessarily when his guest is 20 minutes late for lunch. Brittan, I thought, was suited to the academic life rather than to the rough world of journalism, which abhors a distinction, will not allow an exception and likes nothing better than a good strong read. But I was wrong. In his column in the *Financial Times* he continued to make distinctions and draw attention to exceptions. He became the most respected economic commentator of his time, moving from the liberal Keynesianism of his youth to something more *laisser-faire*, and being consistent only in libertarianism. He was knighted by John Major, and insisted on being called Sir Samuel rather than Sir Sam.

Like Sam, and Peter Jenkins, I had done hardly any journalism at the university. In 1954-5 I had a fourth year to do a post-graduate LL.B. degree. I married young and was virtually a child bridegroom. My wife, Ruth, found a tiny house, a converted stable, at the bottom of G.E. Moore's garden, off the Chesterton Road. This is how I came to know the philosopher, already the recipient of the O.M.

III

Moore was short, slim, blue-eyed, highly agile for his years. Mrs Moore took a kindly, maternal and somewhat bossy interest in her tenants, for she had at least one other couple living in the principal house. She once insisted on selling us a gate-leg table for £10 (I still have it) on the ground that it was genuine Jacobean. Sometimes she would invite us to tea with Moore and herself. Mrs Moore was voluble, and he confined himself to interjections. She was once talking about a table that some of their previous tenants had bought. It is odd how everything to do with Moore seems to come down to tables.

'You see,' she explained, 'they wanted it to have tea on.'

Moore stirred.

'No, no, dear,' he said. 'That's not quite right. Coffee too.'

Occasionally the entertainment was more formal. Tenants, past and present, would be invited to dinner. Moore insisted on grinding the coffee himself. Afterwards he pressed us to Marsala. My exchanges with him were about politics rather than philosophy. He admired Jim Griffiths. I agreed up to a point but said I thought the we-who-have-toiled-in-the-bowels-of-the-earth routine was overdone. Moore looked uncomprehending. To him, Griffiths was a good man; he perceived goodness in Griffiths; there was no room for further argument.

Moore was addicted to baths, which he generally had around lunchtime. His most frequent visitor was Casimir Lewy, the philosopher. The only person about whom I ever heard him speak unkindly was his brother, T. Sturge Moore.

'I wanted to kill my brother,' he said to me. 'He is the only man I have ever wanted to kill.'

'Why was that?'

'You see, I hated him. I have never hated anyone so much as I did my brother.'

Mrs Moore, on the other hand, had a particular detestation of Bertrand Russell.

'Bertie Russell,' she said several times, 'is a bad lot.'

On my asking for further and better particulars, she would reply: 'He has caused a lot of unhappiness in his time.'

IV

Shortly after Christmas 1955 I began my national service in the RAF. Owing presumably to my change of address from Tycroes, Carmarthenshire, to Cambridge, my call-up papers simply did not turn up. I was then working in Messrs Chivers' jam and jelly factory just outside Cambridge and, in the evening, reading law books (and more compendious 'Nutshell' guides) for the Bar examinations. I favoured carrying on in this way for as long as possible. Ruth, however, urged me to turn myself in to the authorities, on the basis that they would be sure to catch up with me sooner or later. I am not sure she was right. But I took her advice, and in late December found myself in a camp in Cardington, Bedfordshire, whence I was conveyed, with 30 or 40 other national servicemen, to the RAF's officer cadet training camp at Jurby on the Isle of Man.

I emerged successful after three, to me, gruelling months only because I impressed the representative of the service's Education Branch at the camp by my ability to speak *extempore* in public. On no account, he said in his report to his colleagues, who were more sceptical of my abilities, should I be lost to the cause of education in the RAF. An education officer is what I wanted to be. Accordingly I spent another, more agreeable month, in theory learning how to be an education officer, at Spitalgate just outside Grantham in Lincolnshire, travelling back to Cambridge every weekend. The commanding officer, like many senior Air Force officers of the period, somehow resembled a pantomime dame. He told us, unoriginally but reassuringly, that one of the functions of RAF Spitalgate was to knock back into us some of the nonsense that RAF Jurby had tried to knock out of us.

Just before the end of this comfortable spell, a wing-commander came from London to ask us where we wanted to be posted. I remember him clearly. He was wearing a check sports coat, cavalry twill trousers (much in vogue in the 1950s), a yellow cardigan, a mauve silk tie and suede boots. He was manifestly a very superior sort of wing-commander. I said I should like to be posted somewhere as near as possible to Cambridge. He said he would see what he could do. Within weeks – this was in late spring 1956, before the Suez operation had got under way – I was informed that I was to be an education officer at RAF Duxford, a famous fighter station (64 and 65 Squadrons; now a museum) 12 miles outside Cambridge. I had fallen on my feet. So I supplemented them with a Lambretta scooter; passed the test; and commuted daily between the fighter station and the matrimonial home.

On some Fridays I used to go down to Lincoln's Inn for one of the several dinners I was obliged to eat to qualify for call to the Bar. The Council for Legal Education drew no distinction between military service in the jungles of Malaya and in the flatlands of Cambridgeshire. Accordingly I had to eat fewer of these ridiculous dinners than I should have been compelled to consume if I had not been doing national service.

I would take with me the *New Statesman* and the *Spectator* to read on the train. The first thing I always turned to was Henry Fairlie's political column in the *Spectator*. On one occasion I remember thinking and asking myself the question: Now, who would you rather be? Would you rather be Mr Justice Devlin (even then the most glamorous judge, though he had yet to be elevated to the Court of Appeal and, briefly, the House of Lords)? Or would you rather be Henry Fairlie? And I answered it: Well, I would rather be Mr Fairlie.

3

Only Poofs Drink Rosé

'The *Sunday Express* is the strongest paper in the group.'
Lord Beaverbrook to the author, 1961

I

In 1959, three years after my conversion on the train from Cambridge to Liverpool Street, I was becalmed as a research assistant at the London School of Economics. I was working for Professor William A. Robson, as he preferred to be called, though he was known in the Senior Common Room as Willie Robson. He was one of the great legal theorists of the mid-century, the inventor of administrative law as an academic discipline. I was helping him with a new edition of his pioneering work on the subject, *Justice and Administrative Law*. It was the umpteenth edition, which never saw the light of day, probably because the accretion of case-law had by then made the book unrecognisable in its original form. The other book on which I was engaged, a new one this time, duly came out under the forbidding title of *Nationalised Industries and Public Ownership*.

Robson wrote all his books and his numerous articles on lined foolscap paper in green ink, but was in other respects entirely sane. He smoked a pipe constantly but nevertheless reproved me for smoking too many cigarettes, as I was undoubtedly doing at the time. His evening parties (that was the phrase used) for his graduate students, who included myself and my wife for this purpose, were famous for their cider cup – or, rather, for the exiguous quantities of cider cup, the only form of strong drink available on these occasions.

I was about to write that he was not a mean man. Yet the truth is that this is exactly what he was. And yet the truth is also that he dispensed small quantities of cider cup to his graduate students, and bought farewell lunches for departing research assistants such as myself at the cheapest Italian restaurants, not so much because of his reluctance to part with his cash as because he thought this was the right way to behave. He was the last of the Fabians: the protégé of Sidney and Beatrice Webb, who had spotted his potential and brought him into the world of the Fabian Society, the early Labour Party and the LSE.

On the academic side, at the LSE, Robson had prospered greatly, deservedly so. On the political side he had exerted less influence. He was never one of the Great and the Good.[1] Committees on ministers' powers, on tribunals, and on many other legal and constitutional subjects sat without the benefit of Robson's presence on them. When life peerages were introduced in 1958, he was not to receive one. He was not perhaps a bitter but certainly a resentful man. He was properly proud of his academic achievements but would have welcomed some public acknowledgment of his eminence to add to the honorary degrees from Scandinavia and the translations into Japanese. Shortly after I had left him, a Labour figure told me he had the reputation in party circles of being 'an awkward cuss'. Even so, I learnt more from him in 18 months than I had at Cambridge in four years. I also met Bernard Crick, whom I continued to see from time to time, and John Griffith, who became a lifelong friend.

The question was: what to do next? I raised this with Robson, who said he had some influential friends at the *Economist* Intelligence Unit. He was sure they could fit me in somewhere. Robson was being as helpful as he could. But I did not want to spend the rest of my life as a researcher. In any case, the organisation he had in mind did not seem to be one thing or the other: neither a proper research body nor truly part of the weekly journal. Though I had been called to the Bar in 1957, I still wanted to be a journalist.

I remembered that in the committee room of the Union at Cambridge I had met Charles Wintour, then deputy editor, later editor, of the London *Evening Standard*. He had invited me to approach him if ever I wanted a job. But he wished, reasonably enough, to see what I had written. In the four or five years that had passed since our meeting I had written hardly anything. In these circumstances it might have seemed odd that I wanted to be a journalist at all. But

---

[1] A phrase deriving from the Introduction to Henry Fielding, *Jonathan Wild* (1743).

so it was. Accordingly I cast round for a suitable vehicle for my talents and lighted upon *Socialist Commentary*, a most respectable monthly journal of Labour revisionism edited by the redoubtable Rita Hinden.

As a subject I decided on Contempt of Parliament in relation to the editor of the *Sunday Express* and the Committee of Privileges (as it was then called, before 'Standards' was added to its title). The case had been about the *Express*'s adverse comments on the generous petrol rations for constituency parties in the aftermath of Suez:

> Tomorrow a time of hardship starts for everyone. For everyone? Include the politicians out of that ... The tanks of the politicians will be brimming over ...

Scandalously the editor, John Junor, had been compelled to apologise at the bar of the House. This he had done with some dignity, as I duly wrote in Ms Hinden's journal. Even so, I had intended to show the piece not to him but to Wintour. However, Junor sent for me first.

II

He was then only 40 but seemed quite old – or perhaps merely formidable. He was tall, heavily built and in his shirtsleeves. His shirts were always white or light blue with, usually, a dark blue knitted tie and a dark blue suit. With the variation of a black tie instead of a blue one, this was the uniform adopted by young Max Aitken and by Lord Beaverbrook himself, though the latter sometimes spoiled the effect by wearing brown shoes. Junor's face was unusually red, whether because of his liking for outdoor activities such as golf, sailing and, at this period, tennis or because it was that colour anyway. His drinking habits were always temperate, judged by the liberal standards prevailing in the Fleet Street of the time. Summer was just beginning and he was sweating slightly.

Though formidable, he could not have been more agreeable, maybe because he had been depicted in the *Socialist Commentary* article as Mr Integrity, the Fighting Editor. About my writing he was absurdly flattering, basing his view as he was on only one, admittedly lengthy, article. He said he had been an editor for five years. He had discovered there were people who could write and people who could not write. It was entirely a matter of chance, of luck. Those who could write were in a minority. I was very fortunate because I could do it. Accordingly he would offer me a job as a feature writer on the *Sunday Express* at the National Union of Journalists' then minimum rate of £20 a week. As this was just under double what I was then earning at the LSE, I accepted without hesitation.

I might have preferred the offer to come from the *Daily Herald*, then still in existence, the *Evening Standard* or even *Reynolds News*. The *Observer* and the *Spectator* were outside my contemplation. I had no ambition to work either for the *Daily Mirror* or, perhaps more surprisingly, for the *Manchester Guardian*. Later, in the 1970s, Malcolm Muggeridge was to be surprised that I had never worked for the *Guardian*. He assumed that our paths would have crossed at some stage. I replied that something inside me had told me we should not get on; in much the same way as I have sensed with certain women that, though we are superficially compatible and capable of lively conversation, we are not really meant for each other. I think I was probably right about the *Guardian* at any rate.

When I left the LSE for the *Express*, Robson was disbelieving.

'No one could possibly be called John Junor,' he said. 'It is clearly a pen-name. Pen-names,' he added sapiently, 'are much used in Fleet Street.'

The *Sunday Express* was then approaching the height of its success, selling four million copies. When I met him in New York in 1961, Beaverbrook told me it was 'the strongest paper in the group', which then included the *Daily Express* and the *Evening Standard*.[2]

It was nevertheless a dull paper, made so by deliberate policy on Junor's part. As a feature writer, almost a freelance feature writer even though employed by the *Express* group, I found the only free or loose page was page eight. All the others were mortgaged to some regular columnist or recognised feature article. I also discovered that virtually the only subjects on which Junor was interested in hearing from me were bishops and the royal family.

The royal family was Junor's favourite standby. Indeed, by the standards of those days he allowed himself or his writers to be remarkably outspoken, even impertinent (I am talking about the early 1960s, rather than the year 2000). Thus: Prince Charles

---

[2] For my meetings with Beaverbrook in New York, see pp. 49ff. below.

should not go to Eton, or should do a proper job; Princess Margaret should do more to earn her money; and the Queen was quite excessively rich (this a field which Bernard Harris had made peculiarly his own).

Though Beaverbrook possessed no very favourable views about the Royal Family, he felt, if anything, even more strongly about the bench of bishops. He was a Presbyterian. It was not clear whether he wanted England to adopt his own church in place of the Church of England (Wales already having its own disestablished Anglican church) or wanted no established church of any description. From the evidence, he was not at all clear himself. What was clear was that he disliked bishops, could not stand them at any price.

It seemed to me that attacking the Royal Family slyly, or assaulting the bench of bishops more vigorously, was hardly full-time work, especially as the result of the effort put into it was likely to appear in printed form every six weeks or so. However, relief was at hand in the form of the 'Crossbencher' column. It was certainly the one most quoted by Tory MPs – and most feared by them. This was so despite the column's justified reputation for getting its predictions wrong, exposed in a sketch by Gerald Kaufman on the 'satirical' television show *Not So Much a Programme*.

The occasion was the mysterious illness of Hugh Gaitskell in 1962-3, from which he was to die early in 1963. The column had asserted that Gaitskell would undoubtedly recover. Sir (as he then wasn't) David Frost concluded a recital of 'Crossbencher's' previous incorrect predictions with the words: 'Sorry, Hugh.' The column in question had been written by Wilfred Sendall, who was then coming to the end of that particular writing spell. He was much distressed and felt almost personally responsible for Gaitskell's death. Part of the responsibility was mine. He had asked me, as his junior colleague and the paper's resident expert, so it was thought, on the Labour Party, what Gaitskell's health was like. I replied, not unreasonably on the evidence then available, that he was as strong as a horse. So I felt guilty too, though more on behalf of Sendall than of Gaitskell.

In the week I joined the paper in summer 1959 Sendall was on holiday. I was told by Junor that I would have to write the 'Crossbencher' column for that week. At the same time he said he had forgotten I was coming. It all seemed a bit of a muddle. In Sendall's absence and my non-appearance, the column would presumably have been written by Robert Pitman, then literary editor, later assistant editor.

III

Pitman was a Londoner, very much so, who had been at Worcester College, Oxford, and later taught English at the Sloane School, Chelsea. While still a schoolmaster, he had written for *Tribune*. Following a familiar path of the 1950s, he had journeyed to the *Express* group. Indeed, so wholeheartedly had he gone over to the Beaverbrook side that even Beaverbrook's friend and admirer Michael Foot was no longer prepared to speak to him. Oddly, perhaps, Foot continued to speak to – and have lunch in the Gay Hussar restaurant with – Robert Edwards, who had enjoyed a similar career as editor of the *Daily Express* and later of the *People*.[3] Junor had a wary respect for Pitman on account of his intelligence, his writing ability and, not least, his ability to decode the strange, garbled messages which would issue from Arlington House, Cherkley, the Waldorf Towers, Montego Bay, Cap d'Ail or wherever Lord Beaverbrook happened to be resting his head at any given moment.

'Bob has a genius for seeing what's in the old man's mind,' Junor would say.

This, by the way, was what he usually called Beaverbrook, occasionally varying it to 'the old bugger'. It was never 'principal reader', which was for cables. Still less was it 'the Beaver', which was mainly used by people who did not know him but wished to appear familiar with what the Victorians called 'affairs'.

Other 'executives' were not so fortunate as Pitman in their dealings with Junor. Late one Friday afternoon he was discussing Sunday's possible leaders with me. He interrupted our talk to contact someone on the intercom, then the distinguishing feature of the offices of all Fleet Street figures with any pretensions to authority. It was clear he was speaking to Arthur Brittenden, the foreign editor. The conversation was of course audible.

'Have you read Sam White's column in the *Standard*?' Junor asked.

'Not yet, John, I'm afraid.'

'What time is it, Arthur?'

'I don't follow you, John.'

[3] See Robert Edwards, *Goodbye Fleet Street* (1988), *passim*.

'I asked you what time it was.'

'Half-past five, John.'

'Your watch agrees with mine, I see. And what position do you hold on this paper?'

'I'm not quite with you, John, I'm sorry.'

'I asked you what position you held on the *Sunday Express*, Arthur.'

'I'm foreign editor.'

'The foreign editor of the *Sunday Express*, at half-past five on a Friday afternoon, has not yet read Sam White. May I suggest you read the column to which I refer, which may contain ideas that may interest you or your gifted correspondent in Paris? And when you have read it, would you be so kind as to give me a buzz?'

My predecessor as 'Crossbencher', Wilfred Sendall – though there was a short interregnum by Douglas Clark – made the mistake of working through Thursday night and producing his column at half-past ten or so on Friday morning. He persisted in this error, which allowed Junor to indulge in more bullying.

'This column is piss-poor, Wilfred,' he would say. 'I see no method of salvaging it. You must rewrite it completely, and have sandwiches and Pepsi-Cola for your lunch in the office.'

For some reason he always specified Pepsi-Cola. To such a dedicated luncher-out as Junor this must have seemed a harsh penalty indeed. For he could not only have bullied but, despite his temperate habits, have lunched for England as well. His instructions to journalists about lunch were precise and embodied his own practice with Ministers such as Quintin Hogg and, more surprisingly perhaps, R.A. Butler: always to choose first from the table d'hôte menu, which would almost invariably shame one's guest into doing the same; never to order additional vegetables, certainly not potatoes, which were (it was then universally thought) fattening; above all, to have no truck with vintages and wine waiters but to order the house wine. This could be red or white – there was nothing wrong with white wine – but never on any account rosé.

'Only poofs drink rosé.'

IV

My own practice, as opposed to Sendall's, would be to write the column on Friday morning, finish shortly after one, and have a convivial Fleet Street lunch first at El Vino's, then at Shortlands salt beef bar in Fetter Lane and finally at Mooney's Irish pub (often in the company of Paul Dacre's father, Peter). I would then present the finished product to Junor at about half-past three. He might grumble ('No one's ever heard of Iain Macleod') but time was too far gone for major alterations. Though they could still have been made, they would have been inconvenient for the organisation of Junor's Friday.

Yet he preferred, whenever possible, to flatter his journalists. This did not mean he would go on to print their contributions. He had three categories of assessment: 'good', 'very good' and 'brilliant'. Good articles seldom went into the paper; brilliant ones might even be excluded.

'There is only one word to describe your article,' Junor would say to me regularly. 'Brilliant. You know, if I were going to use it I wouldn't change a single comma. Unfortunately Alan Taylor has just come up with a piece, completely out of the skies, brilliant too, although not so brilliant as yours, but unfortunately we've got to use it because Taylor is under contract to us to produce a certain number of articles a year.'

The last bit, about A.J.P. Taylor's obligation to produce a certain number of articles, was true. The second bit, about Taylor's piece appearing unexpectedly, was entirely false. Taylor never had or wanted to have an idea of his own about *Sunday Express* articles. He was given clear instructions beforehand by Junor (whom he privately described as a 'blockhead').[4]

Junor had various journalistic maxims:

An ounce of emotion is worth a ton of fact.
No one ever destroyed a man by sneering.
Always look forward, never back.
Everybody is interested in sex and money (not wholly true of me, as
    a matter of fact).
When in search of a subject, turn to the royal family.
It is not libellous to ask a question.

The last maxim was much followed in Junor's 'J.J.' column, which he began after I had left the paper. But it was legally perilous, as I was to discover later when I asked some questions in

---

[4] For Taylor's relations with the *Sunday Express*, see Adam Sisman, *A.J.P. Taylor* (1994), 260-2 and *passim*.

the *Sunday Mirror* about Reginald Maudling's corrupt dealings.[5] I did not hear him say: 'Never trust a man with a beard.' This was supposed to be another Junorism. What he said to me was: 'No first-class journalist ever has a beard.' He also said: 'No one ever has sex in the morning.'

V

Unlike some journalists, I did not go out of my way to seek Lord Beaverbrook's company. He certainly did not go out of his way to seek mine. There was little reason why he should. Of my existence he was only vaguely and intermittently aware. Ian Aitken (who was not a relation but knew him better than I did) tells me he went under the impression that my name was Watkinson. Though, as will appear, we met several times, he never called me by this or, indeed, by any other name. Our connection, at the beginning anyway, was indirect. One day in February 1960 Junor called me into his office.

'Have you ever heard of Anthony Praga?' he asked.

I confessed I had not heard of him. Junor explained who he was. In the 1930s, it appeared, Praga had written a series of articles for the *Express* in which the plots of well-known, lengthy but unread novels were summarised.

'Like short stories,' Junor said.

The series had been successful. Beaverbrook, at any rate, had been pleased with it. Some 30 years later he wanted to revive the idea. Junor read to me part of his dictated memorandum. He wished for a start to have summarised, in short-story form, *East Lynne*, *Lorna Doone*, *The Scarlet Letter* and *Three Weeks* by Elinor Glyn. He was particularly keen on Elinor Glyn, perhaps on account of her relationship with Lord Curzon or perhaps for some other reason. However, he foresaw trouble owing to her advanced views.

'Elinor Glyn,' he wrote, 'may present difficulties but we should be able to overcome them with tactful treatment.'

The assignment, I confess, did not greatly appeal to me. The prospect of reading *Lorna Doone* was particularly distasteful. This was a book I had been at pains to avoid. It had been on a school reading list and I had failed to progress beyond the first chapter. To

---

[5] See below, p. 126.

read it now, in Fleet Street, at the request of Lord Beaverbrook, would be to suffer some kind of defeat in life.

'What about Bob Pitman?' I asked.

Pitman was then the literary editor.

'Bob is much too busy with other things,' Junor said, which seemed a comprehensive enough reply. 'You are the only other person on the staff with enough literary ability to do this job.'

The flattering effect of this opinion was slightly spoiled by what came next.

'I may say,' Junor went on, 'that this series will appear in the *Sunday Express* over my dead body, but as the idea comes from Beaverbrook we have to go through the motions at first.'

It was one of Junor's several virtues that he was a by no means obedient follower of his proprietor's often incomprehensible in-structions. After they had been deciphered, usually by Pitman, he would sometimes procrastinate or deliberately misunderstand them. However, he was rarely so frank about his intentions as he was on this occasion. I cannot say I was wholly discouraged by the promise of non-publication. I had no wish to acquire a reputation, however slender, as a compressor of the works of Elinor Glyn.

'He wants the first piece to be on *East Lynne*,' Junor said. 'Just to see how it goes.'

I bought a Collins Classics edition of Mrs Henry Wood's work and, hour after hour, sat reading it at my desk. Occasionally Junor would pass by on his errands of encouragement or reproof to his staff.

'You're a slow reader, I see,' he would say, and laugh as if he had made a joke.

Eventually I produced a piece of about 1,500 words which was dispatched to Beaverbrook.

'He thought it was all right,' Junor said some days later. 'Now he wants you to have a go at Elinor Glyn.'

Happily I never did have a go at Elinor Glyn. I pretended to forget the task, the editor made no more references to the matter and Beaverbrook, as far as I was aware, showed no further interest. Elinor Glyn, like *Lorna Doone*, remains a gap in my reading.

Beaverbrook next impinged on my work when a Labour MP, J.P.W. Mallalieu, appeared to be in trouble with his constituency party over a divorce case in which he was involved (in the end there was, I believe, no trouble). On this general issue, as on a few others

– bishops, the royal family, the powers of the House of Lords, access to Ascot – Beaverbrook's views were broadly radical though not entirely consistent. This time, however, he did not require an 'opinion piece' or a polemic but an historical article about the effects of divorce or similar irregularities on the careers of politicians. Over the dictaphone came a list of suitable cases for inclusion. Inevitably that of Parnell appeared on it. He had been brought down, Beaverbrook stated, because at a meeting of the Irish MPs he had said: 'I am still the master of the party.' To this Tim Healy had supposedly interjected: 'Who is to be the mistress of the party?' Collapse of Parnell; or so I was given to understand.

Perhaps rashly, I decided to verify the story in Healy's own published reminiscences. He was clear that the interruption had not come from him but from some other, un-named Irishman. Nor was the remark in the form of a neat question: rather the phrase 'the mistress of the party' had been heard above the general noise of the meeting. I consulted various other political memoirs of the 19th century. They all told the same story. This was decidedly worrying. I faced the choice either of taking Beaverbrook's perhaps first-hand version – first-hand in the sense that the story might have been told to him by Healy himself – or of preferring the accumulated evidence of others. I chose the latter. Junor was alarmed.

'Do you realise,' he said, 'that Beaverbrook is a great historian?'

I produced Healy's reminiscences together with other works. Junor was slightly mollified but still unconvinced. We compromised on retaining the question 'Who is to be the mistress of the party?', attributing it not to Healy but to an unnamed Irish MP. Beaverbrook accepted this version.

'He says he must have been mistaken about Healy,' Junor said.

VI

Some months afterwards I was sent to New York as the paper's correspondent there. The tour of duty was six months. I did not greatly want to go. The United States political system did not interest me as much as the British did. In any case, I was to be based not in Washington but in New York. And though I had spent much of my first 20 years watching black-and-white films about the darker aspects of life in that city, I had no wish to develop any closer

acquaintance with it. Most of all, we had a boy of 16 months and
Ruth was pregnant with another child. The paper had no objection
to my uprooting my family from Parson's Green Lane, London
S.W.6, where we were then living. But we, not the *Express*, would
have had to pay. So reluctantly I set off on my own.

'Scrub the nicotine off your fingers, don't light up unless he gives
you permission and don't argue with him unless you're very sure of
your facts,' Junor advised me. 'If you make a bad impression on
Beaverbrook it could have a fatal effect on your career. After all, it's
his newspaper.'

One of the curious features of life on the *Express* was that it was
only in New York that an employee was likely to come across
Beaverbrook in the leathery flesh. In London senior journalists had
grown grey in his service without having once set eyes on him. In
New York, on the other hand, the most junior reporter might find
himself suddenly called upon to accompany his proprietor on his
constitutional in Central Park, which was less dangerous then than
it was later to become. Indeed, on one of these expeditions a
predecessor of mine, Arthur Brittenden, had succeeded in losing his
– and Beaverbrook's – way. For hours, so the story went, the two of
them had wandered forlornly about, lost. Subsequently an instruction had gone out to the effect that every member of the New York
office must acquaint himself with the geography of Central Park.
The conversation on these tours consisted chiefly of questions from
Beaverbrook about the value of skyscrapers or other buildings
which caught his eye.

'How much would ya say that was worth?' he would ask.

As his companion was usually ignorant of and uninterested in
New York property values, the only possible response was a desper-
ate guess. Oddly, these made-up answers would not anger or even
amuse Beaverbrook but make him appear worried, particularly if
the sums were on the high side.

'Ten million dollars? Ya really think so? Now why d'ya say that?'

'Well, it's in a good position.'

'It's in a good position. But ten million dollars. Ya can't be right.'

Every day he would telephone the office, generally between seven
and eight in the evening. Perhaps he did this to satisfy himself that
the staff had not all departed; on the whole, however, I do not think
this was the reason.

'What's the news?' he would inquire in jaunty and hopeful tones.

Alas, as most members of the New York office spent their time rewriting agency copy or reproducing stories from American newspapers, transmitting the results to London at great expense, there rarely was any news.

'Oh I see,' Beaverbrook would say, disappointed, and replace the receiver.

David English of the *Sunday Dispatch* was more original and enterprising in his approach. My colleagues in the *Express* office warned me against him. In those more spacious days Lord Beaverbrook maintained half-a-dozen journalists in New York alone to keep his readers informed or, more often, entertained about events on the continent. So advice was plentiful. It was also unanimous. English, I was told, was a sharp fellow, very sharp. He would readily pull a fast one and might even, if he thought it necessary, practise deception. I had better keep an eye on English.

Sharp he turned out to be, but in the most engaging way. He looked a decade younger than his 29 years and had about him something of the Artful Dodger. He also had an extensive collection of stories about Old Fleet Street, for before joining the *Dispatch* he had already effectively edited the *Daily Sketch*. He became one of my three closest friends in the city, the others being Peter Hopkirk of the *Express* and Judith Atkins, a former girlfriend of Hopkirk's who was 18 years old and seeing herself through Columbia University by working as a guide to the Rockefeller Center, where the *Express*, the *Dispatch* and the *Mail* all had offices.

English was married, living in the salubrious suburb of Scarsdale. I was a temporary bachelor, living on the upper East Side of Manhattan. We still managed to see a good deal of each other. We would meet at lunch or, after work, in various Third Avenue bars all called P.J. O'Something. Not once did he do anything mean or underhand. Indeed, on one occasion he went out of his way to accommodate me.

Quite early one Saturday morning we both went into our respective offices to find excited cables awaiting us from London. There were brief reports in the English papers that a man had returned to New York from the Peruvian Andes accompanied by a giant earthworm. This bizarre creature was, it appeared, some six feet long and almost a foot in diameter. It reposed in an earth-filled box, perhaps several boxes, in the explorer's apartment. Could we visit it; interview him; above all, secure pictures of the giant Peruvian earthworm? No expense, we were given to understand, need be spared in the enterprise.

English was exhilarated at the prospect. I was not so much apprehensive as horrified. I explained to him that even a grass snake terrified me. The spectacle of a giant earthworm might well tip me over the edge of sanity. He listened with sympathy. Then he became practical. Clearly we must each send cables to our London offices saying that the explorer was denying access to his earthworm. It was of a sensitive nature, specially where journalists and photographers were concerned. We would then perform our customary Saturday-morning tasks and afterwards depart for a lengthy lunch. This we proceeded to do. In the way of newspapers, the giant Peruvian earthworm was quickly forgotten by Fleet Street.

In the summer the *Dispatch* was absorbed by the *Sunday Express*. I worried that the *Express* would replace me with English. This was irrational because I was by then at the end of my term anyway. English said I had nothing to worry about – adding that he found himself in the position of the condemned man offering consolation to the priest. It all ended happily. I returned to London as had been planned. He remained in the United States not to work for the *Sunday Express* but for the *Daily Express* in Washington, smoothly continuing the career that was to end in triumph at Associated Newspapers.

Meanwhile Beaverbrook had been making his presence manifest. In the corner of the office was a cupboard containing stationery. It also contained a supply – about a dozen tins – of Campbell's tomato soup. I asked a secretary why they were there.

'That soup belongs to Lord Beaverbrook,' she said. 'It's the only kind of soup he likes, and one day he couldn't get any, so we have to keep a supply. You leave it alone.'

From time to time the secretary or one of her colleagues would take a foolscap envelope from the cupboard and then maltreat it, screwing it up, scoring it with pencil or even skating on it across the floor. The envelope, it turned out, was to contain copy to be sent to Beaverbrook at the Waldorf Towers. He considered it wasteful not to re-use envelopes. The secretaries reasonably thought it irksome and uneconomic of both effort and storage space to hoard used envelopes. They therefore processed new ones to look like old. Everyone was satisfied.

Eventually a summons to lunch arrived. It was communicated by Raymond, the butler, a red-haired man of uncertain age with protruding eyes, a surprisingly strong handshake and a camp conversational style.

'Oh, the old bugger. He's in such a *temper* these days. I pity you all, I really do. Some of the things, you wouldn't believe.'

On the appointed Sunday, Hopkirk and I presented ourselves at Beaverbrook's suite in the Waldorf Towers. Ian Aitken was already there, arrived from Washington, where he was then the *Express*'s correspondent. Beaverbrook questioned Hopkirk and me about the stories we had lately sent. He appeared satisfied though unenthusiastic. There followed a waddya-think-of session. Though the subject matter of these conversational exchanges might vary, the form was unchanging. First Beaverbrook would ask:

'Waddya think of ...?' – it might be J.F. Kennedy, Nikita Khrushchev or Harold Macmillan.

Whatever the answer might be, he would go on to ask:

'Now why d'ya say that?'

Whether the reply to this question was satisfactory or not, he would conclude with:

'Oh I see.'

A Washington correspondent, one 'Lobby' Ludlow, once got drunk and announced:

'We're going to play the game differently this evening, Lord Beaverbrook. We're going to ask *you* the questions.'

He was afterwards dismissed.

'He is a bad man,' Beaverbrook was reliably reported to have remarked. 'If he spoke to me in that manner, what would he say if he met the President?'

On this occasion there was no encouragement to behave in such a dangerous fashion. At any rate there was no opportunity to get drunk, because no drink was provided. Nor did matters improve at lunch itself. We ate boiled chicken, equally plainly boiled rice, and a mixture of frozen carrots and peas. We drank water. However, the only woman present, Lady Dunn (widow of the Canadian financier Sir James Dunn and later Lady Beaverbrook) consumed steak and a large baked potato. For most of the time Beaverbrook talked about Bonar Law and Lloyd George, whom he called 'George', pronounced 'Jarge'. He summoned Raymond to cool his coffee, which he did by pouring it repeatedly from one cup to another until the required temperature was achieved.

Afterwards, in the sitting room, we were talking in a desultory fashion when a large man appeared in the doorway and advanced towards Beaverbrook with hand outstretched.

'Lord Beaverbrook ...' he said.

'Go away,' Beaverbrook said. 'I can't see ya today. I am much too busy to make any arrangements now. Ya must make an appointment. There are no vacancies on my newspapers.'

He spoke these words gently, almost timorously. Then he raised his voice and shouted:

'Raymond, that man is here again.'

To Ian Aitken he whispered in tones of appeal:

'Ian, get rid of him. Tell him to go away.'

Aitken was fully equal to the situation. He rose and took the man by the arm, leading him gently into the tiny entrance hall of the suite. When he returned, having handed the intruder over to the charge of Raymond, Beaverbrook said:

'He is an Australian. He has been pestering me for a job. I have told him that no jobs are available but he will not listen.'

'He must be a good reporter,' Aitken said, 'to get in here at all, past all those people.'

'Takes more than cheek,' Beaverbrook said, 'to make a good reporter.'

Some weeks afterwards I was working late in the office one Saturday when a telephone call came from Beaverbrook's granddaughter, Lady Jean Campbell, in Montego Bay. She asked me to listen carefully to her instructions. Lord Beaverbrook wished to have dispatched to him quantities of honey, coffee and cider vinegar, all of specified brands with which I was unfamiliar. In fact I did not have the slightest idea of where to obtain these groceries at eight o'clock on a Saturday in the middle of New York. I went to several delicatessens and did the best I could.

However, I rebelled against packing a parcel: partly as a gesture of protest, partly because I have an intense dislike of and am highly incompetent at packing parcels. Instead I left the assortment of groceries on the desk of the then chief of the *Daily Express* bureau, Henry Lowrie, together with a note saying they were to be sent to Lord Beaverbrook clearly marked 'unsolicited gift', a point on which Lady Jean had placed great emphasis. The goods were duly sent off but they were the wrong goods. I had made a mess of things, obtaining 'White Rose' instead of 'Red Rose' coffee – or it may have been the other way about – and making various other more or less fundamental mistakes in regard to the honey and the cider vinegar. Beaverbrook blamed Henry Lowrie.

'The New York office,' he wrote in a letter of reproof, 'is going to rack and ruin.'

VII

I returned to London in 1961. The year before, Beaverbrook had published *Men and Power*. Robert Pitman was asked to review it. In his copy he compared Beaverbrook favourably to Gibbon and Macaulay, maybe Tacitus and Herodotus as well. This was sent to Beaverbrook for his approval. Beaverbrook may have cut out a reference to Tacitus here and Herodotus there as falling into the error of excessive praise. Otherwise he bestowed his blessing on the product of Pitman's labours.

That week Junor was on holiday. Editing the paper was his deputy, Victor Patrick, a large, affable Scotsman, the best cricketer on the paper – apart, of course, from Denis Compton. Having received Beaverbrook's approval for the review of his book by Pitman, Patrick concluded, not unreasonably, that one of his problems at least was solved. The leader-page article, the main article in the paper, would be Pitman's review. There was no need to commission anyone else, or to follow Junor's practice and order not only an article which he would almost certainly print (usually by A.J.P. Taylor) but also one or even two articles to be held in reserve.

Shortly before one on the Saturday, Beaverbrook telephoned Patrick, as he did Junor, to find out what was going into the paper. What, he asked, was going to be on the leader page? Why, Patrick replied, there was no question: Bob Pitman's review of Lord Beaverbrook's book, of course. There was, according to the acting editor, a long silence. Beaverbrook then said he did not like that idea, did not like it at all. The leader page, he went on, was the Sunday pulpit. It was there for the purpose of propaganda (for Beaverbrook did not distinguish between preaching and propaganda). His book on the First World War was not propaganda. It was, on the contrary, a work of history. Accordingly it should be dealt with on the literary page (in those days page six).

So that was that. At one o'clock on Saturday, the acting editor had to find a new leader-page article. Patrick set to work Brian Gardner, Llew Gardner, Bernard Harris and myself to produce, in an hour and a half, 1,000-odd words on subjects of our own choice.

The competition was won by Brian Gardner, with an article entitled 'Is This the End for Hammersjkold?', a reference to the then Secretary-General of the United Nations. The *Sunday Express* of the 1960s anticipated the *Daily Mail* of the 1990s in its affection for the interrogative headline. As an American journalist once observed: 'Not only do your papers not give you the answers. They keep asking you the questions all the time.' Anyway, Gardner's hurriedly composed article proved prophetic, for Dag Hammersjkold was to be killed in an air crash shortly afterwards.

One might have expected Beaverbrook to take a close interest in the 'Crossbencher' column. In his later years, at any rate, he rarely intervened. So I was puzzled to receive, via Junor, a dictated memorandum in the following terms:

> There is a man in the West Country called Bessemer or something like that I believe he is a Liberal I have a good opinion of him I commend him to your attention you might mention him in your political notes.

He usually referred to the 'Crossbencher' column as 'your political notes'. His memoranda were rarely punctuated, as those responsible for taking them down were frightened of putting the full stops and commas in the wrong places, thereby altering the meaning, if any.

An examination of the list of Liberal candidates produced the name of Peter Bessell, who was standing for Bodmin. A colleague said he thought Bessell was in the habit of writing to Beaverbrook about the Common Market, as it was called, and other matters. Further inquiries showed this to be so. Indeed, if anything exceeded Lord Beaverbrook's high opinion of Mr Bessell, it was Mr Bessell's high opinion of Lord Beaverbrook. Unhappily I could think of nothing sufficiently flattering or interesting to say about him. Besides, I did not see why the column should, for no very good reason apart from Beaverbrook's memorandum – in which he did not even get the man's name right – devote space to an obscure

Liberal. Junor, to his credit, agreed with me initially. We decided that for the moment we should ignore Peter Bessell.

About six weeks later, Junor sent for me. He had a concerned expression. He read out part of one of those dictated messages:

> Some time ago [it went] I offered you a piece of advice about your political notes I see that you have not taken this advice perhaps you could give me the reason.

'Look,' Junor said, 'no one's asking you to attack anybody. You're being asked to praise. There's no question of principle remotely involved. Just write a short paragraph saying something nice about this chap. It would make all our lives a lot easier.'

And so I wrote the paragraph. I said that Bessell had inaugurated the Liberal revival at Torquay in 1955 – which was, as it happened, true – and that he would win Bodmin for the Liberals at the 1964 general election. This also turned out to be true. It must have been one of the few correct predictions I made. Subsequently Bessell led an adventurous life as Liberal MP, emigrant to the United States, financial criminal and discredited witness at the trial of Jeremy Thorpe.

Junor fell out with Beaverbrook over support for Harold Macmillan in 1963. He was not inclined to give Macmillan the uncritical support which Beaverbrook wanted. One of his reasons was that he held Macmillan responsible for the jailing of two journalists for refusing to answer questions at the Vassall inquiry. He resigned, and was replaced for a short time by Derek Marks. Subsequently Arthur Brittenden was the heir apparent. But the resignation of Macmillan and his succession by Lord Home allowed Junor eventually to make his peace.

These excitements at the *Sunday Express* office produced a spell of interventionism by Beaverbrook in the affairs of 'Crossbencher' and of his papers generally.

'I haven't enjoyed myself so much in years,' he said.

One Friday afternoon his new secretary, Colin Vines – a put-upon individual who wrote a minor classic of humour, *A Little Nut-Brown Man*, about his master – asked me to send the 'Cross-bencher' copy to Arlington House. I was to follow later.

'Tired old notes,' Beaverbrook said when I arrived. 'Ya political notes were tired,' he added as if to leave no room for misunderstanding on the point.

I did not dissent.

'Tired old stuff on Home and Wilson. Home is not worth bothering with. He has not made good. He is a failure.'

Again I did not quarrel with this judgment.

'What I suggest to you,' Beaverbrook went on, 'is a note on the financial position of the Liberal Party. That will be something fresh. Have ya got a pencil?'

I said I had a pencil.

'Take down these notes. Have ya heard of Lord Sherwood?'

Lord Sherwood, I subsequently discovered when working on a book about the Liberals, had been an obscure benefactor of the party.[6] At this earlier time, however, his name was unfamiliar to me. I admitted as much to Beaverbrook.

'Ya never heard of Hugh Sherwood?'

The gap in my knowledge seemed to present him with endless possibilities for wonder and amusement.

'Ya call yourself a political writer and ya never heard of Hugh Sherwood? Well, ya better learn about Hugh Sherwood, that is my advice if ya wish to be a political writer.'

Beaverbrook dictated some material of chiefly historical interest on the Liberal Party's funds, or lack of them. He then asked how I passed my working day. In the course of my reply I said – not entirely truthfully, I must confess – that I spent a good deal of time making assiduous inquiries on the telephone. This, it soon became evident, was the wrong thing to say.

'Vines,' he suddenly yelled. 'Drat that Vines, where is he?'

Colin Vines appeared.

'Vines, I wish to send an urgent message to the staffs of my newspapers about the use of the telephone.'

Vines stood at the ready.

'Mr Brittenden,' the message went (for during this period of activity by Beaverbrook Arthur Brittenden was editing the paper), 'a member of your staff tells me that he spends a good deal of his time on the telephone have nothing to do with the telephone that is my advice rip out the cord and throw it away two feet after the subject of your inquiry that is the way to beat the agencies and get exclusive news.'[7]

Beaverbrook was quite right, as he was about so many other

---

[6] Alan Watkins, *The Liberal Dilemma* (1966), 44.
[7] Cf. C.M. Vines, *A Little Nut-Brown Man* (1968), 239.

journalistic matters. But the use of the telephone in the *Express* building did not noticeably decline as a result of this message. And modern newspapers are constructed virtually entirely from telephone conversations and flickering screens.

VIII

A more regular and more useful source was the Leader of the Opposition, Harold Wilson. In 1963-4 I would go off on Friday afternoons to see him in his room in the House of Commons. I was not alone. James Margach of the *Sunday Times*, Ian Waller of the *Sunday Telegraph* or, sometimes, Victor Knight of the *Sunday Mirror* would be leaving his room as I was waiting, or waiting as I was leaving. In perpetual attendance in the outside room were Marcia Williams, later Lady Falkender, and her colleague Brenda Dew, both of them typing at a clattering pace, for these were the days before word-processors.

At this point on the Friday I would have switched hats, from political columnist (as 'Crossbencher') to political correspondent, the post now called 'political editor'. Wilson was more interesting on general themes than on what he was going to say or do next week. He often told me that the Conservative politician he feared most was Iain Macleod, with R.A. Butler as runner-up. He would have preferred Harold Macmillan to stay. But when he was succeeded by Sir Alec Douglas-Home (as he had become) rather than by Butler or Macleod – who, as matters turned out, did not reach the starting-gate – Wilson's joy was great. In the election of 1964 Home proved a more difficult opponent than he had been in the House, and Labour won by only four seats.

Wilson was always interested in what I had written in 'Crossbencher'. One week in 1963, before the resignation of Macmillan, I had kicked off (in the argot of the trade, 'led') with the already evident troubles at the top of the Tory Party. Wilson asked me whether I had read the reports claiming that Butler was marooned at his holiday home on the Isle of Mull owing to stormy weather. That was clearly made up, Wilson said. From his observation post in London S.W.1, he knew that the weather off the West Coast of Scotland was not specially bad. In any case, his boatman in the Isles of Scilly (where Wilson had *his* holiday home) would be able to negotiate the seas without any difficulty. No: Butler, who then bore the curious title of First Secretary of State and Minister in charge of the Central African Office, was obviously having a great row with Duncan Sandys, the Commonwealth Secretary, about the Central African Federation. Rab was sulking on his island, refusing to meet his colleagues. This idea struck me as a good one. I returned to the office, modified the column accordingly and turned out to be right – or, rather, Wilson did.[8]

Beaverbrook's last instructions to me concerned Anthony Nutting. I never discovered what Nutting's crime had been. Certainly his behaviour at the time of Suez (the official house-reason) did not seem fully to explain the ferocity with which he was pursued. Anyway, Beaverbrook discovered that Nutting was the Conservative candidate for Oldham.[9] This was well-known – had been known for many months – but it came as news to Beaverbrook. He therefore demanded a paragraph attacking Nutting. I refused to write it not only because the information was scarcely fresh but also because the attack was supposed to mention some divorce proceedings in which Nutting had been involved. There the matter uneasily rested.

Then Beaverbrook died. *Cadit quaestio*: or so one might have thought. But no. In the same week – a few days after 9 June 1964 – Junor called me into his office and suggested that 'as a last tribute to Beaverbrook' I should carry out his final known instruction and attack Anthony Nutting. In the circumstances this seemed to me unnecessary and irrational, not to say bizarre. I said as much; perhaps more. However, the attack duly appeared, written by Douglas Clark, who would do anything Junor instructed him to do. Later in that year I moved to the *Spectator*.

---

[8] See Peter Oborne, *Alastair Campbell* (1999), 115-16; Anthony Howard, *RAB* (1987, pb edn 1988), ch. 14. For criticism of journalists for becoming too close to Wilson, see Anthony Howard, 'Dealing with Mr Murdoch', in Stephen Glover (ed.), *Secrets of the Press* (1999), 260 at 267.

[9] He lost to Charles Mapp, Labour, by 3,931 votes.

4

The Weekly World

For anyone who aspires to a thorough understanding of the City of
London and of Westminster, there is no better training than a
regular job on a 'weekly'.

> R.H.S. Crossman, Introduction to Walter Bagehot,
> *The English Constitution*, 1963

I

In October 1964 I fulfilled the first of my ambitions and succeeded
Henry Fairlie as political columnist of the *Spectator*.

Today we are spoiled for choice in political columns. Indeed, it is
difficult to avoid the things. Every self-respecting paper has at least
one, sometimes more. It was not always so. Fifty years ago the
genre hardly existed. In the *Sunday Times*, James Margach wrote
a well-informed though laboured column under the name 'A
Student of Politics' (of whom Bernard Levin once remarked:
'About time that lad took his finals.'). In the *Observer*, Hugh
Massingham wrote a livelier column as 'Our Political Correspondent'. In 1954 the new proprietor of the *Spectator*, Ian Gilmour,
inaugurated a political column. In December 1954 it was written
by a contributor called 'Trimmer' who in February 1955 revealed
himself as Henry Fairlie. He continued until June 1956, when he
moved to the *Daily Mail*. He died in Washington on 25 February
1990 at 66.

The diarist of the *Financial Times*, in the sole depreciatory
reference to him after his death, called Fairlie 'a great dilettante',
which led me to think that the diarist concerned was either not
much at home with political journalism or ignorant of the meaning
of the word. Fairlie was a charmer, an adulterer, a drinker, often a
beggar man, even (it must be said) on occasion a thief: but a
dilettante he was not. To say that he was a journalist's journalist is

perhaps to imply that he never made an impact on a wider public. This was not so. His genius, in the 18th-century sense – and there was a good deal of the 18th century about Fairlie – was early recognised and rewarded. What he always enjoyed was the professional admiration of his peers. He was regarded in much the same way as Walter Hammond by English batsmen of the 1930s and 1940s – though personally he was a more engaging character than Hammond ever seems to have been.

Fairlie shared Massingham's wit and his psychological insight into politicians. But Massingham looked at them as the novelist he also was; whereas Fairlie saw them more as players in a great historical drama. Between them, they changed political journalism in this country. If Massingham in the *Observer* was the pioneer, it was Fairlie in the *Spectator* who carried the change through, writing at greater length and under his own name. In retrospect, what is astonishing is the short time he took to impose the change. Here he is on Harold Macmillan, a politician who always gave him a good deal of enjoyment and to whom he became close (perhaps too close) in the early 1960s. He is describing Macmillan at a Conservative garden party in the 1950s:

> For the next 20 minutes it is sheer delight. Here – and what other politician has it today? – is style: the style of the man who accepts his position in the world without question. And when the speech is over, and he has wandered round the stalls and tea tables, where does he go when he leaves? Ah! if only it could be the Gaiety; if only Lillie Langtry or Ruby Miller were on again; if only it could be Romano's or the Star and Garter at Richmond. But no, it is 1955.[1]

He enjoyed Aneurin Bevan as well, but was clear about the real reason for his resignation from the Labour government. Later research has shown that Fairlie's surmises were correct:

> For Mr Bevan, though he ostensibly resigned in protest against the health charges imposed by Mr Gaitskell, had in fact responded to a quite different kind of provocation. The removal of Bevin and Cripps had been followed by the promotion of Mr Gaitskell to the post of Chancellor of the Exchequer. For the first time, Mr Bevan had been

---

[1] Henry Fairlie, 'Peeling Edwardian' in Ian Gilmour and Iain Hamilton (eds), *Spectrum: a Spectator Miscellany* (1956), 48 at 49.

superseded by a representative of a generation of Labour leaders younger than himself. His successor to the leadership of the party ... was now threatened by that most dangerous kind of political rival, a man who had time on his side.[2]

Fairlie was most famous for inventing or anyway popularising – for A.J.P. Taylor also claimed paternity – 'the Establishment'. It often happens that writers are remembered only for one phrase which they themselves did not take with great seriousness at the time. Fairlie deserves to be remembered for more: not only as an innovator but also as the author of *The Life of Politics* (1968), which attacks the then and now even more fashionable view that MPs count for little.

He had numerous affairs, notably one with Kingsley Amis's wife Hilly, and remained on good terms with most of the women he had known. One of his former girlfriends used to say that Henry was a very good lover if you managed to get hold of him in the morning. He liked to boast that, in time of need, there would always be what he called 'a hot cooked supper' awaiting him somewhere in North London. His male friends included George Gale, Philip Hope-Wallace, Anthony Howard, Paul Johnson, Derek Marks, Malcolm Muggeridge, John Raymond and Peregrine Worsthorne. Muggeridge and Gale both deserve commendation for actions beyond the call of friendly duty. Gale often looked after one or more of Fairlie's children. Fairlie was once arrested by a tipstaff after appearing on an *Any Questions?* programme and taken to Brixton prison. His wife Lisette said: 'At least I know where Henry is.' It was just before Christmas. He was then living in Lewes, with Malcolm Muggeridge as a neighbour in Robertsbridge, near Battle. Muggeridge bought a turkey and a Christmas pudding for the family and presents for the children. His wife Kitty was one of the few people who were resistant to Fairlie's charm. It came mainly from his wide smile, which would illuminate his whole square, ruddy, high-cheekboned face. Philip Hope-Wallace described it as 'Henry's delinquent ploughboy grin'.

In 1965 he fled to Washington; typically, he was soon in trouble for lacking the necessary work permit. Several reasons were advanced for his departure. One was that Lady Antonia Fraser (later

[2] Fairlie, 'Anatomy of Bevanism', ibid., 225, 227.

Pinter) was suing him for defamation in respect of something he had said about her on the television programme *Three After Six*. But Lady Antonia had no intention of pursuing Fairlie personally. This would have been a profitless undertaking in any event. Another reason given was that he was being pursued by the implacable Inland Revenue. This was more plausible. Certainly he was always in financial trouble and failed to turn up for his first examination in bankruptcy, when the registrar said that the 'usual consequences' would follow. News of his doings in Washington – where he never attained the magisterial status he had achieved in England – was brought to me by friends such as Anthony Howard and Geoffrey Wheatcroft. Another friend, Stephen Glover, wrote:

> Fairlie was unusual [as a columnist] in being practically forgotten in his own lifetime ... He drank too much. I met him once around the mid-1980s in the offices of the *New Republic* magazine in Washington, where towards his end this impoverished, tramp-like figure sometimes slept the night.[3]

At around this time I received a circular letter from one of his American friends, an academic, soliciting a contribution from Fairlie's old friends in England towards a heart operation. He had always had trouble with his heart, which was to be the cause of his death. I duly sent off the sum requested. A woman friend rebuked me for so doing. Why should I, she asked, who had worked conscientiously and saved prudently (that was what she said), disburse my hard-earned cash to a man who was, by my own account, completely feckless in his ways? He was my first hero, I replied.

II

In spring 1964 I was having a drink in the House of Commons press gallery bar with David Watt, the then political correspondent of the *Spectator*.[4] This was an unusual occurrence, for Watt was not a

---

[3] Stephen Glover, 'What Columnists Are Good For' in Stephen Glover (ed.), *Secrets of the Press* (1999), 289 at 296. See also Anthony Howard, 'Henry Fairlie' in *DNB 1986-90*, 130-1.

[4] The political correspondent of the weeklies wrote the political column. That was his chief function, indeed, virtually his only function. He was, however, expected to help in other ways from time to time: chiefly by writing the odd note at the beginning of the paper, in the days when the weeklies ran the 'Notes of the Week' feature, and also by obtaining government or parliamentary documents which might then be read as the foundation of a leader or of a comment by somebody else.

great one for bars or, come to that, for the House of Commons. He had been writing the political column with some skill since 1962, having succeeded Bernard Levin ('Taper'), who had himself succeeded Fairlie. There had been a few temporary columnists, including David Marquand, but the true succession was as I have described it.

Watt was both pro-American and pro-European, views he shared with Peter Jenkins, though not with me. He told me he would shortly be off to Washington as correspondent of the *Financial Times*. I asked whether any replacement had been nominated for the *Spectator* column. He said no, not as far as he knew, and he went on to encourage me to apply for his job. This was kind of him, because we never really warmed to each other. Though he enjoyed an adventurous sex life, there was a prim and disapproving aspect to him. If he happened to be at a bar – as I have said, a rareish event – he was not at all agile in buying his round.

He had first made his name by writing an article in the *Spectator* about his experiences in an iron lung, for he was one of the polio victims of the 1950s.[5] Previously he had been a good games player. He died in 1987, after trying to pick up an electric cable outside his Oxfordshire cottage, which had come down in the great storm of that year. In the August before his death he sent me his Surrey County Club membership card, saying he would be out of the country in that month and I might like to use his card, as I duly did. This was against the county's rules, and showed that Watt was more generous and less priggish than I had taken him to be. Ferdinand Mount always found him engaging as a golf partner.[6]

He had never got on well with the *Spectator*'s then editor, Iain Macleod, who with Enoch Powell refused to serve in Sir Alec Douglas-Home's government in 1963. Indeed, their refusal had produced one of the few scoops of my career, in the *Sunday Express* of 20 October 1963. Ian Gilmour, the new proprietor of the *Spectator*, offered the editorship to Macleod in place of the incumbent, Iain Hamilton. The news leaked to the *Evening Standard* before Hamilton could be told. The row immediately became confused. Had Hamilton been treated discourteously by Gilmour? Whether he had or not, did he deserve the sack? And, even if he did, should he be

[5] David Watt, 'Last Gasp' in Gilmour and Hamilton (eds), op. cit. 28.
[6] Ferdinand Mount, Introduction to Mount (ed.), *The Inquiring Eye; a Selection of the Writing of David Watt* (1988).

replaced by a practising Tory politician (Macleod showed no signs of wanting to give up his seat in Parliament)?[7] Watt did not leave the paper as some others did. But his relations with Macleod in 1963-4 were prickly. He was determined to prevent the new editor from interfering with his column and consequently saw interference where nothing of the kind had been intended.

III

For myself, I had no doubts about working for Macleod. I had met him at a Cambridge Union debate in 1955 and we had enjoyed several agreeable lunches at L'Epicure in Frith Street (sadly no longer with us) in 1963-4. Accordingly I wrote to him, he replied favourably and, after one friendly meeting, he suggested lunch at White's Club to complete the arrangement. White's was always important to Macleod. It fortified his romantic Toryism, performing much the same function in his life as his occasional weekend visits to Randolph Churchill at East Bergholt in Suffolk, which were sometimes prolonged to the Monday or Tuesday. When I arrived at the club at one he had a large dry martini (his favourite drink) in his hand and was seated before a television set which, surprisingly I thought, was situated on the ground floor, virtually in the bar itself. England was playing Australia. Bobby Simpson and Bill Lawry were opening the Australian batting. Macleod bought me a drink and said somewhat peremptorily:

'I forbid any further conversation until 1.30.'

After that he was gruff but friendly enough.

'How soon can you start with us?' he said, almost in a rasp, as if trying to give an imitation of Lord Beaverbrook or, at least, of a tough editor of few words, at any rate spoken ones.

I explained that I had a three-month contract with the *Sunday Express* and could, if necessary, give in my notice that afternoon.

'You do that at once,' Macleod said decisively.

When I did, John Junor was discouraging. Macleod, he said, was a failed politician. The *Spectator* was a failing magazine. No good would come of my going there. This disapproving response was not surprising. All editors are irritated and some angry when a contributor departs for another publication. Junor exhibited this pos-

[7] See Simon Courtauld, *To Convey Intelligence: the Spectator 1928-98* (1999), ch. 4.

sessive characteristic more markedly than most, even though the *Sunday Express* and the *Spectator* were in no respects rivals.

I was more surprised by my father's response. I told him when Ruth and I and our, by then, three children were in Tycroes for our annual two-week summer visit to my parents. He was angrier than Junor had been. Indeed, I had not seen him so cross since my childhood. Though a Welsh Radical – neither a Liberal nor a Socialist – he nevertheless saw Beaverbrook and Express Newspapers as the embodiment of wealth, stability and, above all, security. The *Spectator* was, by contrast, a tinpot little literary magazine which could fold tomorrow, leaving me and my young family without visible means of support. He was thinking of me; whereas Junor had been thinking of the blow to his pride as an editor. I realised this at the time. It did not prevent me from shouting back at him. Understandably he – who valued financial security above all other goods – thought my wife would support him. This she refused to do. In this aspect of life, Ruth told him, I knew more or less what I was doing. She was fully behind the move to the *Spectator*.

An editor's relationship with his or her political columnist (though these days some papers have several such columnists) is almost always delicate. Admittedly it varies a good deal. The factors that can affect it include the nature of the paper; the existence (or not, as the case may be) of an overtly 'political' proprietor such as Beaverbrook; the character of the editor and his or her interest in politics; the character of the columnist; not least, the type of column he or she has been engaged to write. Columnists who write under their own names are rarely instructed to take a given 'line'. Editors are prone not so much to issue instructions as to steer writers away from subjects on which certain of their views are considered dangerous or tend to be repetitious.

The columnist Neal Ascherson, for example, wrote frequently and learnedly on Poland, on Scotland and on nationalism generally. His successive editors at the *Independent on Sunday*, Ian Jack and Peter Wilby, called him 'the supermarket trolley', because whichever way you pushed him he always ended up moving in the same direction. Or suppose that a columnist and his paper are in conflict over the single currency and that he wishes to write a column on the subject. Don't you think (he may be told) that we've heard quite enough about boring old Europe for the time being? After all, we had a leader on it only the other day – last week, wasn't it? Couldn't you do us a light piece on Peter Mandelson instead?

Discussions of this kind never took place with Iain Macleod, in part because whenever possible he avoided discussions on the reasonable ground that they wasted time. When he came to the *Spectator* he abolished the editorial conference. Instead every member of the staff could come and see him whenever he or she chose. There was no need to knock. The editor's room would be open to everyone at all times. This was not perhaps such a valuable concession as it may have appeared at first sight, for Macleod's hours of work were from 10 or 10.30, when he arrived in a chauffeur-driven Daimler provided by the finance company of which he was a director, till one, when he departed for lunch.

These hours suited my own habits well enough but were less convenient for those other members of the staff who spent the whole day at the office. Nonetheless I wished to see him regularly – weekly, at least. He was, after all, the editor; knew a great deal about politics; and could tell me of any other articles in the week's issue whose subject matter might overlap with my own. In reality the last reason was not very important, for the deputy editor, John Thompson (who was later to become editor of the *Sunday Telegraph*) was as well if not better apprised of the contents of the paper than Macleod himself. But the other reasons for seeing him remained valid. He was never less than totally courteous.

'Come in, come in,' he would say.

'I was thinking of having a go this week at ...'

'Go right ahead and do it,' Macleod would reply, often before I had told him what I proposed to do.

This admirably illustrated his quickness of mind and his vaunted speed of decision. Usually he was right about my projected topic; sometimes not. He never turned down an idea flat; and he was always reluctant to embark on what might turn out to be a lengthy discussion. At the beginning of our connection I made the mistake of trying to engage him in such talk during office hours.

'Ha, good to see you,' he would say with apparent enthusiasm. 'What can I do for you?'

'I was just wondering whether we could have a talk.'

At this the editor's expression would become troubled. The eyes would begin to flicker and dart and he would move his head from side to side for, owing to his crippling arthritis combined with the effects of a war wound, he moved the upper half of his body as little as possible, which partly accounted for his power as a speaker. A talk could comprise so many things – resignation, family troubles, offers from other papers, difficulties of various kinds. Who could say where such a discussion might end?

'About what, exactly?'

'The state of politics, I suppose.'

My delimitation along these lines would do little to cheer up Macleod. Politics, he seemed to say, was the last subject he wished to discuss with his political columnist.

'What aspect of politics?'

'Well, you know, your party, and how Alec's doing, and ...'

'Ha, Alec. Alec is a difficult case.'

Sometimes Macleod would add a few words about the difficulty of the case of Sir Alec Douglas-Home, the then Conservative leader in opposition; more often he would not; and we would part with mutual expressions of goodwill which would be renewed when we passed each other on the stairs or in the corridors of 99 Gower Street, where the *Spectator* had its offices before moving to 56 Doughty Street in the same Bloomsburyish part of London.

'Carry on the good work,' he would say, or sometimes, with a vagueness that would have done credit to William Whitelaw:

'Splendid, splendid. Nice to see you.'

Macleod, however, was sometimes uneasy about what I wrote.

'Oh dear,' he would occasionally lament after Edward Heath had succeeded Home in 1965. 'Must you really say that about Ted? Well, if you must, I suppose you must.'

Strangely, our one real row concerned dinner jackets. In the course of making some fairly obvious contrasts between Labour and Conservative conferences of the mid-1960s – the Tories had heavy leather baggage or even trunks, whereas the Socialists, as Macleod called them, had battered suitcases, and so forth – I wrote that of an evening the Tories lost no opportunity of getting into their dinner jackets. Indeed, this was one of the reasons for their possession of such large quantities of luggage. From some cause these light-hearted observations on what Conservatives wore in the evenings infuriated Macleod.

'It simply isn't true,' he said, 'and you know it isn't true. Dinner jackets went out in 1939.'

I was not so much hurt as surprised, both by the vehemence of the response and by its denial of what went on at Conservative conferences. For the truth was that Conservatives, when gathered together by the seaside in the autumn, were forever putting on their dinner jackets. Agents' dinners, Young Conservative balls, South-West receptions, to say nothing of private functions of one kind or another: the list, if not exactly endless, often seemed so. And at all these events dinner jackets were worn. Why had Macleod failed to perceive this? And, whatever the truth of the matter, why was he so angry about it?

Perhaps he thought his party was being traduced. He was always at pains to emphasise the unsnobbish and meritocratic character of the modern Conservative Party, often citing his own career as evidence of this laudable condition. One reason for his anger about the elevation of Home was that it seemed to cast doubt on this view. But Macleod, as I have already said, attached considerable weight to his membership of White's and his long weekends with Randolph Churchill. In any event, he himself certainly possessed a dinner jacket. I had seen him wearing it, and at Conservative conferences moreover. The episode remains mysterious. But it produced no lasting ill-effects as far as relations between Macleod and myself were concerned.

On only one occasion did he evince suspicion of my activities. In the 1965 election for the Conservative leadership he supported and voted for Edward Heath, though he was on closer terms with Reginald Maudling. He had in his younger days been even closer to the third candidate, Enoch Powell. But in the period when I knew him the two of them had become somewhat distant from each other.

'Poor old Enoch,' he would say. 'Driven mad by the remorselessness of his own logic.'

Like Macleod, I was closer to Maudling than to Heath, whom I knew hardly at all, a condition which has persisted to this day. Unlike Macleod, I hoped and believed that Maudling would succeed Home. I did not write in Maudling's favour because I do not like writing articles of this kind. In any case, few Conservative MPs would have taken much notice of what I had written. On the afternoon of the result I saw Maudling in the Members' Lobby of the Commons.

'That was a turn-up for the book,' he commented in his affable way.

He then said he was withdrawing from the contest, even though Heath had not polled well enough to win outright on the first ballot.[8] I returned to Gower Street with the news. Macleod was, for once, spending the afternoon in the office. He knew the result but not Maudling's plans, or lack of plans. I told him of the withdrawal after the first ballot. Far from commending his political columnist for his zeal, he looked exceedingly angry:

'I hope you haven't been telling Reggie anything of what I've been saying. It would be very damaging,' he added, to leave no misunderstanding on the matter.

As Macleod had not said anything to me of any substance about the Conservative election, I was able to assure him with sincerity that on this subject I had been silent. The spurt of suspicion and anger was untypical. The omission to confide in me over the election was, however, characteristic of Macleod's dealings with myself. No doubt he was discreet to the point of taciturnity partly because he wanted to be able to tell his colleagues that he had had nothing to do with whatever it was his political columnist had written. Perhaps again he did not want me to feel I was being pointed by him in any particular direction. Not that he was distant exactly: he was uninformative. The principal reason, I believe, was that he saw his period as an editor not as a continuation of politics by other means but as respite from them.

In these circumstances it was normal for him to take more pleasure in his personal column 'Quoodle' and his articles of war-time and other reminiscences than in the leaders or the rest of the overtly political pieces in the paper. Macleod wrote most of 'Quoodle' in longhand – and sometimes in bed – on Saturday afternoons while watching sport on television. One of his engaging characteristics was to convince himself subsequently that all the items in a 'Quoodle' column had been not only thought of but actually composed by himself. This was a characteristic he shared with both Kingsley Martin and R.H.S. Crossman. In fact about a quarter or a third of the column (the proportion varied from week to week) was contributed by other members of the staff. As a rough guide it is safe to assume that anything written about art, music, the theatre, the cinema, non-political books or the law, though not of course sport – the blind spot of most editors – was by someone other than Macleod.

---

[8] Contrast with Michael Heseltine's – perfectly proper – behaviour in 1990, when he continued in the contest, withdrawing with Douglas Hurd in the third ballot in favour of John Major.

Not that Macleod wrote as politicians customarily do. Real writers write in words; most literate people in ready-made blocks of words; and politicians, commonly, in whole prefabricated sentences or sometimes paragraphs. By this test Macleod was very close to being a real writer. Certainly he was a journalist of considerable technical accomplishment, being able to pen short and easily understandable sentences without producing a jerky or staccato effect. And, like most columnists, he had his favourite targets, notably Harold Wilson and Sir Hugh Greene, then director-general of the BBC.

His dislike of Wilson was, as he confessed, irrational. He simply did not care for the man. For George Brown he felt affection, for James Callaghan a growing admiration. 'The best man they've got is Jim,' he would sometimes opine, for no very clearly stated reasons. But he made no effort to understand Wilson. Wilson did not reciprocate. At least I never heard him say an unkind word about Macleod. Indeed, he regarded Macleod with a wary respect. When he was elected leader of the Labour Party in 1963 he said Macleod would be his most dangerous opponent – that if the Conservatives had any sense they would choose him to lead their party. But Macleod was prone to dislikes of this kind. Another example was Roy Jenkins, who irritated him by his displays of aloofness (or perhaps by getting the better of him) during debates on successive Finance Bills after 1967.

Sir Hugh Greene and the BBC were different. While Wilson was referred to as 'the little man', though he was an inch or so taller than Macleod, the BBC became 'Auntie'. For Macleod to use this nickname at this particular time was in a way strange. The satire trade, though not perhaps flourishing, was still being plied with vigour and a certain amount of profit – as I was to discover when I wrote scripts, chiefly for John Bird as Harold Wilson, for the television programmes *BBC3* and *The Late Show* in 1966-7.[9] Macleod claimed to disapprove of the protests which some of his colleagues had made in the earlier period, 1961-3. Nevertheless he remained convinced that the BBC was dominated by the Left. This was inevitable because the Left were usually more intelligent and more politically conscious. It was only a result of chance, he would add, that he was not on the left himself.

[9] *BBC3* was the name of a 'satirical' programme rather than of one of the Corporation's services.

He had a genuine dislike of monopoly and what he termed 'the nanny state'.[10] This was paradoxical. For at times he would declare: 'I am a Tory.' He never, as far as I am aware, described himself as a Liberal who found himself in the Conservative Party for the want of any more comfortable resting-place. Furthermore, in his political life he was always happiest at those departments which provided him with ample opportunities for action – the Ministries of Health and Labour and the Colonial Office. He was rarely in practice averse to paternalism or, at any rate, to interventionism. At the core of his political thought, nonetheless, there was ambiguity: as perhaps there has to be with any successful politician within the British system. He did, said and wrote many courageous things. But I am sure that by canonising him the young Conservative Left misunderstood his real political nature.

IV

Macleod soon made his peace with the new Conservative leader and returned to the opposition front bench in the Commons. Obviously he could not and did not want to continue as editor. Ian Gilmour offered the post to Nigel Lawson. I did not know him but had admired him as City editor of the *Sunday Telegraph*, no doubt because of his predilection, in his weekly column, for politics and economics rather than for stocks and shares. He had early determined on a political career and in 1963 became special assistant – more accurately, speechwriter – to the Conservative Prime Minister, Sir Alec Douglas-Home. After Home had narrowly lost the 1964 election, Lawson briefly returned to freelance journalism before taking up his new duties in January 1966.

We had already enjoyed an affable lunch at a Chinese restaurant in Brighton during the party conference season of autumn 1965. Though I have always had a healthy appetite myself, I was nonetheless surprised at the amount he ate. He said it was essential that the political columnist of the *Spectator* should be – or should give the appearance of being – on what he called 'the inside track'. I did not dissent. My principal informants were then R.H.S. Crossman and C.A.R. Crosland, of whom Crossman told me everything and

---

[10] The phrase has stuck. It was much used, with some justice, of the Labour administration of 1997. It was coined in 'Quoodle', *Spectator*, 3 December 1965, in relation to the proposed 70 mph speed limit on motorways.

Crosland nothing. Harold Wilson used to believe that those leaks from his distinctly talkative Cabinet which appeared from time to time in my column in the *Spectator* and, later, the *New Statesman* came from Crosland. That, at any rate, was what I was told by Gerald Kaufman, who was Wilson's man of business in the press gallery of the Commons before becoming an MP himself. But then, Wilson was capable of believing all kinds of extraordinary things about who was leaking to whom. He was convinced, for instance, that in the late 1960s Nora Beloff, the political correspondent of the *Observer* – intelligent and industrious but neither young nor beautiful – was enjoying a series of affairs with youthful MPs who were, he thought, plotting against him and who included John Mackintosh, David Marquand, David Owen and Brian Walden.[11] Anyone who believed that would have believed anything.

There was nothing intrinsically unbelievable in the notion that Crosland was telling tales. Earlier in this chapter I wrote that Henry Fairlie was my first hero.[12] Anthony Crosland was joint first. Their joint positions dated from the middle Fifties, when I was 23, Fairlie was writing his political column in the *Spectator* and Crosland had just published *The Future of Socialism*. He said that Socialism was not about nationalisation but about equality: not equality of opportunity but equality of outcome. He believed that the economic problem was solved. He did not foresee higher unemployment, a world-wide economy, a capitalist system which was not nearly so tame – so subject to governmental or union control – as he had supposed that of the 1950s to be.

He was also a convinced libertarian, a position which is even more suspect in the Labour Party of today than his economics are. Nevertheless he was an inspiring figure to my generation and to the generation slightly before mine. Anthony Howard was right when, reviewing a biography of him, he wrote that Crosland's heroic stature derived as much from his personality – languid, insolent, socially fearless and often offensive – as from the originality of his writing.[13] He was always polite to waiters:

'Would you mind terribly? ... when you have a moment to spare ... gosh, you are clever ... thank you so much.'

---

[11] Peter Oborne, *Alastair Campbell: New Labour and the Rise of the Media Class* (1999), 116.

[12] See above, p. 64.

[13] Anthony Howard, 'Exciting Friend', *New Statesman*, 3 May 1999.

In the middle of one of these displays I could see that the beneficiary of his attentions was becoming annoyed. Crosland could see it too. He asked me what the matter could be.

'He thinks you're taking the piss,' I replied.

Crosland was perplexed. He had been trying to be nice. Like Evelyn Waugh, he sometimes found it difficult. He once had a memorable row with the novelist at the Oxford Union. Waugh had assumed from his appearance, manner and accent that he must be a Tory. Michael Foot, who had his feline side despite his affection for dogs, used to call his way of speech 'Tony Crosland's bogus Oxford accent'. And yet surrounded by people who spoke more or less as he did (in fact rather less than more), in a restaurant or wherever it happened to be, he would say:

'For God's sake let's get away from these awful Tory voices.'

Though he was never a great House of Commons man, disliking the place as he did most male institutions, from Oxford colleges to London clubs, one of his qualities was his ability to patronise Conservatives in days when they could afford to be more patronising than they are now. This ability may have been modelled on his mentor, Hugh Dalton; or he may have developed it independently. Some of us enjoyed the performance. Crosland's colleagues on the floor of the House tended not to. Like the waiter, they thought they were being patronised.

This was the first tragedy of Crosland's political life. He loved the old Labour Party, the party of Comrade Chairman, of composite resolutions and of moving the reference back. It was the only institution he did love. But he was never accepted by it; still less taken to its heart. The second tragedy lay in the refusal of two successive Prime Ministers, Harold Wilson and James Callaghan, to make him Chancellor. Arguably it was an even greater tragedy that Denis Healey was never made Foreign Secretary. He had trained himself for the post more assiduously and more self-consciously than Crosland had trained himself to be Chancellor. A Labour government of 1966-70 with Crosland at the Treasury, Healey at the Foreign Office and Jenkins at the Home Office could conceivably have won the 1970 election.

In 1959 I had written to Crosland from the London School of Economics, pointing out that abolishing the grammar schools without simultaneously 'doing something' about the public schools would hinder rather than help the egalitarian cause. He replied fully and courteously, saying he agreed. In office in 1965 he took a different course, with malign consequences that are with us to this day. We did not fall out about this. Crosland did not talk much about the Cabinet or about his departmental duties because he had a highly-developed sense of honour. Perhaps it was over-developed. Certainly he never really understood political journalism properly.

At around this time Ian Aitken, the political correspondent of the *Guardian*, invited him to lunch. Naturally they discussed education policy. Aitken thought the discussion was on 'lobby terms': he could reveal what the Minister had told him provided he was neither identified nor quoted directly. This Aitken proceeded to do in his newspaper with complete propriety – though it did not take much political acuity to identify the source. Crosland, however, thought (or said he thought) that the conversation over lunch had been confidential. He talked of reporting Aitken and the *Guardian* to the Press Council, later the Press Complaints Commission. I told him not to be so silly. He took my advice.

Nigel Lawson assumed his new duties in January 1966. Iain Macleod had been concerned to avoid turning the paper into a Conservative party organ. Lawson followed Macleod's policy in this respect, as he did in most others. Relations between him and Ian Gilmour were not, however, quite so easy as those between Macleod and the proprietor. Lawson was prickly, tending to regard any suggestions by the paper's owner as proprietorial interference. Gilmour, for his part, complained that Lawson had been brought in as Macleod's successor partly because of his distinction as a City editor. He had expected Lawson to attract advertising. Lawson appeared more interested in the political scene and in broader questions of economic management.

However, he enjoyed happy relations with his staff. He made no attempt to impose his views on me. With Hilary Spurling (later to become a distinguished biographer) as his literary editor, he strengthened the paper's coverage of literature and the arts, areas in which his predecessor had been largely uninterested. He continued to rely, as Macleod had, on the administrative and journalistic skills of his deputy, John Thompson. But he played a more active part in the day-to-day running of the paper than had Macleod. For example, he reinstated the editorial conference. This did not prove an unqualified success – in fact it turned out to be rather a waste of time – for Lawson, like many accomplished journalists, though unlike most aspiring politicians, was not a ready man in speech, being prone to silences, hesitations, gropings for the word he wanted. These were characteristics he was to retain throughout his later political career.

Contrary to the reputation for energy and decisiveness which he acquired, he was also inclined to dilatoriness and procrastination. He would never produce the paper's leading article, which he normally wrote himself, until the last minute had passed. The *Spectator* was then printed at Aldershot. One of the small staff would rush with the completed article to Waterloo station, modestly rewarding the guard for handing the envelope to another member of the staff on Aldershot platform, or for throwing it out of the train if it was an express. Occasionally the plan would miscarry and the week's leader would end up either somewhere on the South Coast or back at Waterloo. If this happened, Lawson would dictate the leader from his copy (or 'black') to whichever of his colleagues happened to be manning the presses at Aldershot.

Our greatest adventure concerned what came to be known in political circles as 'the D Notice affair'. It began when Chapman Pincher, the defence (or, some would have said, the spy) correspondent of the *Daily Express*, produced a front-page lead story alleging that the security services were interrupting and reading certain overseas cables.[14] On 21 February in the Commons Harold Wilson, the Prime Minister, accused Pincher and the *Express* of having breached two D Notices. These (the 'D' stands for Defence) are communications from the Services, Press and Broadcasting Committee to newspaper editors. The committee is one of those semi-official bodies whose precise status is unclear and which the English love to include in their constitutional arrangements. Its function is to warn newspapers and broadcasting services against publishing certain kinds of stories. These warnings are embodied in D Notices, which can vary not only between the general and the particular but also in their timespan. They are advisory only, and provide no defence against prosecution under the Official Secrets Acts. Indeed, when the *Sunday Telegraph* and Jonathan Aitken were prosecuted unsuccessfully under these Acts in 1971 in respect

---

[14] It was never entirely clear whether they were doing likewise with domestic telegrams. H. Chapman Pincher, known in Fleet Street as Harry Pincher, was originally a botanist and zoologist and the author of, among other books, *Breeding of Farm Animals* and *A Study of Fishes*.

of a story about the Biafran war, it emerged that the paper had sought advice and was told there was no cause for concern.

In 1967 the row showed no sign of abating. Wilson appointed a committee of inquiry consisting of Lord Radcliffe, the chairman, Selwyn Lloyd and Emanuel Shinwell, whom I was later to describe in the *Spectator* of 3 March 1967 as 'an unlikely and slightly hilarious trio'. It seemed to me that, if people were to arrive at any conclusion abut the justice of Wilson's accusation, they ought to be given the opportunity to read the D Notices for themselves. Accordingly I trotted off to Shell-Mex House, where the secretary of the D Notice Committee, Colonel L.G. ('Sammy') Lohan, had his office. The colonel was a self-created 'character' with a large ginger moustache who prided himself on not behaving as a conventional civil servant would. He was a friend and confidant of Pincher: a relationship which Wilson was later to use unscrupulously to try to discredit both of them. Lohan made no difficulties about dictating the D Notices to me. I wrote them down in my notebook, returned to the office and included them in my political column of 3 March 1967. They were as follows. The first was dated 27 April 1956:

Will you please in the national interest make no reference to the following:
(i) Secret intelligence or counter-intelligence methods and activities in or outside the UK.
(ii) Identities of persons engaged in intelligence or counter-intelligence duties, whether actively engaged in such duties or in a clerical or administrative capacity, and of whatever status or rank.
(iii) Any information from which the number, duties or type of staff or other details of the organisation of MI5 or MI6 could be ascertained.
(iv) Any information from which could be deduced the addresses where our Intelligence Services operate.
(v) Special methods of training the Intelligence staff.
In conclusion may I ask you to bear in mind that the task of Intelligence Services in a democratic country is far from easy and earnestly request you, when in doubt, to act on the principle that as little publicity as possible should be given to their activities?

The second D Notice was dated 30 October 1961:

The Services, Press and Broadcasting Committee request that in the interest of national security you will make no reference to the following:

(1) The nature of the cyphering work carried out in government communication establishments or by named persons employed in those establishments.

(2) The various methods used in the interception of foreign communications for secret intelligence purposes. In this connection the committee request that you will not refer to the fact that on occasions it is necessary in the interest of defence for the services to intercept such communications.

I have been asked also to emphasise that the methods or systems of official cyphers used by the British and other governments should not be referred to without prior advice.

Both D Notices were signed by Admiral George P. Thomson, the then secretary of the committee.

There was a tremendous row which lasted several days. On the Thursday afternoon, when the *Spectator* was already available in Fleet Street, I took the receiver off the hook and went to bed. My parents were agitated at the thought of my going to jail or, indeed, of my being in trouble of any kind. My wife remained stoical. I felt fairly sure that to publish a D Notice was not to breach the Official Secrets Acts, because the notice was not official information within the meaning of those statutes. But the point was certainly arguable.

Nigel Lawson was later to accuse me of having 'landed him in it'. This was at a dinner in December 1998 to mark Sir Samuel Brittan's 65th birthday. I had no wish to mar a pleasant social occasion through a dispute with my next-door neighbour at the dinner table; so I let it pass. But in fact Lawson was kept fully informed and approved the publication of the D Notices. As he put it at the time, in a typically Lawsonian formulation:

'There is no D Notice on D Notices.'

He was, however, under a misapprehension, not about this, but about whether the *Spectator* was part of the D Notice system. He thought it was not. I did not know whether it was or not. It turned out, when inquiries were made, that it was indeed part of the system, but that Iain Macleod had been in the habit of reading D Notices and then chucking them away.

After a few weeks had passed Lawson and I were summoned – or, rather, invited – to appear before Lord Radcliffe and his two colleagues. I felt flattered to appear before the greatest committee-sitter in the history of British government and public administration. But I did not tell my parents, who would have been even more worried than they were already. On 11 April 1967 Lawson and I presented ourselves to the hilarious trio. Part of my evidence went:

Radcliffe: Now, I would like to come to Mr Watkins's part in this, because there does not seem to be a common ground on the pure question of fact as to what happened. Mr Watkins, when you went to Colonel Lohan's office you did not take copies [of the two D Notices] with you?

Watkins: No, I copied out pretty well in total the D Notices in my notebook.

Radcliffe: I must ask you this to begin with: did you copy out those parts of those which were headed either 'Private and confidential' or 'Secret'?

Watkins: I honestly did not notice what was on the top. I assumed it would probably have 'Private and confidential', but I certainly did not observe at the time that one was marked 'Secret' and the other, I understand, 'Private and confidential'. I copied out the body of the text, as it were.

Radcliffe: I thought you might have done that. I want Mr Lawson to remember that they in fact do all carry either the words 'Private and confidential' or 'Secret' on them. But you were allowed to copy out a number, if not all, of the existing D Notices?

Watkins: No, the two that were in dispute or the two that were relevant to the particular political point I was examining.

Radcliffe: Yes. We are given to understand there were two people in the office, Colonel Lohan and an assistant?

Watkins: Yes, an assistant or secretary, a middle-aged woman.

Radcliffe: But we are given to understand that they both gave you a warning to the effect that these D Notices were confidential documents and that they were not to be published?

Watkins: No, what happened was this: I asked Colonel Lohan in the morning, having talked on an 'off the record' basis with him about the dispute in relation to the *Daily Express*: 'Can I come along and see these D Notices?' And he said: 'All right, but you should have copies in the office.' I made no inquiries whatever in the *Spectator*. I went along that afternoon, took out a notebook, and he certainly did not say anything about non-publication. The woman said, either to me or to Colonel Lohan, something to this effect: 'Mr Watkins does realise that these notices are confidential?' To which Colonel Lohan said; 'I do not think we need worry about that, there are copies back in the office.' I said nothing, and continued to copy them out, and said 'Thank you very much', and went away and put them in my article.

Radcliffe: Had you any doubt, when you had finished, that in fact they were confidential communications?

Watkins: Oh none at all, of course not.

It seemed to me that Lord Radcliffe had manoeuvred me into admitting I had done something wrong, as in his mind no doubt I had. I resolved to clarify my position. The opportunity came later, when Nigel Lawson was being questioned by Selwyn Lloyd:

Lloyd: I take it that you would accept that you should not publish a private and confidential document, and that if you feel you want freedom to do that you should contract out of the system?

Lawson: I think clearly if one accepts a system on a plainly understood private and confidential basis, that is one thing and one adheres to it; on the other hand, it could be that the confidentiality of the documents was on the same basis as the advice in the documents, in other words that there was a request, with the same authority, not to publish them.

Watkins: May I just interpose here, because I want to clear up an answer which I gave to Lord Radcliffe earlier? I think it is necessary to distinguish two senses of 'private and confidential document'. One case, it seems to me, is where one has entered into a system or into a relationship with the person who gives you the document. The other case is where the document has 'Private and confidential' stamped upon it, or indeed 'Secret', or indeed 'Top secret'. And the classification which the originator of the document chooses to put upon it, whether 'Confidential', 'Private' or whatever, should not I think necessarily inhibit a journalist or an editor, although of course he will take account of it.

Radcliffe: Of course, I accept your distinction, but I was thinking about the first of the classes which you referred to, in which the terms of dealing with the possession of the document are clearly set out. Thank you very much, we are much obliged to you both.

The editor and I retired to a pub at the Trafalgar Square end of Whitehall for a well-earned *restoratif*. My exchange with Lord Radcliffe was subsequently cited unavailingly by Lord Wigoder QC at the Old Bailey when he was defending in an Official Secrets Acts case. Lord Radcliffe and his colleagues exonerated the *Daily Express* but condemned the *Spectator*. The Wilson government agreed with them about the latter but disagreed about the former: so strongly, indeed, that a White Paper was hurriedly put out denouncing the work of the learned Lord of Appeal. This was approved by the House of Commons in a shameful whipped vote. Altogether it was a sordid but comic episode in our public life. I am, however, proud of the part which Nigel Lawson and I played in it and, if the circumstances were to recur, would do the same again.[15]

VI

In these tribulations, which I enjoyed, really, there was an unfailing source of cheer and consolation at the *Spectator* office. This was George Hutchinson, the general manager. By trade he was a political journalist. We had first met in 1959, when I entered the press gallery as Wilfred Sendall's assistant at the *Sunday Express*. Though political journalists are – at any rate, were – friendly to newcomers, much friendlier than the industrial correspondents used to be in those remote days when they were a power in the land, nevertheless Hutchinson had been exceptionally helpful. So had James Margach of the *Sunday Times* and Hugh McCartney of the *Glasgow Herald*, Scotsmen all.

At this time Hutchinson was going through a period of professional difficulty. He was the political correspondent of the *Evening Standard* (this was a time before the term 'political editor' had been invented). The *Standard* had, however, acquired Robert Carvel, the esteemed political correspondent of the soon-to-be defunct third London evening paper, the *Star*. He resolved the difficulty in typically Hutchinsonian manner by doing nothing. Eventually the *Standard* made him diplomatic correspondent. He then became press officer at Conservative Central Office, for which he was (as he, a stickler for correct usage, would have said) appointed CBE. I

---

[15] See Report of the Committee of Privy Counsellors appointed to inquire into D Notice matters, Cmnd 3309 (1967), paras 73-80 and Evidence, 270-8; Peter Hedley and Cyril Aynsley, *The D Notice Affair* (1967); Edmund Heward, *The Great and the Good: a Life of Lord Radcliffe* (1994), 162-9.

used to telephone him in those days with fairly routine inquiries of one sort or another.

'Have no fear, Master Watkins,' he would say. 'You shall have the answer to your question within the hour. It shall be done. It must be done.'

The hour would pass. There would be no reply from Hutchinson, not even a message from somebody else on his behalf. The day would pass with silence from Central Office. The next day would go by likewise. At this stage I would ask somebody else, or look up the answer in a book. Hutchinson had a genius for procrastination which would have qualified him instantly for honorary citizenship of South-west Wales. In fact he was a Scotsman who had been brought up in Staffordshire and served in Arctic convoys during the war. The only trace of Scottishness that I could detect was his pronunciation of 'billiards' and 'girl'. He wore highly polished brogues, tweed suits and, always, a hat, for the sole purpose, it often seemed, of raising it to women or, indeed, to anyone who he thought warranted this courtesy. At 12 o'clock or so on most mornings at the beginning of the week, Hutchinson would put his head round the door of my small office and say:

'Master Watkins, we have each of us done a good morning's work, and I feel we should reward ourselves with a glass of refreshment.'

As I would have arrived at the office at half-past 10 at the earliest, usually later, I could scarcely be said to have done a good morning's work. Nevertheless I did not demur. I would then go into Hutchinson's larger office next door to mine, where he would point to a tray on which rested two glasses, a jug of tap water and a bottle of Teacher's whisky assembled by our excellent joint secretary, Cecilia Hurst.[16] Even in those days, when I had not relinquished whisky completely, I did not want to drink the stuff shortly after 12 in the morning. But I thought it would have been churlish to refuse, so I sipped away. On his subjects, Fleet Street and the Conservative Party, Hutchinson was one of the most entertaining and informative conversationalists I have ever known. There was no one quite like him at my next port of call, the *New Statesman*.[17]

---

[16] Cecilia Hurst was to marry Alastair (later Sir Alastair) Goodlad, MP.

[17] See Geoffrey Wheatcroft, 'George Hutchinson' in *Absent Friends* (1989), 67 ff. Reviewing this book in the *Sunday Telegraph*, the distinguished military historian and journalist Sir John Keegan said that Hutchinson was not worth writing about. On the contrary: he was a most interesting and a slightly mysterious man who wrote two valuable books, one on Harold Macmillan, the other on Edward Heath.

5

Great Turnstile

[Henry Fairlie and John Raymond] took me for a drink to El Vino's which I had never been to before ... The lunch break went like a flash. For the first time in my life the hours between one o'clock and three o'clock passed without any thought of food. Never before had I enjoyed myself so much. Peregrine Worsthorne, *Tricks of Memory*, 1993

I

The *New Statesman* had never formed part of my plans, such as they were. I had assumed, for no very good reason, that one of the Sunday papers (I should have preferred the *Observer*) would invite me to write a column. While I was still on the *Spectator*, however, I had enjoyed a brief flirtation with the *Financial Times*. A lugubrious character called Bill Rodger took me out to lunch several times. I even had two meetings with the editor, Gordon Newton, one in the Garrick Club, the other in El Vino's. On the latter occasion I asked him what he would like to drink. He looked at his watch.

'As it's half-past 11,' he said, 'I think I'll have some gin.'

We got on well enough, but his enthusiasm for acquiring me – or, rather, my column – waned, partly because I insisted on retaining certain freelance rights (notably, the right to carry on doing scripts for John Bird, John Fortune and John Wells, should they ask me) and partly because news of the possible appointment leaked, which irritated Newton. This was entirely my fault or, rather, it was the fault of a woman friend, a journalist, to whom I had rashly confided the information.

Instead Newton appointed my predecessor at the *Spectator*, David Watt, who was coming to the end of his three-year term in Washington for the *Financial Times*. It was extraordinary that Newton had not appointed him in the first place. Quite apart from his merits as a columnist, he was, I thought, better suited to the *FT* than I was. Together with that paper, he was more inclined than I to take politicians at their own high valuation of themselves. But it appeared that Newton was unaware of or had forgotten Watt's previous existence as political columnist of the *Spectator*. To him, Watt was Our Man in Washington. It was as simple as that. When Watt's previous experience was pointed out to him, the difficulty was overcome.

This episode illustrates a wider truth. Editors rarely know the detailed journalistic backgrounds of those they appoint, even to quite senior positions. They tend to offer a job to someone who is 'very up these days' or is for whatever reason briefly in the news. So it was on this occasion.

My opposite number on the *New Statesman* in 1965-7 had been Matthew Coady. For years he had been a sub-editor on the *Daily Mirror*. But he had always possessed a hankering for what he called 'the higher journalism'. In 1965, when Gerald Kaufman left the *Statesman* to become Harold Wilson's representative in the press gallery of the House of Commons, a vacancy arose. It was filled by Coady. Once in the job, however, he found he did not like it. Certainly it was the cause of some strain. On Tuesday afternoons in the Commons, when the time for writing his column could not be postponed for much longer, he was a nervous wreck. In the circumstances the quality of the column he produced was remarkably high. Hugh Cudlipp, at any rate – chairman of Daily Mirror Newspapers – was an admirer.

Cudlipp was then on the lookout for new writers for the 'Mirrorscope' feature which he planned for the *Mirror*. This was meant to be a serious but, to use the word of the 1990s, 'accessible' survey of important events, at home and abroad. Cudlipp's idea was based on the success which the *Sunday Times* had enjoyed with similar features and on his conviction that the working classes were becoming more serious, more intelligent and more discriminating. It was this conviction that led to his transformation of the old *Daily Herald* into the new *Sun*. Rupert Murdoch was to prove that Cudlipp was quite wrong about the workers and what they wanted.

Anyway, Cudlipp was crossing the Atlantic in an aeroplane with Paul Johnson, editor of the *New Statesman*, and Michael Berry (later Lord Hartwell), proprietor of the *Telegraph*. They had either interviewed or were about to interview Dean Rusk, the US Secretary of State, for a television programme. Cudlipp asked Johnson who this Matthew Coady was and where he had got hold of him. Johnson replied with some surprise (so he told me later) that Coady had been at the *Mirror* for many years before joining the *Statesman*. Cudlipp then pretended he had known this at the time, as he clearly had not. This did not prevent him from asking Coady to return to the *Mirror*, which created a vacancy at the *Statesman*.

To me, at any rate, unexpectedly, Johnson asked me to fill it. He made the offer at a party in Albany chambers off Piccadilly given by Julian Critchley, who had lost his seat at Rochester and Chatham in 1964 and was a journalist and chairman of the Bow Group. He was to return to the Commons in 1970 as Member for Aldershot and North Hants, after 1974 for Aldershot alone. I remember not only Johnson's offer but the presence of several models from the 1950s, of whom the best known was Barbara Goalen. Like most famous people, she was both shorter and thinner than expected. The only exceptions I have known to this universal rule are Tony Blair, Sir Robin Day and Sophia Loren. Miss Goalen was the epitome of Kensington respectability, as models used to be, not only after their spell of fame (as Miss Goalen was by this time) but during it as well. The change occurred in the 1960s. Whether because of such glamorous company or for some other reason, I accepted Johnson's offer on the spot.

At the *Spectator*, Nigel Lawson was flatteringly cross at my departure. He warned me that I would not have so much influence at the *Statesman*, which was almost certainly wrong, and that I would not enjoy as much freedom as I had at the *Spectator*, which was more plausible. For a replacement he turned to Auberon Waugh, then employed as a feature writer by both the *Daily* and *Sunday Mirror*. Hugh Cudlipp once spotted him writing captions to a series entitled 'ABC of Beauty' and remarked: 'Wonderful thing to have an education, isn't it, Bron?'

In the Arab-Israeli War of 1967 the *Mirror* received a tip that Mandy Rice-Davies was tending Israeli soldiers as a nurse. In the Profumo affair of 1963 she had become as famous as Christine Keeler and more sympathetic to the public. Waugh was dispatched to investigate the story and to obtain a picture. He discovered that Miss Rice-Davies, far from nursing injured soldiers, was still plying her old trade of night-club hostess. Reluctant to disappoint his employers, he obtained a nurse's uniform, persuaded her to put it on and to be photographed in it, and wrote a few words on her heroism in the conflict. Everyone was happy.

Before I left the *Spectator* I invited Waugh to have a mid-morning drink in El Vino's, where I would explain the conventions of the trade of weekly political columnist. The essence was that, while there was no obligation to share information obtained from politicians, there was a duty to share knowledge of forthcoming events such as speeches, press conferences and the publication of Blue Books or White Papers. I also wrote a valedictory article in the *Spectator* where I dispensed sage advice about how to go about his tasks. The piece of advice which is, I think, remembered still (at any rate among political journalists who were active at that time) is that he should always be in bed before midnight at party conferences.

I think he was genuinely grateful for this and other counsel. At any rate we got on well together and formed a friendship which has lasted to this day, with not an angry word. He is one of the most considerate and best mannered people I know. But, there is no doubt about it, among others he aroused fear, as he does still. Even so formidable a figure as Philip Hope-Wallace showed apprehension at his approach. The reason lay partly in the reputation of his father, Evelyn, and partly in his ferocity as a writer. The literary agent Pat Kavanagh said: 'Something seems to come over him when he sees a blank sheet of paper.' He also conducted feuds with the husbands or lovers of women for whom he had acquired a *tendresse*: with Harold Evans because of Tina Brown and with Lord Gowrie because of Grizelda Grimond at Oxford many years before.

His feud with Anthony Powell had no such origin. What the origin was remained difficult to establish. Waugh said it derived from Powell's snobbishness and his, in Waugh's opinion, inflated reputation as a novelist. Powell said it derived from his friendship with Evelyn of which Bron, who was frightened of his father, was jealous, and also from envy of Powell's success as a novelist, an occupation which Bron had tried and abandoned. This, at any rate, was what Powell said to a woman friend and myself when we called on him one Sunday afternoon, having spent the previous two nights with Bron and Teresa Waugh at Combe Florey in Somerset. Powell was unaware of this visit. I said that Waugh was a friend of mine and that, whatever Powell's opinion of him as a novelist might be, he was a very good journalist, better than his father.

'Have a care,' Powell advised. 'You may think of him as your friend, but he will turn on you in the end. The Waughs always do. There is a streak of sadism in the Waughs.'

He pronounced 'sadism' in the way the name of the French marquis is pronounced, *sardism* rather than *saydism*. So far Powell's prophecy has remained happily unfulfilled. I have continued to enjoy the friendly relations with Waugh which began in 1967.

II

Paul Johnson, despite his reputation for bellicosity and his choleric appearance – Jonathan Miller remarked that he looked like an explosion in a pubic hair factory – was affable and tolerant as an editor. Nigel Lawson's prediction that I would enjoy less freedom at the *Statesman* than I had at the *Spectator* turned out to be wrong. There were, however, tensions. It was inevitable that there should have been. There was undoubtedly a *New Statesman* School of Labour Party Politics.

Contrary to popular journalistic belief, it was not unilateralist. True, Kingsley Martin became a leading member of the Campaign for Nuclear Disarmament. But even when Martin was editor (1930-60), colleagues such as John Freeman kept the editorial line away from outright ban-the-bombery. Not that the paper supported Hugh Gaitskell's approach, which was not very different from its own in this respect. Indeed, it did not support Gaitskell in any way at all. It was, if anything, even less friendly towards Anthony Crosland. Long before my arrival, it had published an unfriendly profile of him written by the Labour MP and political novelist Maurice Edelman and entitled 'Mr Gaitskell's Ganymede', which was probably defamatory. The Labour politicians whom the *Statesman* supported and who wrote for it from time to time placed themselves on the left of the party but took care not to find themselves too far to the left: Barbara Castle, Richard Crossman, Harold Wilson. There was a clear gap between the *Statesman* Left and the *Tribune* Left under the leadership of Michael Foot, even if a few politician-journalists managed to straddle it.

The *Statesman* Left looked towards the middle classes and was knowing, knowledgeable and somewhat superior. It was familiar not only with the parties of Bloomsbury but with the corridors of Whitehall: an exalted view of this world which took a fearful battering with the failure of the Wilson governments of 1964-70. The *Tribune* Left, by contrast, looked towards the Labour activists in the constituencies and was passionate, committed and somewhat blinkered. It was familiar with chipped teacups in draughty halls and, until his death in 1960, with meetings addressed by Aneurin Bevan: it never truly recovered from his apostasy, if such it was, over nuclear disarmament at the Brighton conference of 1957.

When I arrived at the *Statesman*, it was a month or so from the devaluation of the pound. Wilson's plumage of 1964 was already looking bedraggled. It had never impressed me, though I had always considered him a kindly man. This was one reason I had settled down so comfortably at the *Spectator*. The *NS* not only supported the Labour government. It also supported Harold Wilson as its leader. It did this partly because of Paul Johnson's liking for political heroes – or, when Margaret Thatcher appeared in 1975 (the year of Johnson's conversion), for political heroines. Aneurin Bevan had been a hero, Harold Wilson was one, Tony Blair occupied the position for over two years after May 1997.

Johnson did not try to stifle dissent over Wilson and the government. On the contrary: he encouraged argument. Indeed, I sometimes felt he encouraged it only too much, and that excessive time was spent discussing what the government ought to be doing rather than what ought to be going into the paper that week. True, these editorial conferences never attained under Johnson the monstrous stature which they did under Crossman later on in 1970-2. The Monday conference began at 10.30 with attendant outside experts, from the sparkling Peter Paterson, who wrote on industrial matters as 'Arnold Strang', to the tedious party apparatchik John Hatch, who wrote about African affairs, was ennobled and, as Lord Hatch of Lusby, acquired the reputation of being the most boring member of the House of Lords. Some of these attenders of the conference chose to describe themselves, in their *Who's Who* entries or in other potted biographies, as members of the 'editorial board' of the *New Statesman*. There was no such body. The editorial conference was not a formal institution and possessed no powers of any kind. It certainly had no power to control either the editor or his writers.

Barbara Castle was one of those who liked to claim membership of this non-existent editorial board. Since 1964, however, she had not been coming to the conference because she was a Minister (in

1970 she was to return when Richard Crossman was editor and she was no longer in government). In 1968 she bore the resounding title of First Secretary of State and Secretary of State for Employment and Productivity. As such she decided to reform industrial relations, with the full support of the Prime Minister, Harold Wilson – to begin with, anyway. Her proposals were embodied in a White Paper *In Place of Strife*. The title had been thought up as a deliberate echo of Aneurin Bevan's book *In Place of Fear* by her husband, Ted (later Lord) Castle, an affable character who had been a sub-editor on the *Daily Mirror* and had the distinguished, moustachioed appearance of the third balalaika player from the left in a Hungarian band.

The document incorporated many of the features that were to appear in the Heath government's industrial relations legislation after 1970. But Geoffrey Howe, the architect of the Conservative legislation, placed his faith in the registration of unions and the creation of a new industrial relations court. Mrs Castle placed hers in the power of intervention of the Minister – of Mrs Castle. That was one reason why I opposed the contemplated measure. The other was that I did not think it would get through the Parliamentary Labour Party. Johnson took a different view.

'Harold, Barbara and I are going to see this through together,' he informed a sceptical though impressed editorial conference.

Mrs Castle was not at all pleased about my approach. She summoned me to see her at the ministry. I declined to go, for two reasons. First, Peter Paterson (who took more or less the same line as I did on the proposed legislation) had already been summoned, had obeyed and had simply been hectored by the Minister, surrounded by her civil servants and with a bright light shining in her eyes, though this last may well have been embellishment on Paterson's part. And, second, it was one of my principles never to accept an invitation to visit a Minister in his or her office unless it suited my convenience. This derived from an experience I had suffered with Maurice Foley, a nasty piece of work whom Wilson had for some reason appointed to a junior post in his first government of 1964-6 and who had tried to bully me over a column I had written in the *Spectator*. Accordingly I replied that I should be delighted to meet Mrs Castle as my guest at lunch at L'Epicure restaurant, Frith Street. She recorded the occasion in her diary:

Tuesday, 4 February 1969

Lunched with Alan Watkins. He has been running a series of attacks on me in the *New Statesman* and, as he has obviously been talking to Dick [Crossman] about [the] Donovan [Report], I thought it was time he talked to me. But it was a wretched meal ... he refused to concede that Harold [Wilson] had done anything but 'rush through' my WP [White Paper].

'I think you are a dangerous woman. You are a button pusher like [J.F.] Kennedy and I don't like button pushers.'

'One can push a button to start Vietnamese peace talks as well as nuclear wars,' I pointed out.

'Doesn't matter. I am just against activists. I'm an old-fashioned Whig.'[1]

In this episode James Callaghan, the Home Secretary, took a different view from that of Harold Wilson and Barbara Castle. It is conventional now to assert that Wilson and Mrs Castle were right, Callaghan and those who supported him wrong – and that he would not have suffered as he did in the winter of 1978-9 if Mrs Castle's proposals had become law in 1969. This is certainly arguable. It is nevertheless possible that a Labour government's laws would have met the same fate as those of the Conservative government of 1970-4. By 1972 it was apparent that they were unenforceable, partly through the trade unions' policy of non-registration, and partly through a defiance of the law, supported or at least acquiesced in by the Labour Opposition, in what came perilously close to being a breakdown of civil society. It needed a different age, different conditions and different politicians – Jim Prior, Norman Tebbit and Margaret Thatcher – to impose some kind of discipline on the unions.

III

I had been going to El Vino's spasmodically since 1959 but became a more regular attender after joining the *Statesman*. From Great Turnstile, a passage linking Holborn to the north-east corner of Lincoln's Inn Fields, it was easier to get to than from the *Spectator*'s premises in Gower Street and, later, Doughty Street. El Vino's (officially El Vino but always called El Vino's) was, still is, on the

---

[1] Castle Diary, 4 February 1969: Barbara Castle, *Diaries* (2 vols, 1980-4), I, 601. The best account of the whole episode is in Peter Jenkins, *The Battle of Downing Street* (1970).

south side of Fleet Street at the junction with Fetter Lane. It had been established in the late 19th century to cater not for barristers from the nearby Temple or even solicitors, but for barristers' clerks. The manager in the 1960s was Frank Bower, a large, white-haired, overheated man who liked to wear ornate waistcoats and display a carnation in his buttonhole. A friend of mine referred to him as 'the florid vintner'. He was not universally popular – in fact he was not popular at all but fairly generally disliked – owing to his habit of expelling people or barring them from the premises completely, often on the flimsiest of pretexts. The other reason for his unpopularity lay in his consciousness of being a Fleet Street 'character'; which, his fancy dress apart, he was not. Bower's family had possessed a financial interest in the establishment but by the 1960s control had passed to the Mitchell brothers: Christopher, who supervised the bar, and David (later Sir David), who put in more spasmodic appearances and was Conservative Member for, successively, Basingstoke and Hampshire North-West between 1964 and 1997.

'This is an extraordinary place,' Paul Johnson once remarked, as if he were paying his first visit, whereas he had been there hundreds of times before. 'D'you know, I'm told that one of the waiters here is a Tory MP.'

Johnson, as editor of the *New Statesman*, was one of the emissaries of the higher journalism. The others included (until his departure for the United States) Henry Fairlie, Philip Hope-Wallace, Anthony Howard, Terence Kilmartin, John Raymond, Maurice Richardson and Peregrine Worsthorne. Michael Wharton ('Peter Simple') and Colin Welch appeared more occasionally. Raymond and Richardson, who died at the respective ages of 53 and 71, were journalists of a sort rare then and even rarer today. They were both men-of-letters of extensive learning which they put into their journalism rather than into their books. Indeed, apart from their collections – Richardson's *Fits and Starts* and Raymond's *England's on the Anvil* and *The Doge of Dover*, all three worth reading today – they published little between hard covers. Richardson wrote four books, one of them on his prep-school days; Raymond, one on Georges Simenon. But as journalists they were prolific.

Richardson was a handsome, white-haired man, who bore a resemblance to Randolph Churchill on account of, among other characteristics, his aggressive demeanour and his protuberant, mad, blue eyes. People sometimes mistook him for the son of the former Prime Minister and behaved aggressively towards him. Richardson did not mind this because he enjoyed fisticuffs – or what amounted usually to the preliminaries to fisticuffs which rarely came to anything. He claimed to have missed a boxing Blue at Oxford because he had knocked out the coach to the university team. Far from commending him to the authorities, as it surely should have done, this action appears to have alienated them. This, at any rate, was Richardson's story. He was the cousin of John Richardson, the art critic and historian and biographer of Picasso, who knew him as 'my clever cousin Maurice'.[2] He read Zoology and later English at New College and thought he could have been 'a proper scientist' if only he had been taught mathematics properly as a boy.

In the 1950s he was the *Observer*'s first television critic and coined the phrase 'idiot's lantern' for the television set. In his brief, postage-stamp reviews of crime novels in the same paper, he stretched ingenuity to its limits in finding similes for the stock words. Thrillers would grip 'like a pair of delivery forceps', 'like Pierrepoint's farewell handshake', 'steadily, like a conscientious ant's jaw', 'blindly, like a baby's fist' or (of a Dick Francis racing thriller) 'like Princess Anne's knees'. A plot would creak – this was one of his weaker efforts – 'like a pair of old stays given by Agatha Christie to Oxfam'. Disbelief, instead of being suspended, would be strung up with a strong noose, hung in a closet with the door locked, or garrotted.

Richardson was always short of money because book-reviewing was, as it still is, one of the surviving undemolished houses of old Grub Street, and because he was constantly in trouble with the Inland Revenue. A few weeks before his death in September 1978 I noticed on Terence Kilmartin's desk at the *Observer* an application to open an account with the Royal Linen Bank of Belfast which Kilmartin, as literary editor of the paper, was expected to support, as I assume he did – though this could not, as things turned out, be of much use to Maurice. Fleet Street in those days was a centre for borrowing and lending money, usually in the form of a £5 or £10 note. Quite why relatively prosperous middle-aged men went in for this practice as they did is mysterious: but so it was. Richardson, who was not prosperous at all, certainly went in for it:

[2] John Richardson, *The Sorcerer's Apprentice* (1999), 6, 15.

'I'm taking a Chinese girl out to dinner tonight,' he once said to me. 'Would you mind lending me a tenner?'

I complied with the request.

'I say,' Richardson said, noticing the reasonably full notecase from which I had extracted the money, 'Would you terribly mind making that twenty?'

Again I complied with the request. The money was repaid shortly before his death, of a heart attack, a few days after dancing the night away at the party at the Lyceum for the *Spectator*'s 150th anniversary. Truly did he leave Fleet Street a poorer place, for he was not only a great borrower but, in his way, a great journalist. He was also one of the few who, in the days of typewriters, before the advent of the word-processor, continued to write with a fountain pen, in his case a Parker 51. The nib was never entirely to his liking, and he was forever visiting the Parker shop on the ground floor of Bush House off the Strand, where he was known to the girls as 'Old Nibby'.

John Raymond was an even more old-fashioned character, though he was 16 years younger than Richardson. He was one of the leading critical reviewers of the 1950s; I would say the best. The others were Cyril Connolly and Raymond Mortimer in the *Sunday Times*, and Harold Nicolson in the *Observer*. Raymond appeared in the *New Statesman*, where he wrote the 'Books in General' feature in tandem with V.S. Pritchett. Sometime in the mid-1970s, when Claire Tomalin was the literary editor of the paper, I suggested to her that the feature should be revived. By this time Raymond was writing for the *Sunday Times* and the *Daily Mail*.

'Oh do you really think so?' Ms Tomalin replied. 'I think that approach is a bit *John O'London*' – a reference to the middlebrow literary magazine which flourished in the 1920s.

I still think I was right, both then and now. Weekly papers can usually give more space to literary articles than Sunday or daily papers can. Raymond certainly did not waste the page that was allocated to 'Books in General', a slightly misleading strapline, for quite often only one book would be reviewed. If this was so, Raymond, a man of deceptive industry, would go to the London Library and read other works by the author concerned or read round the subject generally.

Raymond had a face like a Stilton cheese. He was prone to sweating and never looked entirely well. He pushed the mode of dress then prevailing in the higher journalism to extremes, sometimes appearing in a coat, a waistcoat and a pair of trousers from three different suits. Usually he wore a sports coat and a pullover. He always had about him a whole collection of newspapers, periodicals and books from the London Library or from papers which wanted him to review them. Others, such as Philip Hope-Wallace, encumbered themselves similarly. Journalists who could perfectly well afford a briefcase or a bag of some description preferred to inconvenience themselves with quantities of books and newsprint, precariously held. To a certain extent they still do. It is one of the peculiarities of the trade.

Rising early, at six or so, Raymond would complete one or, sometimes, two articles and then embark on the day's conviviality, which might start at El Vino's or at the Bunghole, a wine bar opened in 1968 on the north side of Holborn, opposite Great Turnstile, where the *New Statesman* then had its offices. As he had done a good day's work already, he often managed to be quite drunk by the middle of the afternoon.

This condition caused some annoyance at the *New Statesman* in the late 1950s, when Kingsley Martin was the editor, Janet Adam Smith the literary editor and Raymond her deputy. He built a fortification of books on his desk to prevent him from seeing her – or, perhaps, to prevent her from seeing him. This was the time when several books had been published by or about Lady Diana Cooper and the 'Souls', the high-minded young aristocrats whom Raymond preferred to the contemporaneous Bloomsbury Group, who were also then getting into their stride in the London publishing world. His admiration for the Souls made him identify with their hanger-on, H.H. Asquith. Simultaneously he persuaded himself that Kingsley Martin was Lloyd George.

'Ah, I know you, you wily Welsh attorney,' Raymond would say to Martin (or words to this effect), when he returned to Great Turnstile after lunch. 'You had me out in 1916, but I will have my revenge yet, mark my words.'

Martin, who came from Herefordshire rather than from Wales, took alarm at these oral assaults from the reincarnation of Asquith, whom Raymond did not really resemble much except in his liking for novels, the theatre, the classics and strong drink. Raymond departed the office, though he continued to write for the paper. Thereafter, in the short time that remained to him as editor, Martin would anxiously question possible recruits to the staff about whether they drank, explaining that he had suffered a good deal of trouble lately in that area.

Indeed, 'I know you' was one of Raymond's favourite formulations when he had had too much to drink. This was often followed by: 'I've got you in the diary.' Whether this document existed remains mysterious. He would also sometimes say: 'I advise you to have a care. You are addressing a marshal of France.' This was a reference to his much-prized collection of toy soldiers which he had at home in South Kensington. This he shared with his mother, the musical comedy actress Iris Hoey, who had been famous before the war (his father was the actor Cyril Raymond).

He never married and, during his lifetime, his stories about sexual adventures were never taken seriously by his friends. They were being too cynical, for Raymond certainly enjoyed a fling with Barbara Skelton, the intellectuals' moll of the 1950s, who liked fat men, not only Raymond but George Weidenfeld and King Farouk of Egypt as well. He may also have had an affair with the American novelist Mary McCarthy.

George Gale was a kind of honorary representative of the higher journalism, even though (after a short initial spell on the *Manchester Guardian*, as it then was) he worked for the *Daily Express*. He had read History at Peterhouse, Cambridge, with Worsthorne. Gale, Fairlie, Johnson, Raymond and Worsthorne formed a group having an existence outside El Vino's, where Gale was never wholly at ease.

Gale's lack of ease had nothing to do with the ambience. He was generously paid, highly intelligent and aggressively disputatious – often, indeed, very rude. But he did not like wine and preferred beer. In El Vino's he compromised by drinking gin. Sometimes, however, he would disappear with a muttered excuse: Gale was a great mutterer and mumbler. After 20 minutes or so he would return. He would have been, I learnt later, to one of the contiguous pubs for a pint or even two pints of beer: for Gale, as I also learnt, was one of those people who were attracted not so much by the alcohol in the beer or even its taste as by the sensation brought about by a large quantity of liquid cascading down the throat.

Philip Hope-Wallace, looking like a large Roman senator wearing a pullover and sports coat rather than a toga, presided over a table in the back room, where he talked about operatic singers, French novelists and German poets. He used to say that the test of whether you were musical was whether you liked Verdi and Handel, both of them composers who had been looked upon as second-rate during his own lifetime. He would often be joined by Howard, Johnson, Kilmartin, Raymond, Richardson or Worsthorne. Even before his death at 67 in 1979, following a misconceived visit to a health farm, the management had put up a small brass plaque in his honour just above his favourite chair.

'Looks like a coffin-plate,' Hope-Wallace said prophetically.

They had spelled his name wrongly, 'Phillip' instead of 'Philip'. Taxed with their error, they replied:

'But we checked with the *Guardian*.'

Henry Fairlie preferred to do his drinking standing up, at the front of the house, near the entrance from Fleet Street. His companion was usually Derek Marks, the *Daily Express*'s best political correspondent of the post-war period, though later he was far from being its best editor. Here the conversation was louder, jollier, more brutish even, accompanied by strong spirits rather than by wine, with much ho, ho, hoing, conducted by tall, heavy men with red braces. Fairlie did not truly belong to this group as Marks naturally did, and he would make occasional expeditions into the back room to sit at Hope-Wallace's table of *savants*.

IV

Since 1964, when I started with the *Spectator*, I had been seeing R.H.S. Crossman every three months or so, usually for lunch. I had long shared most of his views on foreign policy, though I leaned more towards C.A.R. Crosland in domestic affairs. I was closer personally to Crosland but was on excellent terms with Dick. Contrary to his reputation for unpredictability and untrustworthiness, I later found he had been not only a prolific source but a reliable one as well. What he told me at the time tallied with what he put into his diary and, normally, with what could be confirmed from independent testimony. On Tuesday 9 June 1970 he recorded:

> I lunched at the Epicure with Alan Watkins, whom I briefed in great detail on the background to the doctors' crisis. I didn't, of course, tell

him that in less than a week he would know that I am to be his new editor. I wonder what he will think of that.[3]

Later that week, Paul Johnson was courteous enough to telephone me at home in Chertsey to tell me, before the official announcement, of Crossman's arrival and his own departure. I was more surprised by the former development than by the latter. Johnson had long wanted to write books and engage in freelance journalism. Crossman was by now scarcely a journalist at all, having been a Cabinet minister for the entire 1964-70 period.

But he had always wanted to edit the paper more than he had wanted any other job. He blamed Kingsley Martin for frustrating his ambition. The crucial year was 1955, when Martin made it clear to the board that he did not want Crossman as editor and to Crossman that he did not want him hanging about the office. Luckily for Crossman, Hugh Cudlipp had made him the offer of a column on the *Daily Mirror* which he accepted, saying he was now a more influential journalist than he had ever been at the *Statesman*.[4] There is some mystery about Martin's memorandum to the board. It is undated. Crossman's biographer thinks it was written and dispatched sometime in 1955.[5] It was discovered by C.H. Rolph (the pen-name of C.R. Hewitt) in 1972 when he was going through Martin's papers for the purpose of writing his biography. Crossman was 'the best reviewer' Martin had 'ever known'. However:

He neither gives nor inspires loyalty. No one either in political life nor [sic] in this office trusts Dick – by which I mean that they are never sure that his judgment is disinterested in its relation to his other ambitions, or that he will say the same thing to a different audience or person, or that he will keep silent about office affairs if gossip is attractive, or that he will stand by his colleagues in a tight place ... I never talk to Dick without the certainty that he will repeat what I said to other people, including, if it suits him, people who will desire ammunition against the paper ... No one can be so utterly charming, but he has no sense of solidarity or comradeship. He bullies whenever that seems the best way of victory in argument and

---

[3] Crossman Diary, 9 June 1970: R.H.S. Crossman, *Cabinet Diaries* ed. Janet Morgan (3 vols, 1975-7), III, 943. L'Epicure restaurant in Frith Street, Soho, was owned by two Cypriots who wore black coats and striped trousers and did rather good generalised continental food of a kind sadly unfashionable today, with much flourishing of spirit flames.
[4] See Anthony Howard, *Crossman: the Pursuit of Power* (1990), 191 ff.
[5] Ibid., 192.

crushes the ideas and vitality of less powerful colleagues ... I have the greatest respect for his intellectual integrity – in conversation. But if he were in charge here I fear the results ... I have never worked on the paper with anyone so brilliant but so impurely motivated.[6]

This short extract gives the flavour of Martin's lengthy though repetitious missive. And, as its precise date is a matter of speculation, so also is there something of a mystery about whether it was ever properly considered by the board. Certainly nobody seemed to remember it when the board opened negotiations with Crossman in 1969. Paul Johnson was, with Jock Campbell (Lord Campbell of Eskan, the chairman), one of the principal negotiators at the time. In his note on the editorship of the *New Statesman*, 1965-72, dated 3 May 1972, he tells us that if the board had known about it, the negotiations would not have begun. Crossman was both a Minister and Member of Parliament for Coventry East. He demanded the right to contest the next election, which would have been held at the latest in 1971. This the board conceded. According to Johnson, however:

One proviso on which the board unanimously insisted, and without which the appointment would not have taken place, was that Mr Crossman should withdraw from Parliament as soon as possible after the election, and in any event within 12 months. This he accepted without argument and it was later put in writing.[7]

Crossman's biographer differs slightly:

His determination to continue as an MP provoked the first complication in his relationship with his new employer ... No evidence of any formal commitment survives, but clearly the paper's board expected that Dick would resign from Parliament on taking up the editorship.[8]

Though the board had no responsibility towards the citizens of Coventry, it was manifestly conniving with Crossman to deceive them – the deception being that, health permitting, he would remain Member for Coventry East for the duration of the next Parliament. Clearly the board or its representatives should either

---

[6] Kingsley Martin, Memorandum to the Board of the *New Statesman* about R.H.S. Crossman, n.d. but probably 1955, reproduced as Appendix to Paul Johnson, Note on the Editorship of the *New Statesman* 1965-72, 3 May 1972.

[7] Johnson, Note on the Editorship of the *New Statesman*.

[8] Howard, *Crossman*, 300.

have insisted that he did not contest the election at all or have accepted, with as good a grace as they could muster, that he intended to remain an MP. As things turned out, Crossman chose to stand by his constituents and to let down the *New Statesman* instead. Occasionally he would be troubled by what looked surprisingly like conscience. In remaining an MP, he would muse, he was really helping the paper. He could see old friends in the Lobby; dine in the restaurants; drink on the Terrace; attend meetings of the Parliamentary Labour Party in the committee room upstairs. Why, it would be like having an additional – and rather better informed – political correspondent.

For my part, I did not mind in the least. Crossman was always most generous with any information he had at his disposal. Nor did he normally dispense it, as Kingsley Martin had said he did, with any ulterior purpose in view. He simply enjoyed gossiping and making mischief. What I did mind – and what would have happened anyway, irrespective of whether he had remained as MP – was that the paper became full of political articles. Certainly Crossman's presence at Westminster in the late afternoon and in the evening enabled ambitious Labour MPs, by now in opposition and with time on their hands, to bend his ear with suggestions for articles to be written by themselves.

But quite apart from importunities of this kind, one of Crossman's objects was, as he put it, to 'make policy' for the next Labour government. To this end, he inaugurated an additional weekly conference, to take place on Thursday, something of a *dies non* with most weeklies. Over his 18-month spell the attenders included Thomas Balogh, Tony Benn (whom Crossman called 'Wedgie' and who lasted only a few weeks before withdrawing at his own request), Barbara Castle, Alun Chalfont, Harold Lever and Des Wilson, the Director of 'Shelter'.

Chalfont was then known principally as the former Minister for Disarmament in a Labour government. Before that he had been Alun Gwynne Jones, defence correspondent of *The Times*, and before that a regular officer in the South Wales Borderers. His dress was of the officers' mess or the City boardroom, an area in which he was just beginning to take a lucrative interest, rather than of the higher journalism: a cream silk shirt with generously displayed cufflinks, a discreet tie, a dark, well-cut suit and highly-burnished black shoes.

'Poor old Alun,' I once remarked. 'Hasn't anyone told him? A certain standard of scruffiness is expected at the *New Statesman*.'

In fact he was both a reliable and an accomplished journalist. Without becoming a full-time member of the staff, he took over Francis Hope's functions when the latter left the *New Statesman* to go on a round-the-world trip and, later, to work in Paris for the *Observer* and in London for the BBC. Hope was killed in the Turkish Airlines Paris crash of 1973. He was presumably not short of money because his surname was represented in Crittall-Hope steel-framed windows. His father, Michael Hope, had been at Winchester with Crossman. Francis had been to Eton, had read History at Oxford and was a Fellow of All Souls. His curly dark hair, arrogant eyes and aquiline nose should have appeared over a Regency cravat. The eyes were deceptive. He was less arrogant than always amenable and sometimes charming. Of all the journalists I have known, he was also the most reluctant not only to put pen to paper or finger to keyboard but even to make a commitment to engage in such an activity.

'Now, Francis,' Paul Johnson would ask in the days before Crossman's arrival, 'do you think you could do us a piece on the mischief the French are making?'

'Well, it's a bit early, Paul,' Hope would reply. 'We'll have to see how the situation develops.'

'What about next week?'

'It may still be a bit early.'

'The week after that then?'

'I can't promise, Paul. Things may still not have worked themselves out.'

'But we've got to have something on what the French are up to.'

'Oh all right, Paul.'

Crossman began by having a higher opinion of Hope than of any other member of the staff, partly because he had known his father but mainly because he was a Fellow of All Souls. Later he viewed him less favourably, and thought Anthony Howard would be the better successor. His deputy editor was Tom Baistow, a Scot, the ship's engineer, who had served with gallantry in the war and with distinction on the old *News Chronicle*, where his heart still lay, with James Cameron and 'Vicky' the cartoonist. The other main members of his staff were Anthony Thwaite, the literary editor, Corinna Adam and myself. With the exception of Baistow, we were all in our mid-thirties or younger. Shortly after his arrival, Crossman recorded his impressions of us:

> Here they hadn't had to work very hard, here they had merely written to contract without great revisions, without changes, here they hadn't had to come in much at the end of the week … They had an uneasy feeling with me that a new regime was coming up, a rough breeze was blowing through the *Statesman*, they were harassed and therefore could easily blame it on this silly old [he was then 62] politician coming in.[9]

The superabundance of editorial conferences combined with Crossman's disposition to accept articles from stray Labour MPs he might encounter in the corridors of Westminster to produce a highly political paper. I was warned off subjects not because my views, if I had any, were considered dangerous or otherwise unsound but because other people had been engaged by Crossman to write about those subjects. I responded by staking, perhaps over-aggressively, various territorial claims at the beginning of the week. Crossman thought I was

> one of the lighter parts of the paper and he writes it very gaily and amusingly and I don't want at all to lose it, and yet he doesn't want to have any relationship to the rest of the paper, he wants to overlap as much as he likes … I had to say, no, you can't do everything … Tony Howard is much more friendly towards me.[10]

In July 1970 he recorded a 'considerable altercation' with me about Harold Wilson's dissolution honours list. Apparently the cause of the row (of which I have no recollection, though I am sure it happened) was that I wanted to anticipate the list, whereas Wilson had assured Crossman that no list was yet in existence.[11] By August 1970 we had had what I regarded as a big row and he called

> a bit of a tiff with Alan Watkins that [Wednesday] morning. [Wednesday was press day. He] came in just before I was due to leave and dumped an article on my place. And I had asked him on the previous Monday:

[9] Crossman Diary, 3 July 1970: Warwick MSS 154/8/71.
[10] Crossman Diary, 16 July 1970: Warwick MSS 154/8/71.
[11] Crossman Diary, 20 July 1970: Warwick MSS 154/8/71.

'You do the change of government ...'

To my fury old Watkins had merely mentioned [John] Davies and not mentioned [Geoffrey] Rippon at all. I said:

'Look, for God's sake, you have got to put a paragraph about Rippon in.'

And then I rushed off ... So he rings up and I say it has got to be done, and he says he won't. He says:

'You will have to lump it, Dick.'

I said:

'Well, I damn well won't lump it. You write the two paragraphs.'

And he did. And then half-an-hour later said he had handed in his resignation to Jack Morgan [the company secretary]. All this is found in the *Sunday Times* this weekend, much to my annoyance.[12]

We made our peace next morning, the Thursday. Crossman said he did not want to lose me. I did not really want to leave the *New Statesman* unless it was to write a column in the *Sunday Times* or the *Observer*. Neither was then on offer, though whenever I met Harold Evans, the editor of the *Sunday Times*, he would say he would shortly be in touch with a view to offering me employment of some description. But then, Evans used to say that to everybody. Crossman and I compromised by agreeing that I should continue my column on the same basis as before but cease to be a member of the paper's editorial staff. I would be a freelance, paying my income tax under Schedule D. As he flatteringly put it: 'Good writer, rotten staff-member.' We further agreed that I should consult my account-ant, A.P. (Pat) Kernon, who had dealt with my income tax since 1961 and became a good friend.

Kernon specialised in writers and was closely connected with the Society of Authors. He possessed an impeccable bedside – or, per-haps, bar-stool – manner, effortlessly purveying reassurance: 'There, there, don't worry. I can sort it out quite easily if you forward the necessary papers to me.' On this occasion his advice was unequivocal: first, not to accept the freelance arrangement for less than I had been paid before and, second, to insist on continuing to receive directly reimbursed expenses. Crossman jibbed at both demands. He was particularly reluctant to carry on paying ex-penses. Freelances, he maintained, did not in the nature of things have their expenses paid. I replied that it was impossible to write

---

[12] Crossman Diary, 29 August 1970: Warwick MSS 154/8/71.

a political column of the kind he wanted without taking the occasional politician out to lunch. After some pouting on his part, we settled on the terms Kernon had advised me to demand. I have been a freelance ever since, though not what I call a genuine freelance: I have always entered into contracts whereby a cheque or cheques arrive monthly through the post.

Our new relationship was confirmed happily with a column I wrote immediately after the great row, on the future of Harold Wilson.[13] It was the result of lunch with Roy Hattersley, who told me that, if Labour had won the recent election, as most people had expected the party to do, Wilson's plan was to resign at some time during the 1970 Parliament: he did not intend to soldier on and on. I was pleased with the piece both at the time and subsequently, for it marked the beginning of the winding path which was to lead to Wilson's supposedly 'mysterious' resignation in 1976.[14] Crossman was pleased as well:

Of course we made the paper with 'Mr Wilson's Future' by Watkins, which was a cautious, careful piece, saying something which nobody else had thought before, that really one shouldn't assume that Harold would stay the course for the next full five years … Nobody had said this before and it made a great sensation. It was his own idea and I leapt at it straightaway on Monday [the day of main editorial conference] and I was clearly right to do so. I don't think I terribly pleased Harold.[15]

Among the papers which followed up the article was the *Daily Telegraph*. In its 'Peterborough' column it referred to 'Mr Crossman's reflections by proxy' in the current *New Statesman*. I was angry not only because I was being accused of taking dictation from Crossman but, more annoyingly, because I was not even mentioned by name. It was as if I had been compared to a wooden spoon wielded by Crossman to stir the pot. I determined to secure a correction and apology rather than damages, in which I was uninterested.

Accordingly I communicated with the solicitors who aroused more fear in Fleet Street than the Lord Chief Justice: Messrs

[13] Alan Watkins, 'Mr Wilson's Future', *New Statesman*, 21 August 1970.
[14] See Alan Watkins, *The Road to Number 10: from Bonar Law to Tony Blair* (pb edn 1998), 203-8.
[15] Crossman Diary, 31 August 1970: Warwick MSS 154/8/71.

Goodman, Derrick. My case was not dealt with by the great man himself, Lord Goodman, who doubtless had other preoccupations, but by his senior partner, John Montgomerie. Goodman wrote later that Montgomerie 'possessed one of the shrewdest legal minds in the country ... was as taciturn as a Trappist monk, hardly uttering a word when he regarded it as unnecessary'.[16] He moved swiftly and without fuss. Within days, a gratifying correction and apology appeared in the 'Peterborough' column, saying that I would be the last person to be anybody's proxy. The *Telegraph* paid Lord Goodman's bill.

I do not regret taking the action I did and, in similar circumstances, would do the same again. Auberon Waugh and others believe that journalists should never have recourse to the law of defamation. In practice they are more likely to avail themselves of it than most other professions. They are more sensitive than politicians or even actors and actresses, rivalled only by academics. Even so, a solicitor's letter produces a spectacular effect in a newspaper office. Editors put work aside, 'executives' are summoned, anxious conferences convened. Such a letter is often the only means available to force a newspaper to behave even half decently.

One of Crossman's sources was Neil Marten, the Conservative Member for Banbury. They tended to travel to London together by train, usually on Mondays. Marten was much to Crossman's liking because he was sceptical, irreverent, independent. More: he was, like Crossman, opposed to our membership of what was called the European Common Market, which was then still in doubt (we were to join formally on 1 January 1973).

Once Marten told Crossman of some impending changes at Conservative Central Office whereby the selection of parliamentary candidates would be more rigorously controlled, awkward elements being ruthlessly eliminated. Crossman told me and suggested, perfectly legitimately, that it might provide a good subject for a column. Having made inquiries, I found that the changes were largely procedural and not nearly as draconian as Marten had indicated to Crossman. I persisted nonetheless in writing about Central Office and Conservative candidates. Crossman was disappointed with my efforts.

'But this isn't what I told you,' he said.

---

[16] Arnold Goodman, *Tell Them I'm On My Way* (1993), 366 quot. Brian Brivati, *Lord Goodman* (1999), 156.

'What you told me, Dick, wasn't true.'

'Never said it was true,' Crossman replied, looking like an affronted infant. 'Only said it was interesting.'

His dismissal by the board in 1972 resulted in a depreciation of his virtues as an editor. Crossman's *Statesman* was the first paper to question the privileged financial and fiscal position of the Royal Family. In those days this was regarded as risky journalistically. Over 20 years were to elapse before the correctness of the paper's views on the royal finances was generally acknowledged. It was even acknowledged by Her Majesty, who made various concessions. Admittedly these had less to do with the *New Statesman*'s small campaign of the early 1970s than with the diminished status of the Royal Family in the 1990s – and with Phillip Hall's unchallenged researches into the subject. Nevertheless, Crossman should be given some credit for having spotted its importance before anybody else.

But what he was most interested in was the Labour Party's attitude towards the Common Market. In the early 1970s, he would muse – though 'muse' is an inappropriate word for Dick's noisy reflections – the pro-Marketeers occupied the same position as the Bevanites had in the early 1950s. They had not only an internal party organisation such as the Bevanites had possessed then but also a leader, a Bevan of their own in the person of Roy Jenkins. Clearly, Crossman would continue, the internal organisation, the party within a party, must be destroyed, and its leader, though not perhaps formally expelled from the party, forced out of any pre-eminent position within it. The party of Wilson, he would conclude, must not make the same mistake as the party of Attlee. That mistake was to be weak, to display tolerance of dissentients.

Coming from Dick, who had himself, with Bevan, benefited from the tolerance of Attlee (though not of Morrison), this was rich, not to say fruity. This most audacious of poachers had briefly been transformed into the most assiduous of gamekeepers. The chosen instrument for destroying the Marketeers and discomposing Jenkins was to be a referendum on whether we should join the Market. This device had been thought of – or been taken up – by Tony Benn, or Anthony Wedgwood Benn as he was still called. Crossman joined in with all the enthusiasm of a puppy that had just been presented with a particularly bouncy ball to play with.

He was forever urging me to write about the referendum before it had become party policy. He went so far as to arrange an interview on the subject with Benn. Or perhaps – I never got to the truth of the matter – Benn had asked Crossman to fix the meeting. I did not much like the arrangement, but went reluctantly at the appointed time to Benn's house in Holland Park, London, W.11.

Benn was charm itself – he was always a well-mannered man – as he ushered me into his basement workroom containing tape recordings rather than books. He showed me to an armchair with a side table beside it on my right. On the table rested an impressive composition consisting of a cut-glass tumbler, a small cut-glass jug of water, some ice (which may have been in a cut-glass dish, but I have now forgotten) and a bottle of Chivas Regal whisky, a concoction much esteemed in the United States and part of the Seagram drinks empire, a contributor to the fortune of Caroline, Mrs Benn.

'I'm sorry,' I said, 'but I don't terribly like whisky.'

'I thought all journalists drank whisky,' Benn said and, with evident irritation, for his plans had been impeded:

'What *would* you like?'

I said some lager would be fine. Benn moved out of the room and yelled:

'Caroline, do we have any lager?'

'We finished the last bottle on Tuesday,' she shouted back.

Benn then made arrangements for the beer to be obtained from some nearby off-licence or shop. Anthony Howard said to me afterwards that I should have drunk the whisky without making a fuss.

After this diversion, Benn said he thought the people wanted the chance to express their opinion on the Common Market. He was then speaking as an opponent of entry. In the 1960s, as WedgBenn of MinTech, he had been in favour on the ground that Europe was the only countervailing force to deploy against the power of the multinational companies.

In 1972 he was successful in making the referendum part of Labour policy. Roy Jenkins resigned the deputy leadership on that account. He later wrote to me saying he had no regrets about doing so, after I had written that he had. He served in the Labour Cabinet of 1974-6, left for Brussels in 1976, delivered his Dimbleby lecture urging the need for a fourth party in 1979 and helped form that party in 1981. So Crossman succeeded in his object of forcing Jenkins out of the Labour Party – though it would be equally true to say that Jenkins would have taken himself off in any event.

The early 1970s were distinguished by a rise in the self-assertiveness and in the power of the trade unions. The National Union of Journalists was the larger union catering for journalists – the other was the Institute of Journalists. The NUJ, which many regarded as being hardly a trade union at all, was blown along by the winds of the times; and those members of the staff of the *New Statesman* who were already members of the union, virtually the whole of them, followed in the wake. They decided to set up a 'chapel' or branch of the union at the paper. The board reluctantly agreed to negotiate with the chapel about wages and conditions. Crossman rightly held himself aloof from these proceedings, which mainly concerned money.

In January 1972 Crossman underwent an operation for cancer of the intestine. Ten years previously he had had a gastrectomy, as a consequence of which he wore a large black truss. I can remember him parading up and down in it in the sitting room of his suite at the Imperial Hotel, Blackpool, during the party conference of 1970. He also claimed that, because of this first operation, he never suffered from hangovers. Though the second operation had been as successful as the first, he was away from the office for two months.

As often happens during these interludes, the board, led by Jock Campbell, decided to dismiss him. Strictly, they decided not to renew his contract. Before Crossman knew about this, the editorial staff (including me, theoretically a freelance) fulfilled our Christian duty by visiting him at his farmhouse – as it was always called, though in fact it was a substantial 17th-century manor house – at Cropredy, near Banbury. Half-a-dozen of us left Paddington like a rugger party or, perhaps, an anti-rugger party. We bore as a suitable present for a convalescent two bottles of Krug champagne which I had purchased from El Vino's out of NUJ funds.

Crossman perfunctorily accepted the wine and immediately secreted it somewhere in the kitchen regions of the house. We did not expect to be given a glass. Apart from anything else, it would not have been cold enough. What we did expect, having journeyed all the way from London on a particularly bleak February afternoon, was something more substantial than the tea and biscuits which Dick proffered. We certainly did not expect what was virtually a tirade on his part about the inadequacies of the paper during his absence. He had been particularly impressed by the *New York Review of Books*, which he had been reading but which was not, in any real sense, a direct competitor of the *NS*.[17] A well-intentioned visit to the sick had been transformed into an unexpectedly disagreeable editorial conference. Tom Baistow, who had been in charge of the paper, said he had not come all the way to Banbury to have its inadequacies pointed out to him. When we left, everyone was disappointed: some of us, including myself, thought the sooner Crossman went, the better for all concerned.

His departure was not long coming. Again, as often happens on these journalistic occasions, the deed was done over breakfast, in this case at Lord Campbell's flat in Eaton Square. Campbell told him that his contract would not be renewed after the end of 1972. Under its six-months-notice provision, he would have had to be told at the end of June. Campbell thought Crossman might have preferred to be told immediately – it was then mid-March 1972 – and to resign because of ill-health. This Crossman refused to do. He preferred to say he had been dismissed. Instead of giving him a day to pack his belongings (the normal newspaper practice, a whole day being on the generous side), the board allowed him to stay at his desk for the next few weeks.

There ensued a controversy conducted largely by Crossman which delighted the political classes but did the *Statesman* little good. The board maintained that Crossman had bullied and alienated the staff.[18]

V

Crossman hoped we would come out in his favour and possibly even threaten a strike. He was deluding himself in both expectations. We issued a statement loftily deprecating the way in which the business had been handled by the board and then moving on rapidly to a demand that we should have a say in the choice of Crossman's successor. On 20 March 1972, 12 of us met Campbell and two of his colleagues in the boardroom. He (I quote the minutes):

agreed to recommend to the board that a committee should be formed

---

[17] Cf. Howard, *Crossman*, 310. Howard wrote that Crossman 'summoned' us to see him. My own recollection is that we went voluntarily, though obviously prior arrangements would have been made; which rendered Crossman's boorish behaviour all the more hurtful.

[18] Throughout these events, 'the staff' was used, both by the board and by ourselves, to mean not the staff defined strictly – that is, those who had contracts of employment – but, rather, those who were members of the NUJ chapel.

under his chairmanship to consider the selection of the next editor and to make recommendations and nominations to the board, the committee to consist of six people, three from the editorial staff, and three from the board (including himself).[19]

The board's representatives were Jock Campbell, Hugh de Quetteville (the managing director) and Paul Johnson; the staff's were Corinna Adam, Benedict Nightingale and myself. The committee contained at least three persons of hot temper: Ms Adam (then Mrs Neal Ascherson), Johnson and me. But we continued to work together with remarkable harmony and came up with a shortlist of six: Francis Hope, Anthony Howard, Peter Jay, Karl Miller, John Morgan and Bruce Page. We then interviewed them. Howard created a favourable impression, with Campbell particularly, by arriving with a handful of notes about the past, present and future of the paper; Page was less reassuring to the staff element, making the comparison between a weekly journal and a boat crew, and stating that you produced a much better crew if you sacked the old oarsmen and started off with a new lot.

We faithfully reported to the chapel what each of them had said. We then had a vote, which produced: Howard 8, Hope 3, Page 1. Howard had won a clear absolute majority; we recommended him to the board's representatives on the joint committee. They – without consulting the board as we had consulted the chapel – said Howard was their man too. He was then rapidly appointed editor by the board.

Afterwards Crossman, who wished Howard well, said to me that if what had happened at Great Turnstile had happened instead at Transport House, I would have written a column mocking a transparent fix. Certainly the process would have been messier if the board members of the committee had produced their own candidate, or if the board had produced someone else again. But neither happened. Paul Johnson told me afterwards that, left to its own devices, the board would have come up with Anthony Howard in any case.

At all events, it was a pioneering exercise. When we began it, Alexander Irvine, then a rising lawyer at the commercial bar, later Lord Irvine of Lairg, warned me I was engaged in a dangerous enterprise which might well land me in trouble. The cautious Scot advised me to have nothing to do with it. He did not see how a board

[19] In the possession of the author.

could relinquish power as that of the *New Statesman* was reported to have done. But it did; and by the end we had set a precedent.

In 1975 both the *Guardian* and the *Observer* used staff participation to choose Peter Preston and Donald Trelford to succeed, respectively, Alastair Hetherington and David Astor; in 1978 the *New Statesman* used the mechanism set up in 1972 to choose Bruce Page to succeed Anthony Howard. In the decades that followed a staff voice in the choice of editor became as quaint, as remote in time, as long hair for men and platform shoes for women. Modern management would as soon consult the horoscope column as the staff about who should be the new editor.

Anthony Howard was the last editor to preside over a paper which was, in its way, and for a time – from the 1930s to the 1970s – part of Western civilisation. He was the most conscientious and industrious editor for whom I have worked, his only rival in both these qualities being John Junor. Letters were answered by return of post, manuscripts read all the way through. Unlike most literate editors, he read the whole paper, not just those parts of it that had been written by himself. He also encouraged the young: in those days, Martin Amis, Julian Barnes, Tina Brown (who rapidly went on to better herself), James Fenton, Christopher Hitchens, Francis Wheen. Nor did he spurn the elderly: when Auberon Waugh took his *New Statesman* column to the *Spectator* in 1976, Howard replaced him with Arthur Marshall, so reinaugurating his career.

His defects were that he was uninterested in the details of party policy and – what is not at all the same thing – the principles of political action. In this he resembled Malcolm Muggeridge and A.J.P. Taylor, both of whom had a horror of abstract argument. His aversion to 'policy' came as a welcome relief after the Crossman interlude. In one respect, however, he reversed Crossman's policy. In the 1975 referendum on our membership of the Common Market, the paper urged a Yes vote. I wrote a column entitled 'Why I Shall be Voting No'. Howard said this was very useful, as it demonstrated that the *NS* was not a propaganda-sheet.

VI

My most colourful colleague, of a sort, during the 1972-6 period was Tom Driberg, later Lord Bradwell, who did occasional stints on the diary. He would appear in the Colony Room, better known as

Muriel's, in Dean Street with a succession of leather-jacketed young men, usually called Terry, whom he would invariably introduce to the assembled company as 'one of my constituents'. He would then provide Terry with a handful of loose change and direct him to the fruit machine in the corner, while he gossiped with Maurice Richardson and Francis Bacon.

He would also attend the fortnightly *Private Eye* lunches at the Coach and Horses pub, not far from Muriel's. He was a regular attender in the 1960s, but stopped coming some time before his death at 71 in 1976. Oddly enough, Richard Ingrams, the then editor, did not make him unwelcome on these occasions, despite his well-advertised aversion to homosexuality. Certainly Driberg did not contribute much in the way of gossip or information. His principal activity was to point out, or engage in arguments about, solecisms, whether syntactical, ecclesiastical or social, as in: 'My dear Richard, I am astonished that you don't appear to know the correct way to refer to the younger daughter of a marquess.' The real reason why Driberg was such an assiduous attender at these lunches was that he had conceived a passion for Patrick Marnham, a regular attender likewise. Marnham, a resolute heterosexual, did not respond favourably to these advances.

Luckily Driberg nurtured no such feelings for me. So when I was looking for a flat in London in 1973-4 it was with a feeling of security that I accepted his invitation to visit his own flat in the Barbican for purposes of seeing what was on offer. He was very proud of his collection of modern books, which had been valued for him by Cyril Connolly. He seemed less proud of the books themselves than of their valuation by Connolly. I thought he would have done better to go to a proper bookseller but refrained from saying so. As I was leaving he indicated a patch of greenery in the middle distance and said, as if pointing to a further attraction of the property, that the girls of the City of London school played games there.

'Rather a Proustian scene,' he added.

This was distinctly odd. I should not have expected Driberg, of all people, to find the spectacle of no doubt scantily clad schoolgirls disporting themselves diverting or even remotely interesting. Perhaps he simply found them a pretty sight, reminding him somehow of the French novelist in question. Who could tell?

Anthony Howard was a great one for trying to get the latest news into the paper. As it reached, say, Scunthorpe on Saturday (if Scunthorpe was lucky), it seemed to me often deleterious to change an article merely to take account of something that had happened on a Wednesday. Howard took a different view, as he was entitled to do. Driberg agreed with me. Unfortunately a diary, consisting as it does of different paragraphs, is easier to mess about with than 1,300 more or less connected words. Accordingly Driberg was sometimes asked to change or replace a paragraph. He complained but complied. 'It's too bad,' he would lament, '*too* bad.' As he was being paid £60 for his efforts, not particularly good money even for those days, my sympathies were with Driberg.

At around this time I was writing a profile of Max Aitken. Driberg, as an old *Daily Express* man, seemed an obvious person to consult. We had dinner at the Ganges restaurant, where he characteristically informed me that milk was the correct accompaniment to Indian food and, more characteristically still, that this invaluable advice had been imparted to him by 'the Great Beast', Aleister Crowley, who had been a friend of his. At half past ten or so I announced I would have to leave shortly. My son, who was then 15, was alone in the flat I had recently acquired. 'So you have a son?' Driberg said. 'Of 15? Do, please, bring him to see me. I have all kinds of books and pictures that might interest him.' I declined on his behalf, explaining that he was busy with examinations and chiefly interested in cricket. No responsible parent would have done anything else – though curiously enough I now feel that Driberg really did want to show him his books and his pictures, for the old monster had his kindly side.

At the beginning of 1976 I left for the *Observer*. Further and better particulars of my departure are to be found in Chapter 7, because they fit in more conveniently at that point.

6

Forward with the People

Publish and be damned.
Attributed to the Duke of Wellington,
used by Hugh Cudlipp as the title of
his history of the *Daily Mirror*

I

It is difficult now fully to understand how popular journalism in the quarter-century after the end of the war was dominated by two papers, the *Daily Mirror* and the *Daily Express*. The *Daily Mail* was a dowdy aunt to the *Express*'s always vivacious, sometimes shrill and usually silly young woman. The *Mirror* hardly bothered to acknowledge the existence of the other tabloid, the *Daily Sketch*, which went out of business in 1971, in theory merged with the *Daily Mail*. It is, like the *Sunday Graphic*, the *Empire News* and the *Sunday Dispatch* (though unlike the *News Chronicle* and *Reynolds News*), largely unlamented. The *Sun* had not yet been thought of.

By the late 1960s, for reasons that lie outside the scope of this book, both the *Mirror* and the *Express* were running out of puff. This was so of their Sunday versions as well. I had already worked for the *Sunday Express* and was glad to have done so, though I had no wish to repeat the experience. I admired the *Mirror* from a distance, even if I was not so admiring of Hugh Cudlipp's 'shock issues' as most of my colleagues were. But I had never had any ambition to work for the organisation. Accordingly it was a surprise when, in 1968, Michael Christiansen, the editor of the *Sunday Mirror*, asked me to write a political column there in addition to the one I was already writing in the *New Statesman*.

I accepted at once, partly because the paper was supposed to be influential in Labour circles, partly because of the difficulty involved in writing a popular political column (even more difficult than writing a gossip column in a broadsheet) and partly because of the money. In fact £60 a week was not specially generous. I had already, in 1966-7, been earning £100 a week for writing scripts for John Bird and others in the television programmes *BBC3* and *The Late Show*. As for its supposed influence, I discovered that virtually all the Labour MPs I spoke to during the week would have read my contribution to the *Statesman* on the previous Friday, while hardly any would have read what I had had to say in the *Mirror* on the Sunday. This did not bother me in the least: it was exactly what I should have expected.

Having accepted the job, I told my editor, Paul Johnson. With commendable candour, he said that, if I had asked him first, he would have refused permission, but that as I had made a commitment he had no alternative except to allow me to fulfil it. However, he insisted that the words 'Alan Watkins is political correspondent of the *New Statesman*' should appear at the end of my column. This is a condition which editors invariably make when a member of their staff (as I then was on the *NS*) or a contributor in a contractual relationship with their paper is given permission to write for another paper. And, equally invariably, the editor of that other paper is reluctant to accept the arrangement. Christiansen compromised by seeking out the smallest typeface he could find.

In those days the *Mirror* organisation was famous for idleness, for eccentricity and for extravagant expenses claims.[1] I charged no expenses at all to the *Sunday Mirror*. If Paul Johnson had been more grasping by nature, he would have insisted I did – or said it was unjust that the *NS*, though prosperous enough in those days, should have to bear the entire cost of my entertainment of various politicians.

The *New Statesman* was a well-managed concern both then and later, in 1973-6, when I was on the board of the Statesman and Nation Publishing Co Ltd as the staff representative. We had the security of owning the freehold of our premises in Great Turnstile, at the north-east corner of Lincoln's Inn Fields and overlooking the gardens of Lincoln's Inn. Jock Campbell, the chairman, brought Neville Vincent of Bovis (a perfectly agreeable character) on to the board with a view to our selling the freehold to Bovis, who would,

[1] See Keith Waterhouse, *Streets Ahead* (1995), 35 ff.

so Campbell and Vincent assured us, lease part of the premises back to us at a favourable rent. Paul Johnson, Anthony Howard and I refused to accept these assurances, though we did not express our position so bluntly at the several board meetings which discussed the matter. At all events, the sale did not occur. Later, when the three of us had ceased to have any connection with the paper, the Great Turnstile freehold was foolishly sold, after which the *New Statesman* led a peripatetic life before settling down near Victoria station.

Anyway, the *NS* continued to pay my expenses and the greater part of my salary. The only *Mirror* expenses story I know concerns Jeffrey Bernard during his brief spell on the *Mirror Magazine*. He claimed one sum to 'Entertaining Mr Sloane'. Unfortunately the man who was handing over the cash was an *aficionado* of the London stage and at once spotted the reference to Joe Orton's play of the same title. He told Bernard to go away and think of something else. The *Mirror* had a greater reputation for eccentricity than the *Express*. Lord Beaverbrook did not approve of odd behaviour. He certainly did not approve of strong drink and, like Rupert Murdoch later on, and Independent Newspapers from January 2000, would not allow it on the premises of his newspapers. The *Mirror* was an altogether more lax outfit.

The pattern was set by Jack Nener, who was editor from 1953 to 1961, and by his deputy, Dick Dinsdale. The latter was a Yorkshireman who, in the numerous stories that circulated about them, played the feed to Nener, a foul-mouthed, bow-tied Swansea boy. Usually Dinsdale-and-Nener conversations were overheard in the lavatory, as in:

'What we need in this paper, Jack, are a few Young Turks.'

'I can see we could do with a few new faces about the place, but why in fuck's name do they have to be Turkish?'

The sub-editors, like most people who work long shifts in unchanging company, had a number of catchphrases or joke sentences. One of them – it comes from the film of *Tom Brown's Schooldays* rather than from the book itself – was:

'Flashman, you are a bully and a liar, and there is no place for you in this school.'

Nener was overheard asking:

'Who's this Flashman, then, Dick?'

'Flashman? Flashman? I don't think we've got anyone of that name on the paper, Jack. Is he a reporter or a sub?'

'I don't give a fuck what he is, but get rid of him fucking quick. He's a bully and a liar.'

II

Perhaps the best illustration of idleness on the *Mirror* in the 1960s was Roland ('Roly') Hurman, the industrial correspondent. Hurman had a gingerish moustache and dressed in a dark blue, double-breasted, brass-buttoned blazer, a check shirt, a striped tie which laid claim to some association or other, and cavalry twill trousers. When Derek Marks became editor of the *Daily Express* in 1965, Hurman left the *Mirror* to accompany him, ostensibly in some factitious post, in reality as the editor's drinking companion. This was an ancient office in Old Fleet Street comparable to one in a medieval (or, for that matter, a post-medieval) court. The incumbent's duty was to accompany the editor to El Vino's or the pub whenever the editor felt like having a drink. Accordingly his work at the paper could not be too important or take up too much of his time and, most of all, he could present no threat to the editor's position.

Roly had spent a long time preparing himself for this sinecure. At the *Mirror* he would arrive at his office from deepest Surrey at half-past 11 or so to find his assistant, Len Jackson, who was older than he was, already hard at work. Hurman would flick through the morning papers, perhaps even make a telephone call. Had Len got the Frank Cousins ban-the-bomb story under control? He had? Good. And what about Bill Carron and the engineers' union? They were always up to something or other. That was being attended to as well? Excellent. Then Roly would look at his watch.

'Bless my soul, it's five to 12 already. I must rush.'

And Roly would stroll down Fetter Lane – the *Mirror*, before its move to Holborn Circus at the north end of the same street, occupied the ramshackle Geraldine House, near the Public Record Office. He would reach El Vino's at midday. At three, when the bar shut, the company would cram themselves into a taxi or even two taxis and make for the Forum restaurant at the top of Chancery Lane. This was owned by a Spaniard and (rather like L'Epicure in Frith Street) served continental food with an Italian bias. At half-past four or so the company would disperse. Roly would make the short journey to his office to find Jackson still hard at it. After a few inquiries about progress on Cousins, Carron and other subjects, Roly would look at his watch.

'Good heavens, it's five to five. I must dash.'

And he would amble down to El Vino's again, where he would remain until between seven and eight, when he would take a taxi to Waterloo.

III

Michael Christiansen, the editor of the *Sunday Mirror*, was not such a regular attender, though he enjoyed visiting the place from time to time, usually with one or two 'executives' from the paper. After one such occasion they returned to the paper for a game of putting in the editor's office. One of them was prevailed upon to lie on the floor with a golf ball balanced on his forehead. The editor, it was explained to him, was a most proficient golfer who would now strike the ball to the other end of the room without causing any injury to the prostrate journalist. Christiansen took his stance, swung his club, struck and hit his colleague on the side of the head. Luckily he survived, but putting in the editor's office was never again quite so much fun.

Michael Christiansen was the son of Arthur Christiansen, the most famous of all the editors of the *Daily Express*. Moodily smoking a cigarette, Michael was one of the journalists featured in David Bailey and Peter Evans's picture-book of the 1960s, a seminal work in its way.[2] The others were Mark Boxer, Quentin Crewe, Robin Douglas-Home, Malcolm Muggeridge, Robert Pitman, Jocelyn Stevens, Kenneth Tynan, Godfrey Winn and Francis Wyndham. This was distinctly odd because Christiansen, though a highly regarded newspaper professional, was a figure neither of fashion nor of controversy. Unlike his father, he was tall, bulky and bald; and, unlike him, he did not regard himself as a superior sub-editor who took his instructions from on high as his father had from Beaverbrook. He was his own man, who tried to run his own newspaper. Even so, the International Publishing Corporation was a highly political organisation. Though it lacked a dictator like Lord

[2] David Bailey and Peter Evans, *Goodbye Baby and Amen: a Saraband for the Sixties* (1969; pb edn 1970).

Beaverbrook, it possessed both a Central Committee and a party hierarchy.

Hugh Cudlipp was then chairman of IPC, having recently ousted Cecil H. King. Cudlipp maintained an office in the Holborn Circus building where he dispensed homely wisdom and, King having earlier persuaded him to relinquish whisky, dry white wine under the mistaken assumption, shared with many other wine drinkers, that it was a non-alcoholic beverage. I had earlier consulted him about a profile of R.H.S. Crossman which I was writing for the *Spectator*. In the last two decades of his life, the 1980s and 1990s, we met often in the Garrick Club, where his wit, his ability to conjure a metaphor or simile out of the air, was marred only by his refusal to acknowledge that he was deaf. In the period during which I was working for him our paths did not cross once. This was probably as well, because he could be an appalling bully.

He also had his amiable, even kindly side. He was admired by two journalists who, one might have thought, would not have thought so highly of him in the normal course of events: Malcolm Muggeridge and Auberon Waugh. Waugh looked up to him, oddly perhaps, for his 'South Wales radicalism'.[3] Muggeridge was grateful to him for being the only editor to offer him regular work – Cudlipp was then editorial director of the *Daily Mirror* and the *Sunday Pictorial* – when he had been made unemployed by the BBC and other organisations following his attack on the Queen in 1957, which would have passed unnoticed in 2000.

IV

The political adviser to the Daily Mirror Group was then Lord Ardwick. He was one of the several *Mirror* journalists ennobled or otherwise honoured by Harold Wilson in the 1960s. As John Beavan he had enjoyed a distinguished career with the *Manchester Guardian* and been editor of the *Daily Herald* in 1960-2, before taking up his advisory position with the *Mirror*. He was a capable journalist who could write a fluent leading article for any paper in under half-an-hour. He was a good-looking man with a fine silver head but seemed to have been squashed from above by a heavy weight. After completing a sentence in conversation he would utter a sound somewhere between a hiss and a sigh. We never got on. He

[3] Phrase used to the author by Auberon Waugh.

clearly did not care for me. I thought him snobbish, affected and, in his writing, the purveyor of any conventional wisdom that might be lying around.

It was one of his articles which was the cause of my solitary conflict with the *Sunday Mirror*. The conflict came about also on account of the absence that week of Michael Christiansen. Our habit was to meet every Thursday morning at half-past 11 or so at a recently established Davy's wine bar in Hatton Garden across Holborn Circus, for 1968 was not only the year of revolutions but also the year when wine bars sprang out of the pavement all over London. When I told Christopher Mitchell of the older-established El Vino's that he would have to wake up his ideas, he replied:

'You look after your business, Mr Watkins, and I'll look after mine.'

I remember Christiansen describing the Vietnam War as a cancer eating up the West – it was certainly one of the causes of the great inflation of the 1970s – when all around us young men and women were laughingly recounting the latest episode of *Monty Python*. But that week there was no meeting because the paper was being edited by Joe Grizzard, an affable enough cove whose strongest suit was certainly not politics. I told him on the telephone that for the coming Sunday I would be writing about opinion polls. This was one of the subjects I would produce for the benefit of editors when I did not have any very clear idea of what I *would* be writing about. Another was 'the government and the press' or 'ministers and the media'.

On this occasion I did not write about opinion polls but about the conflict in the government – it was now 1969 – between, on the one side, Harold Wilson and Barbara Castle and, on the other, James Callaghan and several ministers over the implementation of the proposals for trade union reform set out in Mrs Castle's White Paper *In Place of Strife*. In my column I took the same line as I had in the *New Statesman*: that, despite Wilson's majority of nearly a hundred, the proposed legislation would not get through the House of Commons because the Labour backbenchers would not put up with it.[4] Nor did they. I was undoubtedly remiss in not telling Grizzard of my change of subject, though whether that would have made any difference to the outcome is more doubtful. For that week

[4] See above, pp. 91-2.

Beavan had decided to make one of his by then rare incursions into print and deal with that same subject.

The *Mirror* was even more loyal to Wilson than the *New Statesman*. Indeed, Cecil King's hostility to the Prime Minister was one of the reasons why Hugh Cudlipp had been able to mount a successful coup against him in 1968. The manifestly crazed nature of that hostility made the reason more valid still. Beavan, one of nature's toadies, not only supported Wilson and Mrs Castle. He also wrote that the Prime Minister always had his way: for the theory of prime ministerial power – in abeyance in the 1970s, revived under Margaret Thatcher, dead with John Major and restored by Tony Blair – was then at the height of its popularity; and Beavan was always inclined to pick up ideas he had come across in *Encounter* or the *Political Quarterly* and serve them up in simplified form without examining them any too closely.

At all events, by that Friday afternoon the acting editor of the *Sunday Mirror* had on his desk (this was in an age before word-processors) two articles, each taking the opposite view. A good editor would have made a virtue of necessity, presented both pieces under some such strapline as: 'Crisis in the Cabinet: two leading political writers give you two different views.' But Grizzard, who pushed lack of inspiration to the level of genius, was not adept at this sort of manoeuvre. Late on Friday afternoon he telephoned me at the *Statesman* to tell me that he would not be using my column that week because I had misled him and because John Beavan had written an article on the same subject as I had chosen.

I left the office at more than my usual gentle pace, turned right into Holborn and reached the Mirror Building in what was, for me, record time. I attained Grizzard's office without obstruction. Thirty, even 20, years afterwards this would have proved virtually impossible owing to the omnipresence of 'security'. I shouted at him. He shouted at me. I shouted back, but louder. I said that I was a friend not only of Christiansen (which was true in the journalist's sense of 'friend') but also of Cudlipp (which did not become true till later) and that next week he would find himself in 'big trouble', which was the phrase I used at the time. Grizzard was clearly disturbed. I left. He then complained about my behaviour to various Fleet Street friends of his, including Mike Edwards of the *Daily Mail*, who told my friend Peter Paterson, then of the *Sunday Telegraph*, that the general view in the pubs and wine bars of the district was that I had behaved appallingly towards a much-liked figure in the trade.

No doubt I had. But I did not offer any apology. Nor was there big trouble for me or for Grizzard. I did not complain to Cudlipp. When I next met Christiansen after his return from his short holiday, he mentioned that he had been told there had been 'a spot of bother' during his absence. He said he hoped the whole matter could now be forgotten. It clearly was not: otherwise I should not be writing this. However, I acquitted Beavan of any part in the incident. He had submitted his article, I had submitted my column and the acting editor had chosen to publish the article rather than the column.

Indeed, I was sorry that I did not get on better with Beavan than I did or – what is not at all the same thing – think more highly of his abilities than I felt able to do. His intellectual pretentiousness, it seemed to me, derived from his failure, for whatever reason, to attend a university after his spell at Manchester Grammar School. I was also very fond of his lifelong companion Anne Symonds, who for many years worked as a political correspondent for the BBC's external services. When I first began in the Commons, she was kinder and more helpful than almost anyone else.

V

In the column that did not appear, Barbara Castle and Richard Crossman inevitably figured. Mrs Castle was set on the trade union legislation. Crossman adopted an altogether more ambiguous attitude; as, indeed, did several other leading members of the government, notably Roy Jenkins. With many twists and turns on the road, they began by promising to travel with her but fell by the wayside; whereas James Callaghan had been against undertaking the journey in the first place. Crossman had always been on close political terms with Mrs Castle. In the 1950s they had been part of the sensible Bevanite Left, the *New Statesman* Left, as distinct from the silly Bevanite Left, which included such figures as Harold Davies and Hugh Delargy, with Michael Foot occupying a position somewhere in the middle. They had now fallen out over coercive legislation against the trade unions. I decided to write next about the *froideur*.

There was no trouble this time. But in the interests of delicacy

– as seen by the *Sunday Mirror* sub-editors – such sentences as 'Barbara was fond of Dick' were transformed into 'Barbara was fond of Richard.' Crossman never used the name 'Richard', signing himself 'R.H.S. Crossman' and being called 'Dick' by anyone who knew him even slightly. (Compare C.R. Attlee and C.A.R. Crosland, who so signed themselves and were called 'Clem' or 'Tony' but never 'Clement' or 'Anthony'.) This disagreement did not prevent them from going on a cruise with their families as guests of Charles Forte on his yacht in sunnier climes. It was an extraordinarily silly thing to do. They managed to keep it quiet until I told the story in the *Sunday Mirror*. Even then, there was scarcely any fuss. Thirty years later there would have been questions in the House, tribunals, inquisitions, calls for the resignation of two members of the Cabinet who had accepted for two weeks the hospitality of a leading businessman and financier. Crossman wrote in his diary:

> I was working at Alexander Fleming House [he was then Secretary of State for Social Services] this morning, when Barbara, looking very distressed, put her head into my room and said she'd had a terrible weekend. She asked me to come and see her, so at 6.30 I went along. I knew that one of the things she wanted to talk about was a very unpleasant piece which Alan Watkins published in his column last week, saying that I had remained uncorrupted by a fortnight with Barbara on Charles Forte's luxury yacht. The secret that he was our host had at last leaked out, though ever since Barbara said she wanted a veto on the story the whole of our family has been religiously careful not to speak about it. Alan Watkins has never even approached me on this and I have an uneasy feeling that he must have known it all along.[5]

In her own diary Mrs Castle has no reference to a call on Crossman on that day, 16 June 1969, but on 23 May refers enthusiastically to the beginning of the cruise:

> On board at last! *Maria Luigi II* is sheer luxury. As Anne [Crossman] put it, it really does make life easier to have four crew looking after six people! [Mr and Mrs Castle, Mr and Mrs Crossman and their two children.] Charles has even sent us Gino from the Café Royal to wait on us, which he does day and night most deftly. I feel uneasy about

---

[5] Crossman Diary, 16 June 1969: *Diaries*, III, 518.

the whole thing but no one else – not even Harold [Wilson] – sees any harm in it.[6]

VI

Reginald Maudling, by contrast, was genuinely corrupt. To a certain extent, he has been written out of Tory history. In 1962-3, when the leadership of Harold Macmillan was increasingly shaky, it was he rather than R.A. Butler, still less Iain Macleod, who was thought to be the likely successor. And yet, such is the fickleness of political fashion, that when Macmillan did resign in October 1963, the contenders were R.A. Butler, Lord Home and, initially, Lord Hailsham, with Reginald Maudling nowhere. When Home resigned in July 1965, Maudling was the favourite to succeed him but the election was won by Edward Heath. Though Heath did not win by a sufficient majority to satisfy the Conservatives' complicated rules (which, in amended but similar form, did for Margaret Thatcher in November 1990), Maudling withdrew from the contest.

Throughout 1964-70 he was in opposition and his thoughts turned to making money. It is still part of our political culture that it is regarded as permissible for former Conservative ministers to go into the City or whatever it may be. Indeed, such a course is expected of them. But if former Labour ministers take the same path, it is looked upon as reason for the utmost suspicion. Former Conservative ministers are sympathised with for 'having no money', even though to the outside observer they may appear to have quite enough of the stuff to be getting on with, as in: 'Poor Douglas (in relation to Douglas Hurd), he has no money.' Former Labour ministers are, by contrast, expected to be grateful for having been ministers at all and to devote the rest of their lives to the back benches, the House of Lords or making public nuisances of themselves in other ways.

Reggie was then Deputy Leader of the Opposition. He was even keener on making money than most former Conservative ministers (in 1962-4 he had been Chancellor). But his personal tastes were not extravagant. Unlike Iain Macleod, who was a member of White's Club, he did not aspire to the Tory *beau monde*. He was

---

[6] Castle Diary, 23 May 1969: *Diaries*, I, 659.

solidly bourgeois and highly intelligent. He liked good wine, whisky and Havana cigars. He was not, however, at all fussy. I once asked him, in Annie's Bar in the Commons, what sort of whisky he liked. 'Large ones,' he replied. His colleagues blamed his wife Beryl for his financial greed. This may have been unfair of them. He was certainly devoted to and very proud of her, a former actress who supported numerous theatrical good causes, including the Yvonne Arnaud theatre in Guildford. So it may be that Maudling's dealings with the corrupt architect John Poulson and others did good in the end. Looking back, I find it astonishing that during this period Maudling was only in his early fifties. We got on well together and used to have a drink once or twice a week at the House of Commons bar to which I have just referred.

Annie's was a resort which was re-established by Robert Maxwell when he was Labour Member for Buckingham in 1964-70 and chairman of the Common Services Committee. His other beneficent action was to make the Terrace of the Commons open to lobby journalists, a privilege that was withdrawn in the 1990s because of 'abuse'.[7] Annie's great days were to lie ahead, in the 1976-9 period, after James Callaghan's government had lost its majority and its survival depended on the Deputy Whip, the Wakefield MP Walter Harrison. He secured that survival and yet remains strangely unhonoured by the People's Party. He and the Scottish nationalists, on whom the continuation of the government partly depended, were regular customers. As I said at the time:

'Every night is Burns night in the SNP.'

So also, at an earlier time, was Reggie Maudling a regular customer. I attacked him in the *Sunday Mirror* not for his connection with Poulson but with Jerome Hoffman and the Real Estate Fund of America. The most corrupting element in political or in any kind of journalism is personal friendship. Maudling was a good acquaintance merely. I like to think that if C.A.R. Crosland, whom I did regard as a friend, had entered into a similar arrangement, I should have attacked him in similar terms. In fact Crosland would have been the last person in the Palace of Westminster to become involved with the Hoffmans of this world and their Funds. So the

[7] What this meant was that some journalists, in contravention of lobby rules, reported what they had seen. The rule is that correspondents have ears but no eyes. They can repeat what they have been told but not what they have seen: in this case summer high jinks, pretty girls suspended by their ankles over the Thames, that kind of thing.

question did not really arise. At all events, I had no hesitation, was assailed by no doubts, about attacking Maudling for his attachment to Hoffman.[8]

In so doing I availed myself of John Junor's comforting but legally unsound maxim: It is not libellous to ask a question. I asked whether it had been wise for a former Chancellor to involve himself with Hoffman. Maudling responded by dispatching a solicitor's letter. The *Mirror* board, I learnt much later – while I was writing this book – took alarm. They feared a repetition of the 'Liberace' case in which the paper had been compelled to pay damages of £8,000 and £27,000 in costs to the United States performer after a derogatory column about him by William Connor ('Cassandra').[9] Hugh Cudlipp even went so far as to visit Maudling with the intention of mollifying him.

I was summoned to a meeting of the board, mostly wearing dark suits with lapels you would cut yourself on if you were not careful. At the head of the table was the more genteel figure of Edward (later Sir Edward) Pickering, chairman both of Daily Mirror Newspapers and of the IPC Newspaper Division. In due course he was to become chairman of virtually every body having any connection with British journalism. I sometimes thought that, if there were to be a committee in journalism with disciplinary powers comparable to those of the Law Society or the General Medical Council, there, seated at the head of the tribunal which was about to deprive me of my licence, would be the bespectacled, undertaker-like figure of Ted Pickering.

On this occasion, however, he was affability itself – as, indeed, he always was when we used to meet at the Garrick Club in the 1980s and 1990s. The board, he said, had decided to settle with Mr Maudling and to apologise to him. This, he went on, implied no criticism of me. In fact I was held in universally high regard. I said they could grovel to their hearts' content provided my small bank balance and slightly more valuable house in Chertsey, Surrey, remained inviolate. So assured, I was shown the apology. The *Mirror* lawyer, Phillip Levy (one of the men with sharp lapels), added that, though he had no wish to be offensive, if 'a London jury' – I remember the phrase distinctly – had to choose between Mr Maudling and me, they would unfailingly prefer Mr Maudling. I did not dissent from this view.

[8] See Michael Gillard, *A Little Pot of Money* (1974), 150.
[9] See Hugh Cudlipp, *Walking on the Water* (1976), 231-8.

Shortly after the apology appeared, Reggie's path again crossed with mine in Annie's Bar. He said he hoped there were 'no hard feelings' on my part. He had had no choice but to take the action he did. I replied that I did not feel at all bitter; as indeed I did not. I did not add that he had been satisfied with a payment of something over £500, even in those days not a large sum. It suggested that he did not regard the libel, if libel it was, as specially serious. My own view was, as it remains, that he would not have taken the case to court and that the Mirror board threw in the towel even before they had been touched by a glove, because they were – understandably – terrified of a libel trial.

VII

I do not think the Maudling affair had anything to do with my being deprived of the column in 1969. It was, indirectly, the consequence of IPC's acquisition of Odhams Press in 1961. With it came the *Daily Herald*, the Labour Party's (strictly, the TUC's) official newspaper, which Hugh Cudlipp did not specially want, because its liabilities, journalistically speaking, exceeded its assets. But Cudlipp, more out of good will towards Labour than anything else, agreed to keep the paper going, with his old friend Sydney Jacobson (an intelligent and modest man) as editor.

In 1964 it was decided to transform the dowdy old *Herald* – for such it remained, despite the best efforts of Jacobson and his predecessor – into the sparkling new *Sun*: 'the paper', it was proclaimed, 'born of the age we live in'. Jacobson was the first editor of the *Sun* and remained in his post till 1965, when he was succeeded by Dick Dinsdale, of the Dinsdale-and-Nener stories.[10] The new *Sun* was less arthritic in the political joints than the old *Herald*. The general impression it conveyed was still one of worthiness. Like the 'Mirrorscope' feature in the *Daily Mirror*, it proceeded on the assumption that, as most people became better educated, so would they wish to be better informed about the world.

Rupert Murdoch, who bought the paper in 1969, possessed no such illusions. It was clear from the start that under its new editor, Larry Lamb, there would be changes. So there were. One of them involved the departure of the *Sun*'s political correspondent, Harold

---

[10] See above, pp. 117-18.

Hutchinson, a distinguished-looking man with silvery hair. The *Mirror* chieftains felt uneasy about Hutchinson and thought they ought to do something on his behalf. My column in the *Sunday Mirror* provided a rabbit hutch into which he could conveniently be popped. I made way for an older man and was paid £800, which was neither munificent nor mean but, at just over three months' pay (I did not have a formal contract), probably just about right.

7

In London Last Night

It's going to be tough on some of the guys, the ones who hanker after the old Fleet Street days, El Vino's, all that. The ones who get all misty-eyed over so-and-so who was a great editor, great character, blah, blah, blah. But I don't seriously believe it was ever any different. It was probably kinder, but so was everything.

Doug Lucie, *The Shallow End*, 1997

I

After he had had a few drinks – or more than a few, for he possessed the strongest head of anyone I have known – Ian Aitken would poke me, quite hard, in the chest (which was one of his habits after he had had a few drinks) and say:

'I have known you for many years, and am very fond of you, but I do not regard you as a proper journalist.'

'Why, Ian, do you not regard me as a proper journalist?'

'Because you have never worked for a daily paper.'

This exchange would be repeated roughly once a year, as unchanging as anything in the D'Oyly Carte Opera. Aitken was quite right, of course. I never had worked for a daily paper. Whether this meant I was not a proper journalist was a matter of opinion. On Saturdays at the *Sunday Express* I had reproduced the working practices of many journalists at that time, starting at ten (in fact at 20 past) and finishing between 11 in the evening and midnight. But it was not the same as doing likewise for five or six days a week. People can make a living wage both because of the political weeklies and because of the unique position which the Sunday papers occupy in Britain. Most countries manage perfectly well with a seven-day press, the Sunday editions being more expensive and more varied

editions of the daily version. In this country this method of production does not seem to work. Goodness knows it has been tried often
enough, though never with complete conviction. No newspaper
proprietor or group has simply abolished the Sunday title and
announced that henceforward it will be the seventh-day edition of
the daily paper. Nor has anyone set up a new Sunday paper on the
same basis. Instead schemes have been devised for joint correspondents and the like; sometimes for single editors for both Sunday
and daily operations. But the supposedly unitary editors soon turn
into editors-in-chief, with two other editors appointed each to su-
pervise the daily and Sunday editions, as happened recently with
the *Express*. And the sharing of correspondents rapidly degenerates
into acrimonious dispute about who should be doing what for
whom, as tends to happen with the *Independent* and the *Independent on Sunday*. For some reason, we like our Sunday papers to
be Sunday papers.

II

By 1974 I had already written several leader-page articles for the
London *Evening Standard*. They were usually on political subjects.
As I was also writing a political column in the *New Statesman* at
the time, this could cause editor-envy. The last is a term I should
explain. National newspapers, daily or Sunday, are usually rich
enough to be able to offer exclusive contracts to their more valued
columnists or contributors or (if you want to put it this way) to
impose such terms upon them. Weekly journals, by contrast, are
rarely in a position to compel exclusivity, because they pay relatively so little money. What they like is a small footnote to the
lucrative article in the *Daily Mail* or wherever it may be.

Paul Johnson was, despite his subsequent reputation for intoler-
ance and irascibility, remarkably easygoing: as, indeed, his accep-
tance of my column in the *Sunday Mirror* demonstrated. R.H.S.
Crossman was too egotistical to concern himself much with the
writings of others, even when they appeared in the publication
which he was supposed to be editing. In any case, he was by then a
politician at heart and had lost the journalist's addiction to other
papers. His predecessor, and the person on whose grave Dick was
stamping, Kingsley Martin, had never possessed it either, though
he was not a politician. When an unfamiliar item of news was

presented to him as the possible subject of a leading article, a diary item or whatever, he would say: 'But it wasn't in the *Guardian*.'[1]

Anthony Howard was a dedicated and indefatigable reader of newspapers. On holiday he was capable of driving 20 miles or so to acquire a day-old copy of the *Daily Mail*. He did not miss much. In addition, he was the most possessive, the most jealous, of editors. He once incurred the considerable wrath of the Labour MP Eric Heffer by advising Heffer, who contributed occasional articles to the *New Statesman*, as he did to several other publications, not to write for the *Spectator*. Heffer said, not unreasonably, that he would write wherever he chose – all the more freely in view of the small fees paid by the *Statesman*. We were having dinner at the Imperial Hotel, Blackpool, during a Labour Party conference. Heffer's indignation was assuaged only by the intervention of his saintly wife Doris.

'Oo Eric,' she said, 'pipe down, and don't make a foos.'

III

Howard never liked my contributing to the *Standard* but was prepared to put up with it. Inevitably I had some contact with the paper's editor, Charles Wintour. He was the son of a major-general who had been educated at Oundle and at Peterhouse, Cambridge, and had himself done distinguished service in the Army during the war. In the mid-1950s, when he was deputy editor of the *Standard*, he had returned to Cambridge as a visiting speaker in a Union debate. In those days these debates were – perhaps still are – supposed to be either 'funny' or 'serious'. This was one of the funny occasions. In his speech Wintour spoke of an un-named friend of his who was said to treat every girl like his sister, 'thereby adding incest to injury'. Later that evening, in the committee room, it was Wintour who first placed my hesitant foot on the path to Fleet Street.[2]

Though he was one of my first benefactors, and in addition possessed a sense of humour of sorts, we never warmed to each other. I soon discovered that he rarely warmed to anyone else of the male sex. With women he was different. It was not that he was a womaniser exactly, though he certainly possessed (in the

[1] Information from Paul Johnson.
[2] See above, p. 40.

obituarist's hallowed phrase) an eye for an attractive woman. He encouraged and was in turn looked up to by a succession of gifted women writers: Anne Sharpley, Barbara Griggs, Valerie Jenkins (later Grove), Mary Kenny. Though he got on reasonably well with Anthony Howard, who appreciated his prefectorial qualities better than I was able to do, it was Howard who coined the name 'Chilly Charlie', after 'Cheerful Charlie (Your Chin-up Boy) Chester', the radio star of the 1940s and 1950s.

Some journalists attributed his coldness to the death of one of his then young sons in a traffic accident when he was on his bicycle. However, Milton Shulman, the *Standard*'s theatre critic and much else besides, said Wintour had always been like this. This terrible episode was, in Fleet Street mythology, also held to account for Wintour's hold over Lord Beaverbrook or, at any rate, for Beaverbrook's indulgent attitude towards Wintour. He had, according to the story, been closeted with his proprietor when the news was brought in the form of an urgent message for Mr Wintour. Beaverbrook had said that Mr Wintour was with him and that they were not to be disturbed – with the consequence that he learnt of his son's death later than he should have done. Beaverbrook was prostrate with contrition, or as near as he ever got to that position, thereafter treating Wintour with noticeable deference and consideration. Wintour was understandably reluctant to recall the event in detail, confining himself to confirmation that he had indeed been with Beaverbrook when he had received the news of his son's death.

Wintour was aware of his reputation for chilliness. Shortly after being made editor of the *Standard*, he thought it would be a good idea to put in an appearance in El Vino's for a small glass of chablis (then 2/6 or 12.5p) just to show he had no side. This was on a day when Alfred Hinds had escaped from prison once again. Hinds was a professional criminal who specialised not only in burglary but also in escaping from prison and challenging the authorities in the courts, where he represented himself, sometimes with success. In a gentler age, he was accordingly something of a public hero. With his latest escape the *Express* had been beaten by the *Mail*: Lord Beaverbrook was cross. He tried to get in touch with the editor of the *Standard* to remedy matters and was told he was in El Vino's. Beaverbrook was put through on the telephone. After some introductory pleasantries he said:

'Mr Wintour, may I give you a piece of advice?'

Wintour indicated that there was nothing he would like better.

'Mr Wintour, my advice to you is this. You will not find Alfred Hinds in El Vino's public house. Good day to you, Mr Wintour.'

IV

In September 1974 Wintour asked me to write about political television during the second general election of that year. This was the election in which William Whitelaw, the Secretary of State for Employment and Chairman of the Conservative Party, accused Labour of 'going round the country stirring up apathy'. It was one of several 'Willieisms' for which he was famous and which bore a resemblance to the sayings of William Deedes. Other examples of Willieisms were: 'It is always a mistake to prejudge the past.' And, in connection with some dispute or other between the Church of England and the Conservative Party: 'Of course, the Archbishop of Canterbury is a very religious man.'

The Sayings of Deedes were, if anything, even more on the surreal side. They had both been in the Conservative government before 1964, Deedes in the Cabinet, Whitelaw at that time outside it. In 1974-86 Deedes was editor of the *Daily Telegraph*. When the young Charles Moore was leaving that paper in 1983 to edit the *Spectator* (which was not then part of the *Telegraph* group), Deedes said farewell with the words: 'Good luck, Charles. Always glad to have you back. Whatever you do, don't burn your boots.' Another of his maxims was: 'You can't make an omelette without frying eggs.' Of the then Foreign Secretary he observed: 'Say what you like about Peter Carrington, he weighs a lot of ice.'

This was the election in which Labour won a majority of only three, having functioned as a minority government in March-October 1974. Harold Wilson and his entourage were disappointed at the result. They did not expect a large majority of the kind that had been obtained in 1966, but they had looked forward to something comfortable, not a majority that was likely to disappear within the next few years, as it duly did on account of adverse by-elections. The result certainly fortified Wilson in his long-held resolve to resign on or around his 60th birthday.[3] Whether he would have held on for longer if the result had been more favourable, possibly scuppering

[3] See Alan Watkins, *The Road to Number 10* (pb edn 1998), 203-11.

James Callaghan's chances of succeeding him, is a matter for speculation.

Covering this election as seen on television was the nearest I had come to what Ian Aitken called real journalism. The copy had to be written either late that night or early next morning. I would then dictate it to the *Standard* copytaker at about 8.00 am. For over 10 years, writing the political column in the *Spectator* and, since 1967, in the *New Statesman*, my practice had been to compose late on Tuesday evening, between 9.30 and 12.30 or so, after a heavy day at the House of Commons and a light supper at home. I could not follow that regime today – would not want to try – and can now only wonder that I managed it from 1964 to 1976.

As soon as I joined the *Observer* in 1976, the pattern changed. Writing a political column, or any other article about contemporary happenings, is easier in a Sunday paper than it is in a weekly, because the problem of being or, at any rate, appearing up-to-date is so much easier to solve. In a weekly you are writing on a Tuesday and typing on the Wednesday morning, with a deadline at lunchtime on Wednesday, for what may not hit the newsagents of Scunthorpe until Saturday. Thursday is still the heaviest political day of the week, despite the shifting of Prime Minister's Questions to the Wednesday (where it is now the one prime ministerial appearance of the week).

The trick, I found, was to anticipate the events of Thursday and of late Wednesday by fixing a fortnightly rather than a weekly frame of reference in my mind. I was lucky. James Fenton, my immediate successor at the *NS*, was less so. Writing in the early stages of the Labour conference of 1976, he devoted his column, or part of it, to attacking the Chancellor of the Exchequer, Denis Healey, for lacking the courage to face his own party. Healey had decided not to come to the conference when Fenton wrote as he did. He was intending to go to an international gathering instead. On the way to the airport he changed his mind, and Healey and the *New Statesman* arrived simultaneously in Blackpool, where he proceeded to give a defiant performance to the discontented delegates.

'Of course, Tony's got no choice except to sack James,' Peter Paterson remarked to me.

I told Paterson not to be uncharitable: that but for the grace of God either of us could have done the same as Fenton, who went on until 1978 as one of the best of the paper's political columnists. In practice I took to getting up at six to write the article for that day's *Standard* on the political television of the previous day.

V

I could have asked Milton Shulman, the theatre critic, for advice about his own habits in the matter: but in my experience it is better to discover one's own way. I am sure that, if I had asked for counsel, Shulman would have given it, enthusiastically, volubly and at length. He was perhaps the most talkative man I have ever known. On the short side of medium, strongly built, with glasses (which looked as if they ought to be dark but usually were not) and grey sideboards and a taste for expensive, slightly garish suits and attractive women, he appeared more Italian, from, say, Milan, than Jewish, from Toronto. He had a whole string of Jewish jokes which he told as a regular guest on the wireless programme *Stop the Week* in the 1970s and 1980s. In earlier decades – in the 1940s and 1950s – he might have become a national figure.

Before the war, he had practised as a barrister in Canada, where he had also performed as a crooner known as 'Whispering Milt'. In the war he had served in Europe in the Canadian Army and ended up in Intelligence, becoming the leading authority on the German Order of Battle. In 1948 he published *Defeat in the West*, an account of our postwar arrangements which became a classic in its genre. In the 1990s a friend of mine visited a German library where he was told:

'We are very proud of our section on military thought. We have on our shelves all your great English classics: General Fuller, Liddell Hart, Milton Shulman ...'

The work also drew him to the attention of Lord Beaverbrook who, on appointing him film critic (a job he did before settling down in the theatre), asked him whether he knew any actresses. On being told that he did not, Beaverbrook was relieved, advising him to persevere in this state of chastity, or ignorance. Shulman used to say that Beaverbrook was the only other person he would have preferred to be. He had possessed wealth, power and, perhaps above all, women. I was not so sure myself. Shulman himself lived in a flat in Eaton Square, London S.W.1, with his attractive wife Drusilla Beyfus, herself a journalist of distinction.

But he was not at all rich. Indeed, he took some pains to make clear that he was not. The flat in Eaton Square was, he would explain, rented on favourable terms from some post-1919 legislation within whose compass it fell; while he himself had a large overdraft at the bank brought about by his daily bet, which cost him £11. It was of a 50p each-way Yankee: a combination bet on four horses consisting of six doubles, four trebles and one accumulator. If it came off, it was, of course, highly profitable. With Shulman, as with most gamblers, it came off rarely: hence the overdraft. He was a patron of the betting-shop rather than of the Turf. At a racecourse, he used to say, all you could see was half-a-dozen horses dashing past the winning-post in a multi-coloured jumble and you would then have to ask: 'Who won?'

At this period he was just over 60. He still played tennis to a high standard. He claimed that, as he grew older, he became more accomplished at two activities: sex and tennis. His sexual claim I told him I could believe, just about, on account of greater experience, increased tenderness and so forth. Of his tennis claim I was frankly incredulous. Shulman maintained that the activity was much like sexual intercourse, in that what was lost in rude vigour was more than made up for in a more polished technique. I remained sceptical.

VI

In fact I did not ask Shulman for his advice about how to write a television column because it did not last for very long, ending as it did with polling day in October 1974. However, I must have given a certain degree of satisfaction, because Wintour asked me to succeed Simon Jenkins as author of a weekly column about London. Jenkins is a gifted writer, marred only by a quality of cockiness which almost everyone who worked for the *Economist*, as he was to do in 1979-86, possesses as a sort of stigmata. He took his column seriously, being knowledgeable about both London local government and London architecture. In 1976-8 and 1990-2 he was editor of respectively the *Evening Standard* and *The Times*. But he was more an author and columnist than an editor. As John Junor, who was rarely generous to younger journalists who might become his professional rivals, remarked at the time:

'Simon Jenkins? Don't talk to me about Simon Jenkins. Interested in the preservation of old buildings and young women. Doesn't make him an editor.'

However this may have been, I did not follow Jenkins's approach to the London column. To be honest, I cheated. I wrote about what interested me rather than about the problems of London. If I could conjure up some connection, real or apparent, with the metropolis, so much the better. The column for which I received the largest postbag was on the, as I thought, declining form of the Arsenal Football Club, on the general lines of: 'Wake up, Bertie Mee!' Mee was the club's manager at that point. I also interviewed Anthony Crosland, the then Secretary of State for the Environment, ostensibly on the problems of London housing, though the interview could just as well have been about the problems of housing anywhere.

This was my first and last essay in this form of journalism. No doubt it fulfilled a useful function for some years after it was invented by W.T. Stead, the 19th-century editor of the *Pall Mall Gazette*, who specialised in interviewing famous people who had made the Atlantic crossing. Today the interview has become not only largely superfluous but almost wholly corrupt, at any rate in the broadsheet press. It is used as a vehicle of free publicity for authors, actors and musical performers – for books, films, operas, concerts and recordings.

Sir John Mortimer is a good writer and a delightful man. He is also a prolific author. Accordingly he gives more or less the same affable interview every year. Jeanette Winterson is perhaps less productive. But a new book by her will be accompanied by lengthy interviews in the literary pages of several papers. The status of the professional interviewer, far from being diminished, has been enhanced – though it is fair to say that the leading practitioners, such as Lynn Barber, Susan Barnes (the inventor of the modern genre) and Terry Coleman, on the whole interview people who they think are interesting rather than those who have something to gain from being interviewed.

Even so, one of the deleterious consequences of the modern fashion for interviewing is that the distinction between the interview and the 'profile' has all but broken down. The profile was revived, in what to modern eyes looks unacceptably skimpy form, in the *Observer* of the 1940s, when newsprint was still rationed. It was developed in the *New Statesman* of the 1950s, where it probably reached its peak. Gradually 'quotes', whether from the person being interviewed or from his or her friends or enemies, insinuated themselves into the article. They are much esteemed by sub-editors as a badge of authenticity. In reality anonymous quotations are virtually useless. The fashion came over here with profiles of members of the Kennedy administration in United States newspapers or in magazines, which were even more influential. Thus: 'Says a Pentagon insider: "He has a diamond-sharp brain." ' This tells you nothing whatever, except that some un-named person wishes to ingratiate himself or herself with the incoming holder of office. My interview with Crosland was intended solely as an interview. I was about to go on a week's holiday, and it could conveniently be inserted into the *Standard* during my absence. Crosland agreed to participate, provided he could see the finished product before it went into the paper.

Normally I do not like showing articles to people before they appear in print. Surprisingly few make it a prior condition of their co-operation. One who did was John Biffen, whose profile I was writing in the *Observer*. He made one or two small corrections of fact, so to that extent the exercise was, I suppose, justified.

I went along to Crosland's room in the House of Commons encumbered by the somewhat unwieldy tape recorder belonging to my son, who was then 15. Tape recorders were more cumbersome in those days. After Crosland had been chatting away for a quarter of an hour or so on the problems of London housing – or of housing generally – he noticed that the tape recorder was no longer functioning. This he pointed out to me in his usual forceful manner. At that moment Tony Benn, who occupied the adjoining office, literally put his head round the door.

'Ah, Wedgie,' Crosland said, 'the very man. You understand these physical things.'

The breakdown having been explained to him, Benn fiddled a bit with the machine, pressed a few buttons and announced:

'It's perfectly easy. You simply reverse the spools.'

Crosland thanked him for his help and he withdrew, apologising for having disturbed us. Crosland had taught Benn at Oxford. He had a high opinion of him as a practising politician, though not as a political theorist. Indeed, Crosland and I once played the game of allotting functions to politicians – debating in Parliament, speaking at meetings, orating at party conferences, broadcasting on the wireless, appearing on television, writing articles, organising support on the back benches and in the party at large – and then marking them out of ten for each function. Benn easily came top, with Denis Healey in second place, followed by Barbara Castle, with Crosland himself well down the list. He referred to Benn by his family nickname 'Jimmy'.

'Nothing wrong with Jimmy,' he would say, 'except that he's a bit cracked.'

We completed the interview. I typed it laboriously from the recording, cut it, added a beginning and an end, sent one copy to the *Evening Standard* and another to Crosland, and went off on holiday. I had been at the hotel a few days when the telephone rang. It was David Lipsey, then Crosland's man of business in Whitehall. Crosland, it appeared, had not merely shown the interview to senior civil servants but caused it to be circulated throughout the department. As a consequence no fewer than 47 'corrections' were not being requested so much as officially demanded. For instance 'squatting', then much in the news, had to be changed to 'unlicensed occupation'. Lipsey added that unless I made the changes required my 'personal relations with Tony would be affected'. I was not disposed to accept threats of this kind from Lipsey or, indeed, from anyone else, and informed him that, unless Crosland had any syntactical, grammatical or factual errors to correct (as he did not), I proposed to publish and be damned, which I duly did.

There was no fuss of any kind. My relations with Crosland remained unimpaired. But Roy Jenkins would not have behaved as Crosland did: or, if he had, he would have told his civil servants to mind their own business. Perhaps that, rather than party management from, successively, Harold Wilson and James Callaghan, was the reason why Crosland never became Chancellor. Having told this story in the *Spectator* of 23 January 1999, I received a letter from Ann Carlton (Mrs Denzil Davies). She suggested that Lipsey had been responsible for the whole episode: that it was he and not Crosland who had circulated the interview with me throughout the department. She hazarded this solution because she too had been working there at the time, in a position similar to the one which Lipsey occupied. Perhaps she was right, and I have been doing an injustice to Crosland.

Though there were no repercussions following this interview, other columns caused trouble. One of them was on the A6 murder case which, in the early 1960s, had resulted in the execution of James Hanratty. He was found guilty at the Bedford Assizes of murdering Michael Gregsten, a government scientist at the road research laboratory. He was also supposed to have raped and tried to murder Gregsten's girl friend, Valerie Storie, who had been left paralysed. Gregsten was married to somebody else, and Miss Storie was one of his younger colleagues at the laboratory.

What had not been explained – and has not been explained properly to this day – was what a minor urban criminal with no record of serious violence, such as Hanratty, was doing in the remote Thames valley field where he first came across the couple in their car. Precisely the same question might have been asked of whoever it was who had committed the murder, whether Hanratty or somebody else. I suggested that whoever it was had been put up to it.

I wrote this very carefully, and was surprised to be told that a firm of solicitors representing one of Mrs Gregsten's relations had written to the *Standard* in menacing tones. I was even more surprised to learn that the person behind this letter was Raymond Blackburn, a Labour MP from 1945 to 1951 (the last year as an Independent), who went to prison for fraud and was consequently deprived of his career both as a politician and as a solicitor. However, he had continued to act as a kind of freelance solicitor. I had once come across him, to all appearances a practising lawyer, in Bow Street magistrates court. He told me, I remember, that the most important part of the proceedings was the application for search warrants conducted by a procession of policemen. He was also a great writer of letters to the papers. And he had involved himself, sometimes successfully, in various cases of a public-law character.

Here he seemed to be acting as a kind of solicitor's nark. Whether he was employed or retained by the solicitors who had written to the *Standard* on behalf of Mrs Gregsten's connections or by the connections themselves was not immediately apparent. From other evidence which it would be tedious to go into, I concluded that it was the former. In either case, the Law Society should have been concerned about Blackburn's activities at this period. Though they could not discipline him, for he was no longer a solicitor, they could certainly make their displeasure known to those solicitors who were using his legal services.

Wintour was not at all interested in this aspect of the matter. Indeed, I doubt whether he realised what had happened. All he was concerned about – all most editors are ever concerned about in comparable circumstances – was that the paper had been compelled to pay out money. Here it had been £600, a small sum even in 1975 for a serious libel. Wintour wrote to me saying we had been lucky to get away with so tiny an amount and that I must take greater care in future. In fact I had taken great care. If the *Standard* had chosen to display the courage which the *Observer* was to demonstrate in 1988, in the case of *Meacher* v. *Trelford and Others*, the paper might well have succeeded, as the *Observer* did on that later occasion. If it had succeeded, or even defended the action, successfully or not, a good deal of the speculation about the murder would have been avoided. Our law of defamation is in many respects unfair and absurd. But a three-week trial in the Queen's Bench Division of the High Court is still one of the best ways of arriving at the truth about anything: much better, certainly, than any parliamentary or departmental inquiry.

The editor wrote me another letter at around this time. He complained I was not writing enough about London. This, as I have already indicated, was a just criticism, though its manifest justice did not make me any more inclined to change my ways. I ought to get down to County Hall more, he wrote (when I did not get down to the institution in question at all). In particular, I ought to form a liaison – a journalistic liaison – with Lady Lewisham. Simon Jenkins had been a great friend of hers when he had been writing the column; she had proved a most informative source. Raine, Lady Lewisham, had been Mrs Gerald Legge and was to become the Countess of Dartmouth and, later, the Countess Spencer. I had not met her (nor have I yet), but by all accounts she was a difficult woman. I had no intention of seeking her out on the whim of Charles Wintour or, indeed, of anyone else.

VII

I was not altogether sorry to part company with him and the *Standard*. It was not a blow when he told me I was being replaced by Mary Kenny. Though the money I had earned had come in useful, I was being paid more to write the political column in the *New Statesman*, as I had since 1967. And for Miss Kenny (Mrs

Richard West) I possessed personal affection and professional admiration. She was Irish, and had left her convent school without going on to a university, though she was clearly clever enough to have done so several times over. Like many Irish people, she had the gift of both writing readably and writing well. She was very much a *Standard* journalist, whose admiration for Wintour was exceeded only by his devotion to her. Then and subsequently, she reproached me for my failure to appreciate his finer qualities. For myself, I tended to echo Anthony Crosland, who used to remark:

'Why does everyone go on so about Charles Wintour? All those smart parties and first nights do not affect the truth that he is just another Beaverbrook editor.'

This was not Miss Kenny's view of him. He had helped her. In the 1960s, when she began to work for the *Standard*, she was in tune with the spirit of the age. Auberon Waugh observed that it was her historic function to introduce a whole generation of shy old Etonians to the joys of sex – the young men in question being employed largely on the now defunct feature 'In London Last Night'. This was a gossip column about the famous or notorious persons who had been spotted at parties during the previous evening. An acquaintance of mine from Cambridge days, David Stone (now dead), invented a character called Venetia Crust, as Adam Symes, 'Mr Chatterbox' of the *Excess*, invented Imogen Quest in *Vile Bodies*. Stone likewise was given the sack.

She was also responsible for adding a phrase to the language. In the early 1970s Neal Ascherson and his wife Corinna Adam, then working respectively at the *Observer* and the *New Statesman*, gave a party at their Georgian house in Bethnal Green. Mary Kenny was one of the guests. Others included Christopher Price, MP, Peter Paterson, James Fenton, Jonathan Dimbleby, his wife Bel Mooney and Corinna's mother, Ruth Adam. Another guest was a Ugandan diplomat with one leg. During the course of the evening he disappeared into an upstairs room, accompanied by Miss Kenny. After the lapse of some time the hostess, Mrs Ascherson, remarked to Fenton:

'If you go upstairs, James, you'll find two people talking about Uganda.'

Subsequently the phrase 'talking about Uganda' became a great favourite with *Private Eye* as a synonym for sexual intercourse. Further variants included 'having Ugandan discussions' and 'taking a close interest in African affairs'. Dictionaries and other works of reference give incorrect accounts of the phrase's origins. The true version is the one provided above.

Miss Kenny, however, did not write a London column. It was not presented as such but as a new, European column. In 1975 we were cemented by the referendum into the Common Market, as it was then called. She travelled to Hamburg to meet Helmut and Hannelore, to Lyon to meet François and Yvonne. She discussed their problems in earning a living and making ends meet. She was a wholly admirable successor.

VIII

In 1974 I separated from Ruth, to whom I had been married for 19 years, and removed myself from Chertsey in Surrey to Islington in North London. My son, who was then 14, came with me by his own choice, while his two younger sisters remained with their mother. Though I had been fairly prudent and was paid a living (though hardly a munificent) wage by the *New Statesman*, moving out of the matrimonial home is always an expensive business. To tide me over I thought I needed an additional £5,000. I knew two rich men, perhaps a few more, but two whom I liked and regarded as occupying that no-man's-land between personal friendship and journalistic usefulness: Ian Gilmour and Harold Lever.

For some reason I chose Lever as my potential benefactor. I had known him for a decade or so, since Labour had come to power in 1964. At this time he was Chancellor of the Duchy of Lancaster and a member of the Cabinet whose chief function it was to proffer shrewd financial advice to the Treasury. He was an affable character who had made his money through a practice known as 'bond washing' which was later made illegal. He told me that, through his financial activities, he had once held the monopoly of the importation of bathroom sponges, a commodity of which he was completely ignorant, except for their use in bathrooms.

He looked like a Lancashire comedian but was funnier. He lived in a flat in Eaton Square, London S.W.1 with his pretty and engaging Lebanese wife Diane, whom he said he would still have married even if she had not been as rich as she was. Inside the flat, he spent most of his time in a silk dressing-gown. When visitors asked, as they sometimes did, whether he was unwell, he would reply that he was perfectly all right, thank you very much, but saw no reason to change into a suit or anything else when he had no intention of going out. He liked to say that, compared to most rich men, he led a simple life. He had a flat in Central London and took an annual holiday in Deauville in Normandy. That was all: he did not possess a yacht, a racehorse, a country estate, a Rolls-Royce or even a mistress.

When I called at the flat in Eaton Square, Lever was full of solicitude for what he took to be my personal difficulties. He said that there was 'nothing worse' than domestic trouble. It meant you could not work, could not get on with anything. I agreed. On the other hand, he continued, warming to the subject, it did not do to be too comfortable either. Perfect, harmonious domesticity could easily turn into lassitude and a consequential failure of the will. I agreed with this too, omitting to add that at that moment it was the least of my difficulties. Moreover advice, however good and however well-intentioned it might be, was not what I needed. What I needed was money, preferably in the form of an interest-free loan. Somehow I managed to steer the conversation round to the subject.

Ah yes, Lever said, money. I would clearly be in need of some of that if I intended to set up a separate establishment in London. Presumably I was not in search of anything too grand? Not at all, I replied: three rooms, a kitchen and a bathroom would suit my requirements admirably. Just so, Lever mused, just so. Well, his advice would be to go to the bank. Bankers were the people to go to if you wanted to borrow money. It was their business, after all. He believed Barclays were a most reliable concern. I said I already had an account with them. Excellent, said Lever. I should just trot along to my bank manager. The current rate of interest was – what was it? – 17 per cent. As he waved a genial good-bye he said:

'And don't forget, if you're ever in any trouble, don't hesitate to come and see me.'

IX

In the end I did not have to visit the bank. I found that, taking out a mortgage, I could afford a flat costing £13,000. This, it should be remembered, was 1974, when the price of property was going down owing to the pressure which the banks were exerting on developers. This was a consequence of the 'secondary banking crisis' of that year. At any rate, I was able to afford a flat of the size I needed in Baron's Court, in Battersea or in Islington. I sought my son's opinion. He advised Islington, because it would be best for watching the Arsenal Football Club, of which he was then a devotee.

In June 1974 we moved in. As I was already a perfectly competent cook, we managed quite well. We occupied the flat on the first floor. Completely by chance, Frank Johnson moved into the ground floor flat at the same time. A few years later, by chance likewise, Matthew Engel, the *Guardian* writer and *Wisden* editor, took over the second-floor flat. I liked to think we were a nest of singing-birds. Certainly the presence of Frank Johnson around the place made the move more easy and less painful than it might otherwise have been. Johnson was a very funny man who kept my son and any other friends who were introduced to the premises in a constant state of amusement.

X

At this period I took to patronising the King & Keys, formally the Kings & Keys but always called the King & Keys. It was the *Telegraph* pub, though in the silver age of the *Daily Express*, roughly 1955-65, its senior figures – Edward Pickering, Harold Keeble, Osbert Lancaster – went there too. They took over the 'snug' or private bar at the front of the pub. Lowlier colleagues from the *Express* who ventured into the tiny space were instantly glared away. Lancaster had trained the barman to mix a dry martini, a drink to which he was much attached. He performed the same function with the barman of the pub adjacent to the Theatre Royal, Stratford, East London, which was then at the height of its success.

But in practice the King & Keys belonged to the *Telegraph*. The main body of the pub was long and narrow. The landlord was a jovial Irishman called Sean who claimed to have fought for the IRA long ago. It was a complete hellhole.[4] Fights were not uncommon. One of its regular customers was a member of the *Telegraph* staff who (away from the pub, admittedly) was given to assaulting his wife; on one occasion, indeed, going so far as to break her jaw. She was a colleague of his on the paper, a reporter; while he

---

[4] See Michael Wharton, *A Dubious Codicil* (1991), ch. 4.

was an 'executive'. They could often be seen enjoying a drink together.

Another member of the staff, Michael Hilton, the diplomatic correspondent, was of polished manners while inside the *Telegraph* building and sober. In this hellish pub he instantly became an insulting drunk. It happened that a new leader writer, Frank Johnson, who was then even more temperate in his habits than he was subsequently, was having a tentative drink. Johnson was later to become editor of the *Spectator* and the most entertaining parliamentary sketchwriter of his generation. At this point he was newly arrived from the *Sun* after working for, in reverse chronological order, the *Liverpool Daily Post*, local newspapers throughout the country and the *Sunday Express* as a teaboy.

'Here, you,' Hilton said, 'Come over here.'

Johnson duly went, expecting some small compliment on his recent work.

'Why don't you get back to the gutter where you belong?' Hilton said to a Johnson who was surprised, shocked even, but whose confidence remained happily unimpaired.

There was another *Telegraph* journalist who had been dreadfully injured in the war and consequently lacked an eye, an arm and other bodily parts.

'If I were you,' Hilton said to him in the course of a row, 'I'd go home and cut my throat. Except you couldn't, could you?'

On another occasion he said to Sir (as he then wasn't) Peregrine Worsthorne:

'You're nothing but a tinsel king on a cardboard throne.'

Worsthorne was upset by this. His first, late wife Claude, known as 'Claudie', a Frenchwoman by origin, recounted afterwards:

'Poor Perry, 'ee was so upset 'ee was crying. 'Ee was crying cats and dogs.'

If the place had an arbiter elegantiarum, it was the *Telegraph*'s deputy editor, Colin Welch. Clutching a glass of whisky and swaying alarmingly, he would greet a newcomer he wanted to see with the words:

'Tell me, would you care for an aperitif?'

On any weekday evening in the mid-1970s the company might include William Deedes, John O'Sullivan, T.E. ('Peter') Utley, Colin Welch, Michael Wharton ('Peter Simple') and Peregrine Worsthorne. When Frank Johnson joined *The Times* in 1981, I warned him he would not find such a gathering of wit and intelligence as he had enjoyed on the *Telegraph*. So it proved.

XI

Another regular visitor to this deplorable establishment at around this time was Geoffrey Wheatcroft. He was in his early thirties, above middle height, strongly built, extremely good-looking in a somewhat Germanic way, with blue eyes and shortish hair which even then was showing touches of grey. Unlike most Englishmen, he combined sporting with aesthetic tastes. The only person I have known with as wide a spectrum of interests is Stephen Fay – an Irishman, though brought up in this country. Wheatcroft had read History at New College, Oxford, before acquiring a first-class certificate from the London College of Printing. His ambition had been to become a book designer and typographer.

To this end he joined Cassells. But the publishers, impressed by his good looks and air of knowing the world, placed him in their public relations department. He disliked this work. However, he did other work, such as helping George Wigg, the former Labour minister (the so-called 'Spymaster-General') in Harold Wilson's first administration, when Wigg came to write his autobiography. He was famous for once picking up his unemployment benefit money while dressed in a morning coat, on his way to Ascot races. Finally Wheatcroft and Cassells parted company.

Wheatcroft fell on his feet as literary editor of the *Spectator* under the inspired editorship of Alexander Chancellor.[5] He was both an imaginative and a tolerant literary editor, allowing me (after I had left the *New Statesman* and joined the *Observer*) more or less as much space as I wanted and, even more agreeably from my own point of view, giving me books to review which were not solely about contemporary domestic politics but comprehended some of my other interests, such as history, political theory and, above all, sport. In fact it was Wheatcroft who inaugurated my career, if you can call it that, as a writer on rugby.[6]

In December 1975 he played a part in my departure from the *New Statesman* for the *Observer*. I was being paid something under £5,000 a year to write the political column of the *NS*. I considered

[5] See Simon Courtauld, *To Convey Intelligence* (1999), ch. 8.
[6] See Chapter 10 below.

this inadequate. This was partly because the Islington Borough Council was advertising for a public relations officer at an annual salary of over £8,000. It was also partly because Corinna Adam was being paid more than I was, which I considered unjust even though she was formally a member of the staff, whereas I was not. But it was mainly because of the great inflation of the Heath years, which continued merrily on its way when Harold Wilson formed his third administration in March 1974.

Accordingly I asked Anthony Howard for more money. He refused, saying (or, rather, writing in a handwritten letter) that extra cash for me would disturb the delicate salary structure of the whole paper. I told him that in that case I intended to resign. Jock Campbell, the chairman of the board of The Statesman and Nation Publishing Company (of which I had been a member since 1973), informed Howard that, from his experience at Booker Brothers and other great commercial enterprises, his prediction was that I would be in next morning with my tail between my legs, all threats withdrawn. Howard replied that Campbell did not know me as he did and that he was confident I would proceed with my resignation.

It was a coincidence that this was the moment when Alexander Chancellor decided he wanted a new political columnist at the *Spectator* to replace the incumbent, Patrick Cosgrave, who had held the post since 1971 and was thus part of the old regime of Harry Creighton as proprietor and George Gale as editor. Cosgrave had been educated as an historian at University College, Dublin, and Peterhouse, Cambridge. Indeed, he claimed to be 'a trained historian' who could 'handle an archive' too often for general social ease in his presence. After he had left the *Spectator* he became famous for being sick over Margaret Thatcher when she was Leader of the Opposition and he was her 'special assistant', or one of them.

But even at this earlier stage he was quite famous too, in a small way of business. He had written books on Winston Churchill and on Robert Lowell and was to write others. Most impressive of all, he had in the mid-1970s been right more often than any other political commentator. He had correctly predicted that Edward Heath would lose the election of February 1974 and that he would be displaced as Conservative leader and succeeded not by William Whitelaw (which is what most people thought would happen) but by Margaret Thatcher. And he was rarely off the airwaves. Indeed,

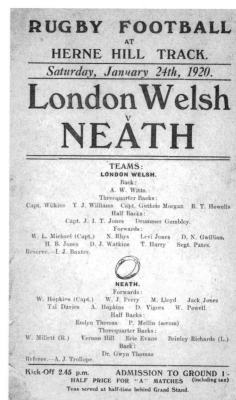

RUGBY FOOTBALL
AT HERNE HILL
(LONDON COUNTY ATHLETIC GROUND).
Saturday, October 4th, 1919.

London Welsh
v.
London Irish.

TEAMS:
LONDON WELSH:
Back:
A. W. Witts.
Threequarter Backs (from):
Lt. Campbell Greenacres E. C. Seward A. Jones T. J. Williams B. John
Half Backs (from):
Capt. J. I. T. Jones J. Thomas J. R. Harper
Forwards:
W. L. Michael N. Rhys H. J. Powell H. B. Jones
H. N. Gwillam D. J. Watkins O. C. Jones W. C. James

LONDON IRISH.
Forwards:
C. R. McGowan (capt.) W. N. McCann H. Brydon R. B. Culbertson
G. N. Cracknell G. E. R. Patey F. Brooks J. W. Murray
Half Backs:
J. B. Gardiner (scrum) P. O. Norton
Threequarter Backs:
G. Doyle A. A. Fryitt W. P. Connolly P. J. Kelly
Back:
S. F. C. Fitzgerald

Kick-Off 3.15 p.m.   ADMISSION TO GROUND 1/-
HALF PRICE FOR "A" MATCHES.   (including tax)

RUGBY FOOTBALL
AT
HERNE HILL TRACK.
Saturday, January 24th, 1920.

London Welsh
v
NEATH

TEAMS:
LONDON WELSH.
Back:
A. W. Witts.
Threequarter Backs:
Capt. Wilkins T. J. Williams Capt. Guthrie Morgan R. T. Howells
Half Backs:
Capt. J. I. T. Jones Drummer Gumbley.
Forwards:
W. L. Michael (Capt.) N. Rhys Levi Jones D. N. Gwillian
H. B. Jones D. J. Watkins T. Harry Segt. Pates.
Reserve.—I. J. Baxter.

NEATH.
Forwards:
W. Hopkins (Capt.) W. J. Perry M. Lloyd Jack Jones
Tal Davies A. Hopkins D. Vigors W. Powell.
Half Backs:
Emlyn Thomas P. Mellin (scrum)
Threequarter Backs:
W. Millett (R.) Vernon Hill Eric Evans Brinley Richards (L.)
Back:
Dr. Gwyn Thomas
Referee.—A. J. Trollope.

Kick-Off 2.45 p.m.   ADMISSION TO GROUND 1/-
HALF PRICE FOR "A" MATCHES   (including tax)
Teas served at half-time behind Grand Stand.

D.J. Watkins's days of glory, 1919-20: London Welsh v London Irish and London Welsh v Neath.

The staff of Blaenau School, nr Ammanford, 1923. D.J. Watkins is on the far left, standing; Violet Harris on the far left, sitting; and Rose Harris on the far right, sitting.

Violet Watkins, 1925.

D.J. and Violet Watkins, *c.* 1930.

Tycroes Youth R.F.C 1947-8. A.W. is seated 1st right.

D.J. Watkins, A.W. and Violet Watkins on holiday in Ilfracombe, 1948.

A.W. walking with a friend, Howard Wade, in the Black Mountains of Carmarthenshire, 1949.

Officers and Committee, Cambridge Union, December 1954. Standing: Robin O'Neill, Evelyn Ebsworth, Neil Crichton-Miller, Richard Moore, John York, Ian Harland, A.W. Sitting: far left: John Waite; 2nd left: Michael Heseltine (President, Oxford Union); 3rd left: Giles Shaw (President, Cambridge Union); far right: Tam Dalyell.

Garland's impression of Lord Beaverbrook and A.W. walking in Central Park, New York, 1961. *New Statesman*, September 1972.

'How much would ya say that was worth?'

Iain Macleod by Vicky, in the possession of A.W.

A.W. awake in Venice and asleep in the Pyrenees, 1982; photographs by Frances Butlin.

Spectator 3 March 1967

POLITICAL COMMENTARY
Mr Wilson and the press
ALAN WATKINS

Shortly after the vacancy in the Pollok constituency became known, a Labour Member concluded that the seat would not be held unless the new candidate was outside the Glasgow Corporation mould traditionally favoured by Scottish Socialists. It occurred to him that a request to editors not to publish. It may be framed in general or occasionally in more specific terms. Though a D Notice is issued by the Committee, it originates in one of the service departments. It may remain in force for many years. It has no legal authority.

The column on D Notices in the *Spectator*, 3 March 1967, which aroused the disapproval of both Harold Wilson and Lord Radcliffe.

OBSERVER
THE FALL
OF
THATCHER
BY
ALAN WATKINS
SUNDAY 17th NOVEMBER

The *Observer* advertises its serialisation of *A Conservative Coup* by A.W., November 1991.

a friend of mine claimed to have heard him presenting 'Thought for the Day' before the eight o'clock news.

Despite this multiplicity of talents displayed by Cosgrave before our admiring eyes, Chancellor wanted to get rid of him. Partly the reason was political: for Cosgrave's brand of free-market, Thatcherite Conservatism, with a heavy overlay of Peterhouse High Tory tomfoolery, was not at all to Chancellor's taste. Partly it was personal: for Cosgrave claimed not only to be a trained historian but to possess close acquaintance with the mighty of the present day in the Conservative Party and elsewhere. This could prove irritating over the months. But it cannot have been anything to do with drink: in those distant days, the mid-1970s, in the silver age of Fleet Street, Chancellor drank as much as Cosgrave, if not more. Either way, it was a close-run thing.

When Chancellor asked me to succeed Cosgrave as political columnist of the *Spectator*, this was convenient for me, in dispute with the *New Statesman* as I was. But it was, I thought, unfair to Cosgrave. I told Chancellor as much, suggesting that he run two columns, one by me on domestic politics, the other by Cosgrave, taking the world as his parish. Chancellor refused, saying he simply did not want to have Cosgrave around the paper any more. I agreed to write the political column at a rather higher salary than I was being paid by the *Statesman*, after I had worked out my notice, which would be in April 1976.

The arrangement never came to pass because Chancellor was unable or unwilling to send me an ordinary letter of engagement which I could countersign and return to him. Instead he turned to the *Spectator*'s lawyers. They produced a document so long and so complicated – providing, for example, for what was going to happen in the unhappy event of my death, serious illness or, possibly, madness – that Chancellor felt he could not decently forward it to me for inspection and signature. He asked me to write my own letter of engagement on his behalf, which he would then sign.

This delay provided Anthony Howard with the chance to ensure that, if I did leave the *Statesman*, it would not be to return to the *Spectator*. The *Spectator* was already engaged in poaching Auberon Waugh from him. To lose me as well to the same weekly rival he would regard as humiliating. He could obviously have solved the whole problem simply by giving me the money I was asking for. But he did not choose to follow this course, whether because, as he had written to me, it would destroy his existing salary structure or because he thought it was time for me to be moving on, for I had then been writing the political column of the paper for eight years.

XII

The *Observer* was looking for a political correspondent to replace the famous Nora Beloff, who had done the job for 12 years. David Astor, who had edited the paper for 23, had given way to Donald Trelford, who wanted to assemble a team of his own. Miss Beloff formed no part of his plans, anyway on the domestic political side. Howard told Trelford and others on the *Observer* that I was on the market. So Trelford and his deputy, John Cole, together saw me one morning in El Vino's. This was a time when Sunday newspapers were increasing their political staffs. The jobs of political columnist and political correspondent, previously done by one person, were being split between two. Later they would be done by three or even four journalists. Trelford and Cole were undecided about whether they wanted one or two people to do the political job. I resolved the difficulty for them by making clear that I wanted to write the political column only, though I was prepared to help out from time to time by writing 'profiles' and occasional leading articles. I still wanted to continue as a freelance, paying my tax under Schedule D.

Trelford said he found this arrangement perfectly convenient, adding that he would pay me at a higher rate than any other freelance on the *Observer*: £100 a week. I did a rapid calculation and found that, with six weeks' annual holiday, this came to £4,600 a year – slightly less than I was being paid by the *New Statesman*. I remonstrated gently about this. Trelford replied he had not really thought about it in that way before. It illustrated (we both agreed) how poorly freelances were paid compared to staff members in Fleet Street, a condition which persists to this day, possibly in aggravated form. We agreed amicably on something around £8,000, which illustrates also the rate of inflation between December 1975 and the present day.

While this was going on I was making notes on a lined foolscap pad; Trelford was doing likewise on a smaller sheet of paper. We agreed to meet the following Friday at the Black Friars, a pub at the junction of New Bridge Street and Queen Victoria Street. It was in the *art nouveau* style, with much copper-work and depictions of jolly friars quaffing great tankards of ale. I never liked the place much, though it had its adherents. It was here that Anthony Howard once detected Patrick O'Donovan surreptitiously pouring a very large glass of gin into his ginger ale when O'Donovan was proclaiming to all that he was on the wagon.

On this occasion Trelford turned up at the appointed time with his letter of engagement. He explained that he had changed his suit that morning and carelessly left the piece of paper setting out our agreed terms in an inside pocket. He hoped he had got all the details correct from his memory. So he had, every one of them. I recall this apparently inconsequential episode because it illustrates Trelford's capacity for concentration and his ability not to get things wrong. I duly countersigned the letter.

At this moment Geoffrey Wheatcroft, whom I had noticed earlier lurking around the doorway and trying unsuccessfully to render himself invisible, entered the premises from the December gloom, as if about to effect an arrest.

'Some gentlemen from the *Spectator* are waiting to see you in El Vino's,' Wheatcroft said.

It was too late. I had already signed for the *Observer*. Nevertheless, we made our way – prisoner and escort – up New Bridge Street, turned left at Ludgate Circus and were soon in the wine bar. Awaiting our arrival were Henry Keswick, the *Spectator*'s proprietor and saviour, and George Hutchinson, its managing director. Though the weather was not specially harsh, they were both wearing hats, heavy overcoats and leather gloves. They looked as my father had when he was about to set off for a rugby international. It soon became evident that their cause was lost. Keswick said that he, like me, had read Law at Cambridge, and had no doubt in his mind that there was a valid contract, even if it was oral merely, between me and the *Spectator*. I did not dissent. I certainly did not want to argue any points about the law of contract. I had broken my word to Chancellor, and that was that.

After the departure of Keswick and Hutchinson (Wheatcroft, I think, stayed), I came across Denis Compton standing at the bar. I had known him when I was working for the *Sunday Express* in 1959-64 and he was a cricket and football correspondent.

'Hear you're in a spot of bother, old boy,' he said. 'My advice is not to worry. These things have a way of working themselves out in the end. God bless.'

8

St Andrew's Hill

THE OBSERVER: Unbiassed by Prejudice – Uninfluenced by Party, Whose Principle is Independence, – whose Object is Truth, and the Dissemination of every Species of Knowledge that may conduce to the Happiness of Society ...   Poster, London, 1796

I

My move from the *New Statesman* to the *Observer* in January 1976 followed the *Observer*'s move from Tudor Street, near the Temple, to St Andrew's Hill, near Blackfriars, a matter of a few hundred yards across New Bridge Street and to the east. The heart of the old *Observer* lay still in the warren-like premises in Tudor Street. And yet the new offices were more ancient not so much in their buildings as in the journalistic history of the ground on which they stood. Printing had gone on in this part of London since the 12th century.

The *Times* had been here, at Printing House Square. When the old *Times* building was pulled down, the new premises were called New Printing House Square. When *The Times* decamped briefly to Gray's Inn Road – before the move to Wapping – it was allowed to take the name New Printing House Square along too: a shocking example of the indulgence of whoever it is that decrees addresses and street names. The *Observer* occupied part of what had been the new *Times* building. It was a good part of the world to be in, with the chastely, perhaps bleakly restored Wren church of St Andrew's-by-the-Wardrobe virtually by the front door, and with the finer church of St Martin's Ludgate and St Paul's Cathedral itself within easy walking distance.

Donald Trelford, the editor, and John Cole, his deputy, had never really made up their minds about whether they wanted a political columnist and a political correspondent or someone who would combine both functions. In the end they had decided to hire me from the *New Statesman* to be the columnist and Adam Raphael from the *Guardian* to be the lobby correspondent. But Raphael could not join until 1 April. So for three months I agreed to do both jobs. I had, after all, done the same at the *Sunday Express* in 1963-4. But I was not happy about the arrangement, even though the *Observer* in 1976 did not go in for 'following up' stories late on Saturday evening as assiduously as the *Sunday Express* had 13 years previously: partly because it was not that sort of paper, but mainly because journalism had somehow changed in the intervening period.

II

My predecessor, Nora Beloff, had been happy enough to do both jobs. I had wanted to succeed her since, I suppose, 1970, and had mentioned the possibility to Trelford, then David Astor's deputy, on the two occasions he had telephoned me in the early 1970s to offer me foreign postings at the *Observer*. He had made clear that the job of political columnist was not on offer, whether to me or to anyone else. And yet it was obvious that a competently written political column was what the paper needed and had, indeed, needed ever since the departure of Hugh Massingham, though Anthony Howard wrote a fortnightly political column in 1971-2, when he was principally engaged with the *New Statesman*.

Miss Beloff was without question a redoubtable figure who was, with Clare Hollingworth of the *Guardian* and a few others, a pioneer among women in serious journalism. If you offered her a drink, she would reply:

'A large whisky, please. I find that a small one just dirties the bottom of the glass.'

Not that she was addicted to strong spirits or, for that matter, to drink in any form. Her greatest vice was to hang around groups of her colleagues who might well be having a drink, listen to their conversations and reproduce in her articles such items as seemed interesting, neither asking permission beforehand nor making acknowledgment at the time of publication. This technique of listening in to the conversations of others meant that, while she did not always get things entirely wrong, she did not usually get them exactly right.

Altogether, indeed, she was famous for grasping the wrong end of any stick that might be in sight. She once wrote that Anthony Crosland was a noted Arabist. When Crosland reproved her, saying that his weakly held views inclined, if anything, towards the cause of Israel, she offered to correct her original misstatement in the next issue.

'Please, no,' Crosland said. 'You'd only make it worse, Nora.'

She once asked me what was Fred Peart's attitude to Israel. Peart was a popular but vague politician who had served in Harold Wilson's Cabinet. I said I did not think Peart had an attitude to Israel (I may have been wrong about this). Miss Beloff was disbelieving. It was inconceivable, to her, that any politician should *not* have an attitude to Israel.

She always seemed more at ease with European than with British domestic politics. She once met by chance the Tory politician Duncan Sandys, who did not know her, in the bar of a Strasbourg hotel. They were both there for a meeting of the Council of Europe, a forerunner of the European Parliament. Sandys asked her to have dinner with him and she agreed. In the course of the meal she said:

'Speaking as a journalist ...'

'Journalist? Journalist?' Sandys said. 'But I thought you were a lady.'

This was Nora's own account.

Certainly her book *The General Says No*, about Charles de Gaulle's frustration of the British Government's plans to enter the Common Market, is a small classic; whereas *Freedom under Foot*, an attack on Michael Foot's policies when he was Secretary for Employment in 1974-6, is hysterical.

Her weekly column showed Nora with a telephone receiver at her ear. She could well have been dictating copy on a Saturday from her desk to the copytakers somewhere else in the *Observer* building. Contrary to the rules (I had some sympathy with her), she preferred dictating to typing. Her 'column' appeared on page 3, a news page. It was not really a proper column at all because not only did it appear on a news page but it was also written partly as a news-story.

III

I was surprised that my successor-column appeared on page 2, a news page likewise. When I remonstrated with Donald Trelford

about this placing, he replied that my *New Statesman* column –
which he had, he said, been proud to acquire – had also appeared
on page 2 and that, in any case, the leader or comment pages were
being remodelled, where I would find safe harbour in due course. In
the meantime, it was an unsatisfactory situation which was not
resolved for several months.

As a discontented temporary dweller in the news pages, I was
thrust into closer contact with the managing editor, Kenneth P.
Obank, known either as 'Ken' or as 'KPO', than I should have liked
in an ideal world. He was famous for his affection for young girl
reporters and for his ferocious temper. Once, after some incident
late on a Saturday evening, the police were summoned, and he was
removed to a cell.

'What a terrible thing to happen,' David Astor said. 'And him a
grandfather too.'

He was also famous for having explained to Astor what a mortgage was. This was at the time of the Orpington by-election in 1962,
when mortgages were much in the news, their high cost seen as a
cause of the Conservative defeat in that contest. Astor wished to
inform himself more fully. Obank explained that the purchaser of
a house (the mortgagor) would borrow most or sometimes all of its
value from a bank or building society (the mortgagee), which would
have the house as its security. The mortgagor would repay the
money over a lengthy period, sometimes as long as 30 years. Astor
listened to Obank's account of these arrangements with growing
disapproval. Did many people on the staff of the *Observer*, he asked,
have these mortgages? Obank said: virtually all of them, if they
were married with children. Astor was shocked.

'But that means,' he said, 'they're all in debt.'

Astor was always solicitous of the welfare of *Observer* journalists.
As a former member of the staff wrote:

> He was never happier than when he could help someone out of an
> illness, an alcoholic problem – we had plenty of those – a mental
> breakdown or a marital tangle.[1]

Sometimes he was, perhaps, too solicitous, solicitude merging into
paternalism. Two members of the staff were having an affair; the
man was married, the woman single. The man's wife complained to

---

[1] John Douglas Pringle, *Have Pen: Will Travel* (1973), 145.

Astor about the liaison. Astor resolved to act and enlisted Obank's support for his purposes. The man, a reporter, would be made a news editor. In this capacity he would be fettered to his desk late on Saturday night and late on Friday as well. He would be worked so hard he would have no time to pursue his illicit relationship. Of course it made no difference at all. Anyone could have foreseen that it would make no difference. The affair continued, and the two journalists duly got married.

Astor was leaving as I was arriving (he did not formally resign until January 1976). He had no opportunity to try to do good to me. Obank proved less fierce than I had been led to expect. His principal defect was meanness with the company's money, so continuing an *Observer* tradition. I had been brought up on the old *Sunday Express* which, despite the puritanism of John Junor and the carefulness of Lord Beaverbrook, had about it a certain expansiveness.

In September 1976 I decided to spend a few days at the TUC conference, which was being held at Brighton that year. I do not suppose I should have gone if it had been in Blackpool. But the visit was certainly justified, with James Callaghan, the new Prime Minister, making his first appearance before the brothers from the branches. (It was at another Brighton TUC conference two years later that Callaghan led the trade union leaders up the garden path, or so they thought, over the date of the election.) I was on holiday at the time, in the middle of my normal break from late August to late September. So the visit could be regarded as a piece of conscientiousness, over and beyond the call of duty.

Such was not Obank's view when I submitted my modest expenses claim. Had anyone, he wanted to know, asked me to go to Brighton? Well, no. And had I asked anyone's permission before going? Certainly not. And had I written anything? No, because I was on holiday. Obank said he would sign my expenses on this occasion but that I must on no account allow the same thing to happen again. Afterwards I never went to another TUC.

IV

My greatest friend at the *Observer* was the literary editor Terence Kilmartin. He had saved David Astor's life in 1944 when they had been ambushed at a crossroads in France, Astor a 32-year-old major in the Royal Marines, Kilmartin a 22-year-old member of the Special Operations Executive. Astor had already been hit in the shoulder. Kilmartin shouted at him to lie flat on his face, and afterwards tended him and others with bandages. Kilmartin was the son of an Irish civil servant. He had, at 16, become tutor to a German family. In this capacity he learnt both German and French. He was recruited into SOE through the influence of his sister, who was older than he was. He joined the *Observer* as editor of the paper's Foreign News Service (one of its few lucrative ventures) in 1949; in 1950 he became assistant literary editor, and in 1952 literary editor, a post he held until 1986. He was unremitting in his pursuit of the highest standards. In the 1960s, when the paper was consciously trying to modernise itself, he refused to allow Astor's request that short notes on reviewers should be placed at the end of their reviews.[2]

He was of medium height, strongly built, with a typically Irish face: a sharp chin and nose and blue eyes set off by a brick complexion. He looked as if he drank more than in fact he did; his consumption was on the generous side of temperate. In many ways he was a man of the 1950s who looked back to his friendships with John Davenport, Philip Toynbee and Patrick O'Donovan, who was still alive (he died in 1991) but rarely came in to the *Observer*, spending most of his time at his house in Hampshire. Kilmartin, with the French about whom he knew so much, disliked drinking white wine as an aperitif unless it was champagne, and much preferred Gordon's gin and tonic – he always specified Gordon's gin.

He translated, among others, Henry de Montherlant, André Malraux and Charles de Gaulle. But he was most famous for translating Marcel Proust, using Scott Moncrieff's translation as a basis. I have seldom been more flattered than when he asked my view of the correct rendition of one sentence. My opinion of the French would have been valueless. He did not want to know it. What he was concerned about was putting it into the right English. For while Terry's 'ear' was perfect, he could not always, so to speak, take the engine apart and put it together again.

He was a resolute heterosexual who married the beautiful Joanna Pearce. She was also a courageous woman who, for the sake of a travel book she was writing, would spend the night in a

[2] Richard Cockett, *David Astor and The Observer* (1991), 245.

shepherd's hut in the Pyrenees while Terry, a hero of SOE, would retire to a nearby hotel. After his death in 1991, she continued his scholarly work, translating the fourth volume of Proust's letters. Shortly before his death (though before he knew he had prostate cancer), Kilmartin said to me that, if he had his time all over again, he would devote it wholly to work of this kind rather than to being a literary editor. He could talk about anything; and you could say anything to him. Of all my friends who are now dead, I miss Terence Kilmartin the most.

V

When I joined the *Observer* early in 1976, I did not know that a decision had already been taken in autumn 1975 to sell the paper. It had been taken by the Astor trustees on the basis that they could not conscientiously (or perhaps lawfully) bear the *Observer*'s losses. Harold Wilson, who was coming to the end of his second term as Prime Minister, suggested to Lord Goodman, who was on the *Observer* board, that the paper should approach the International Publishing Corporation, publisher of the *Daily Mirror* and much else besides. The IPC refused to have anything to do with it. Wilson contemplated direct intervention by the government, though precisely what form this was to take remained unclear.

Wilson resigned, James Callaghan succeeded him, the IMF crisis supervened and there was no more talk of the *Observer*'s being saved by a Labour government – even assuming the talk had possessed any substance in the first place. Instead Callaghan asked the members of the Trades Union Congress whether they would be interested in buying the *Observer*. It was presumably a question expecting the answer No, and No the answer duly was.

In the meantime Roger Harrison, the paper's managing director – a gentle soul whose favoured activity was hitting small balls around courts with rackets – had conceived the idea of inviting Rupert Murdoch to make a bid. Goodman thought this a good idea, as did Astor, who had served with Murdoch on the board of London Weekend Television, when he had formed a favourable opinion of him. In September 1976 Murdoch flew to London.

On 21 October 1976 the news of Murdoch's imminent takeover appeared in the *Daily Mail*. It became known in Fleet Street – it had already been known to some – that he intended to make Bruce

Rothwell editor-in-chief and Anthony Shrimsley editor. Indeed, so confident was Shrimsley of attaining this position that he met my friend Frank Johnson and offered him my job as political columnist. Johnson said he would have to think it over and immediately told me about it. Shrimsley was at this time political editor of the *Sun* and political adviser to Murdoch's News International Newspapers. Rothwell was an Australian whom Murdoch had already appointed editor of the *Australian*. Both had worked for the *Daily Mail*: Shrimsley as political and assistant editor, Rothwell as Washington correspondent over many years.

After the news of Murdoch's takeover had appeared in the *Mail*, it was generally assumed that the source was Donald Trelford, the *Observer*'s editor, whose job was imperilled (not for the last time). Trelford later denied he had had anything to do with it and said he thought the likely source was Shrimsley, Rothwell or both.[3] Whoever the informant may have been, the news had the effect among *Observer* journalists of a fox in a chicken-run. On this occasion, however, the chickens fought back. Several meetings were held, at which Murdoch was excoriated and undying devotion pledged to Trelford. At one of them Clive James, the paper's television critic, said that selling the *Observer* to Murdoch would be like giving your beautiful 17-year-old daughter to a gorilla.

This was more or less the view of the journalists, though John Cornwell, then the manager of the foreign news service, later a noted biographer, thought Murdoch would be a good thing for the paper because he had a lot of money at his disposal. This was also the unanimous opinion of the print unions. In Murdoch they saw endless prosperity for themselves. I presented a *What the Papers Say* programme in the first, critical period. The Granada people asked me to do this precisely because of the crisis and I, perhaps unwisely, agreed. Next day the Imperial Father of the Chapel (the nominal leader of all the non-journalistic unions) complained to the management that my comments had been 'unhelpful'. On 22 October 1976, however – the day after the *Mail* story – Rupert Murdoch issued a statement from the United States:

> In view of the breach of confidence that has taken place, together with the deliberate and orchestrated attempt to build this into a controversy, News International is no longer interested.

[3] Conversation with Donald Trelford, 18 March 2000.

Richard Cockett, in his book about Astor and the *Observer*, describes this withdrawal as 'purely tactical'.[4] Following him, Brian Brivati, in his biography of Lord Goodman, writes about a 'mock withdrawal' by Murdoch.[5] This is by no means self-evident. William Shawcross, in his biography of Rupert Murdoch, nowhere suggests that the withdrawal was simulated. On the contrary: he takes Murdoch at his word:

> Murdoch was not pleased. After all, the *Observer* management had sought him out ...[6]

Whether the withdrawal by Murdoch was genuine or not, other, more bizarre figures now entered the bidding. Robert Maxwell expressed interest, as he always did at that time in any newspaper which might be up for sale. 'Tiny' Rowland was mentioned as a potential buyer: he was to become a real one five years later. Olga Deterding, the heiress, said she was fascinated by journalism and by the *Observer*. Sally Aw Sian, an entrepreneur or entrepreneuse from Hong Kong, offered still more exotic possibilities. Associated Newspapers and the *Daily Mail* prowled on the margins: a member of their staff, a fierce Scotsman called Mackenzie, told me menacingly that we would not be allowed to waste their money.

The most pressing suitor of all was, however, Sir James Goldsmith. To demonstrate his credentials as a proprietor he entertained a delegation of *Observer* journalists to dinner at his London house. In front of each place, beside the wine glasses, was a bottle of chateau-bottled claret. Far from being given credit for his munificence, Sir James was deprecated for his vulgarity. Clearly a person showing such disregard for the conventions of polite society was unfit to own the *Observer*. That was what his guests thought. Informed afterwards of their disapproval, he remarked that it was notorious that journalists liked to drink a lot and that accordingly it was only sensible to indulge their tastes with as little fuss as possible.

Whether at this stage, October-November 1976, Murdoch wanted the *Observer*, the Astor trustees still wanted Murdoch. David Astor and Lord Goodman turned up at yet another staff

[4] Richard Cockett, *David Astor and The Observer* (1991), 280.
[5] Brian Brivati, *Lord Goodman* (1999), 224.
[6] William Shawcross, *Rupert Murdoch* (1992), 180.

meeting. Astor looked uneasy, even shifty, as if he wanted to get home to St John's Wood as soon as he decently could. Goodman was altogether more exuberant. By this time he had clearly decided to turn himself into a character from Dickens, both comic and alarming, sometimes menacing. To this end he had pushed orotundity and circumlocution to a height previously encountered only in the missives from Goodman, Derrick: not a jot ... or a tittle ... nay, not a scintilla ... grievous charges ... our client's reputation ... apologies ... substantial damages ... return of post ...

On this occasion Lord Goodman contented himself with a figure of speech involving, not a white knight, but a man on a white horse. If a man on a white horse were galloping up Fleet Street to save the *Observer*, why, he and Mr Astor would be only too delighted to allow him to save it. They would welcome him as a long-lost brother or a prodigal son. Alas, they had scanned the horizons with the most powerful field-glasses, and no such benevolent figure could be discerned. Men on white horses were, it seemed, in short supply. In default there was no alternative to selling the paper to Rupert Murdoch. So on 12 November 1976 the trustees met in Goodman's flat in Portland Place, London W.1, and decided to recommend a sale to him.

VI

But there *was*, as things turned out, a man on a white horse after all: or, rather, a man with a big Texas hat, even though his company was based in California. This was Robert O. Anderson, chairman of Atlantic Richfield or ARCO, an oil concern. On the same day as the trustees had decided to sell to Murdoch, Kenneth Harris was entertaining to dinner at Rule's Restaurant, London W.C.2, Douglass Cater and his wife, and Lady Melchett.

Cater was a Washington journalist and man-of-affairs who was a friend of Anderson. Harris, a friend of Cater, was an *Observer* journalist, then 57, who had enjoyed a distinguished though unspectacular career as Washington correspondent, high-class gossip columnist (the original 'Pendennis') and, most recently, interviewer at length of the rich, the powerful and the famous. Harris asked Cater whether Anderson would be interested in buying the *Observer*. Cater said he would find out, which he did. On 15 November 1976 David Astor and Roger Harrison flew to Los Angeles to talk to

Robert Anderson. In the meantime Lord Goodman agreed to keep both Murdoch and Associated Newspapers in the bidding.[7] There was no need for Goodman to worry. The deal went through, and Atlantic Richfield proved a model proprietor.

The only journalistic difficulty was: what to do with Harris? He was the saviour of the paper. There could be no question about that. If he had not interested Cater, and Cater had not involved Anderson, the *Observer would* have been sold either to Murdoch – subject to the doubts raised earlier about whether Murdoch was any longer interested – or to the Harmsworth family, owners of Associated Newspapers and the *Daily Mail*. Goodman told Trelford that Anderson was determined to make Harris chairman, vice-chairman, editor-in-chief or even editor. Goodman subsequently claimed that he told Harris that he was not up to any of these jobs:

'I may be the most suitable person in the world to be a prima ballerina, and I may know it, but the fact of the matter is the world will never see me that way.'[8]

I had a certain regard for Harris because he had come to the Cambridge Union in the early 1950s as a visiting speaker from the Oxford Union and made one of the funniest speeches I could remember. He was also a fellow South Walian. Shortly after the ARCO acquisition, when he had settled for the position of associate editor, Harris said to me:

'Someone was speaking to me very favourably of your last column the other night.'

'Who was that, then, Ken?'

'The Prime Minister, actually.'

VII

Cater and, over the next few years, a few other ARCO importees arrived in London to keep an eye on their recent acquisition. They did not affect my work in any way. I dealt with Donald Trelford and the deputy editor, John Cole. I had first met Cole in autumn 1960 at the TUC conference at Douglas in the Isle of Man. It was a famous conference at which Bill Carron, the leader of the engineers' union, had decided to vote both ways in the great unilateralist dispute which convulsed the Labour movement of that time. Cole

[7] Cockett, *Astor*, 282.
[8] Brivati, *Goodman*, 225-6.

was then labour correspondent of the *Guardian*. I was then, in effect, deputy political correspondent of the *Sunday Express*. The *Sunday Express* had no labour correspondent, but the *Daily Express* had the most famous in the land, more famous even than Cole (who was then only 33), in Trevor Evans.

In those days labour correspondents were more esteemed than they were subsequently to become. They covered not only the TUC, as they still do, but also the National Executive Committee of the Labour Party and the whole of the party conference. Whereas the political correspondents to whom I had been introduced at Westminster after 1959 had been uniformly helpful and friendly, the labour correspondents whom I met during the same period exhibited the opposite characteristics. Cole was the leader of a specially unhelpful and unfriendly group consisting of himself, Keith McDowell of the *Daily Mail* and Ron Stevens of the *Daily Telegraph*, who made the closed shops of that time look like welcoming saloon bars.

Cole had made his name through his scoop in the *Guardian* about Alfred Robens's move to the chairmanship of the National Coal Board in 1961. Subsequently he became deputy editor of the paper. On the departure of Alastair Hetherington in spring 1975 he contested the editorship with Peter Preston. Election by the staff produced in 1972-5 the editors of the *New Statesman*, the *Guardian* and the *Observer*. Preston won: some thought because Cole was a Presbyterian from Belfast who was too attached to the Unionist cause. Three days after the election, in which he had been Hetherington's favoured candidate, he was asked to join the *Observer* and accepted the invitation.[9]

If there are good persons and bad persons, Cole was unquestionably among the good. But like many Dissenters, the one thing he would not tolerate was dissent.[10] He saw it as the function of the *Observer* to support the Labour government; saw it as his function to support the Labour government; and saw it as mine as well. Thus, while jokes on my part directed towards, say, Eric Heffer were regarded as acceptable, even, on occasion, amusing, similar comments about Jim Callaghan, Denis Healey or Merlyn Rees (respectively Prime Minister, Chancellor of the Exchequer and

---

[9] John Cole, *As It Seemed to Me: Political Memoirs* (1995), 115.
[10] If he had been a Scottish Presbyterian he would not have been a Dissenter, the Presbyterian Church of Scotland being the established church of that country.

Home Secretary throughout 1976-9) were looked upon by Cole as not quite playing the game, not fair. Indeed, he once used the latter phrase to me in the course of rebuke. I said that, as a political columnist, it was not invariably my job to be fair but rather, sometimes, to express an individual, honest opinion.

'Some people,' he replied in menacing tones, 'might take a different view.'

I was almost as quick tempered as he was. On this occasion I walked into Donald Trelford's office and told him I was not prepared to put up with any more interference by John Cole. Of course not, Trelford replied. No one would expect me to do anything of the kind. The only person who could alter my copy was the editor. He would do so only on grounds of taste or after receiving legal advice. On the other hand, there was Cole's position to consider. He was not only deputy editor of the paper but also, in practice, political editor. He knew a lot about politics – almost as much, Trelford added, as I did. He relied a good deal on Cole's sage counsel in political matters, where he himself was never wholly sure-footed. While Cole had no right to tamper with my copy, he should always be listened to respectfully. Afterwards I could, of course, write whatever I pleased.

Trelford said he understood my difficulties with Cole only too well. Why, only the other week, he went on, he had come into his office grasping the raw copy (the typewritten version) of my column in a shaking hand, protesting it was 'unusable'. Trelford had read it. It seemed unexceptionable to him. Cole pointed to a disrespectful reference to Jim – or it may have been Denis or Merlyn. Trelford then changed course. Certainly what I had written about Jim (or Denis, or Merlyn) was quite disgraceful. There was no doubt about that. Trelford was certainly on Cole's side on the merits of the case. But that was not the point at issue. It was, after all, only a very small reference, almost a peripheral observation. He could certainly ask me to remove it. But would this course be worth the trouble that would undoubtedly ensue? I was notoriously unpredictable. Anything might happen. Far better to leave the column as I had written it. In the meantime, Cole should know that Trelford sympathised with him in his difficulties with me, an awkward customer.

In many ways Cole was a kind and considerate man. Once, when we were both visiting the Lime Grove television studios to appear on a programme, he insisted on our occupying a 'smoking' carriage entirely for my convenience: he was a non-smoker himself. This was in the days when you were allowed to smoke on the Underground and I got through 30 to 40 untipped Gauloises a day.

His loyalty to Labour, or a part of it, did him credit of a sort. Once, in the early 1960s, my friend Peter Paterson, then industrial correspondent of the *Sunday Telegraph*, discovered some piece of skulduggery in the upper regions of the TUC. He told Cole, who occupied the same position on the *Guardian*, that he hoped to write about it.

'And to hell with the trade union movement, I suppose?' Cole said.

The trouble was that it was impossible for me, at any rate, to have any disagreement with John Cole without its turning into a quarrel. He was an illustration of the contemporary usage whereby an argument is synonymous with a row. In 1977 he persuaded Trelford to remove me from the political column and to transform me into the author of a diary on the back page.

VIII

The opportunity arose in this way: Michael Davie, who had previously filled the space with distinction, was off to Australia to edit the *Melbourne Age*. I was chosen to succeed him. Trelford was, I remember, distinctly uneasy when he made the offer. He said in reassurance that he had no intention of appointing anyone else as political columnist while I was going about my new tasks on the paper. What he had in mind, he added, was something along the lines of the *Spectator* diary rather than the unitary piece of 1,600 words or so which Davie had written. With the utmost foolishness, I agreed: both to my removal from the political column and to my writing the new column in the form of a succession of paragraphs, as they are called in the trade.

I can write such itemised columns perfectly well. But they cost me a good deal in effort and worry, because they are rather like a restaurant menu or, indeed, like the meal itself, involving as they do questions of sequence and balance. By contrast, I have always been able to write an article of between, say, 700 and 1,800 words without too much trouble. My more successful pieces in the 'diary' space were on single subjects, where I had decided to jettison the itemised formula for that week. There was one such on the Tony-pandy riots in South-east Wales before the First World War.

James Callaghan, the Prime Minister, had mentioned them in the House. They had once again become a matter of political controversy. The old questions were repeated. Had troops been sent there or not? They had, and they had stayed for over a year. Who had sent them? More complicated, because the decision had involved both Winston Churchill, the Liberal Home Secretary (in Labour mythology, the villain), and R.B. Haldane, the War Minister. Was sending the troops justified? In my opinion, yes, though they overstayed their welcome.

I asked the Home Office's equable, elderly press officer, Donald Grant, whether I could look at the relevant files, some of which were still restricted. Grant replied that I could see the whole lot – provided the Home Office could see the completed article before publication. Accepting official censorship as the price of viewing public documents seemed to me to require the arbitration of the editor.

I duly consulted Trelford. Nothing, he said, could be more straightforward. We would promise to show the article to the Home Office officials after it had been written. On Friday we would send it to them. We would keep our word. If they objected to anything, we would not take any notice at all but publish it exactly as it had been written. This elegant solution illustrated the genius of Donald Trelford as an editor.

Happily, the need to employ it did not arise. The column was duly sent to the Home Office. No objections were made. In fact there was nothing important in the secret papers that was not in the Blue Book which was published at the time and which I dug out of the library of Lincoln's Inn.

It was not merely that the diary, subject to a few exceptions such as the above, did not suit me but also that I might lose the knack of writing a political column – worse, cease to be regarded as a political columnist at all. Robin Day said I had become a gossip writer and urged me to return to serious matters without delay. Anthony Howard (this was before he rejoined the *Observer*) told Trelford he had thrown away a valuable card. Politics were already interesting enough. Labour had lost its majority. Indeed, it had lost it in 1976, shortly after Callaghan had become Prime Minister. The Lib-Lab pact had been formed to see the government through. A general election was confidently expected in autumn 1978. With Cole still deputy-cum-political editor, I was restored to my old duties; not a moment too soon, I thought.

IX

We had also acquired a new editor-in-chief in Conor Cruise O'Brien. The invitation to hire O'Brien came from the Atlantic Richfield people, who had formed a favourable impression of him at the *Observer*-ARCO dinner at Lincoln's Inn, ARCO being the name by which the American company was usually known. This annual function was organised by Kenneth Harris; the guests, who usually turned up in force, included the Cabinet, the Shadow Cabinet, the TUC, the bench of bishops and anybody who was anybody. Lincoln's Inn had no connection with the *Observer*, with ARCO or, indeed, with Kenneth Harris, and was presumably chosen as a venue because it was suitably grand.

Quite apart from the favourable nature of any impression which O'Brien may have created, he was already one of the most distinguished figures in the Western world: author; diplomat; famous for his intervention on behalf of the United Nations in the Katanga conflict; less famous for being Minister for Posts and Telegraphs in the government of the Republic of Ireland; an enemy of Charles Haughey; a non-believer in the cause of a united Ireland. David Astor, who, with Goodman, had stayed on the board at Atlantic Richfield's request, thoroughly approved of the appointment. O'Brien told Astor, Goodman, Anderson and Thornton Bradshaw, the president of Atlantic Richfield (in US company parlance the president ranks below the chairman), that he would first have to meet Trelford to assure himself that the editor 'willingly accepted' his appointment. He saw Trelford in Dublin, who told him that he would be happy to accept him as editor-in-chief, because Trelford 'regarded his role in journalism as that of a craftsman'.[11]

It was never clear whether Trelford was making the best of a bad

---

[11] Conor Cruise O'Brien, *Memoir: My Life and Themes* (1998 pb edn 1999, 364). O'Brien infers that because, of the four people who interviewed him, he knew only Astor, accordingly Astor was responsible for his appointment. But according to Trelford the first move came from Atlantic Richfield, even though Astor approved of – was even enthusiastic about – O'Brien's appointment.

job or genuinely welcomed O'Brien's arrival, as I did. Rather as an extra-marital liaison by one of the spouses often improves a marriage, the arrival of O'Brien made my life easier at the *Observer*. There was now an editor-in-chief who knew as much about politics as the deputy editor, if not more. And he was as interesting to talk to as anyone on the paper, though I could always talk more frankly to Terry Kilmartin. Cole, O'Brien and I would often drink casually at one of the two pubs, the Cockpit and the Red Lion, near the *Observer*. One Christmastime we were having a drink at the former establishment, which was owned by an Irishman from Cork who disliked his native land and loved London. It was full of jostling printers, journalists, secretaries, all talking at the tops of their voices.

'You're hating this, aren't you?' Cole said perceptively to me.

'Yes, but Conor's enjoying himself. Either that, or he doesn't notice the crowd.'

'That's because he's still a politician at heart,' Cole said.

In fact Cole had said to O'Brien with his customary rough honesty that he should not have accepted the post of editor-in-chief because he was not a proper working journalist.[12] Subsequently they got on well. Though Cole was the hotter tempered of the two, neither was someone to bear malice. They were, after all, stuck with each other for the time being. Not least, they more or less agreed about Northern Ireland despite their different backgrounds in that island.

It was Ireland which was the cause of the one row between O'Brien and me; more precisely, it was the dismissal of Mary Holland, the paper's Ireland correspondent. Mary was Southern Irish; had lived and had offspring with a Republican of extreme tendencies; was herself a believer in a united Ireland. She was also a good journalist who had made her name in the *Spectator* of the 1960s with more general articles, when she had been in competition for notice with some very good writers indeed. It seemed to me that with Mary you knew what you were going to get. If you did not like it, you did not avail yourself of her services in the first place. Part of the trouble was that O'Brien had inherited her (as he had, after all, the rest of us) rather than hired her himself. She had

---

[12] O'Brien, *Memoir*, pb edn, 365.

published one article celebrating the character and achievements of the 'blanket women' – relatives of Provisional IRA prisoners who organised demonstrations intended to demonstrate sympathy for the Provos. I wrote to her about this and we had a somewhat acrimonious correspondence. She stuck to her guns and I told Donald Trelford I had no confidence in her objectivity of her coverage of Northern Ireland. John Cole agreed. Donald Trelford acquiesced, for the moment, as he generally did if the opposition appeared adequately motivated. Mary Holland was 'out' of the *Observer* as long as I was still there ...[13]

The *Observer* chapel of the National Union of Journalists then decided to interest themselves in the dismissal of Ms Holland and to haul O'Brien before a meeting to explain himself. Such a demand would be as inconceivable today as the election of an editor. It is still less likely that any editor or editor-in-chief would comply with it. I was appointed to examine him before the meeting was made open to the floor. For this purpose I acquired a blue counsel's notebook, foolscap size, from a law stationer's in Chancery Lane. I did so partly because I dislike taking a note in a small book but partly also, I must confess, because I wished to appear more intimidating than I perhaps felt.

Conor sat at the head of the long table in the boardroom with me on his left. Trelford did not attend because editors were not members of the NUJ – or, if they were (the precise restrictive details I have now forgotten), were not allowed to attend meetings of the chapel. The other members of the staff disposed themselves around the table.

The encounter turned itself into what was, for me, a stimulating discussion of political theory. I said that to believe in a united Ireland, as Ms Holland did, was not a sackable offence. After all, many persons of the utmost respectability, some of them still with the *Observer*, believed in the same cause. Just so, Conor replied. What was wrong was to support or encourage violence. Yes indeed, I said. But that was different from believing in a united Ireland. Not a bit of it, Conor replied. For the only means of securing a united Ireland was through violence. Accordingly, support for a united Ireland entailed the support of violence. There the matter rested – and Mary Holland stayed sacked, though after O'Brien

---

[13] O'Brien, *Memoir*, pb edn, 373.

'had retired as editor-in-chief Donald quietly restored her. This did not surprise me.'[14]

Superficially this episode did not affect the always cordial though never close relationship between Conor and me. We had a drink together, usually with Cole, Kilmartin or Trelford there as well, once a fortnight or so. Conor could drink prodigious quantities, beer or wine (he rarely touched spirits), without showing any ill-effects. I attributed his great capacity to his practice of walking whenever he could instead of using public transport or taking a taxi. He would usually walk from the houseboat in Chelsea, where he lived for most of the week, to St Andrew's Hill near Blackfriars. I considered the walking healthier than the houseboat, which lacked amenities and was cold and from which Conor might easily fall off on a dark night. This was none of my business. I did, however, once ask him:

'Conor, has any doctor ever advised to you to drink less?'

'Oh yes, over the years, three of them.'

'And what do they say now?' (by the time this conversation took place, he was nearly 80).

'They're all dead.'

Still, after the Mary Holland incident I thought – I may have been wrong – that O'Brien regarded me with an element of wariness. He certainly referred to me as 'Vishinsky', after the notorious Soviet prosecutor in the show trials of the 1930s and, later, the foreign minister of the USSR. It was, of course, a joke but somehow, I felt, only half a joke.

X

The great question throughout O'Brien's first period as editor-in-chief was: which party, if any, was the *Observer* to support in the general election that was due in autumn 1979 at the latest? Most people expected it to take place a year before then. John Cole wanted the paper to support Labour; Donald Trelford preferred the paper to take no position; Conor Cruise O'Brien, if he had possessed a vote, would have voted for Margaret Thatcher.[15] I supported Trelford on the ground that the Labour government of 1976-9 had not been notably successful, any more than the government of 1974-6. In any case, the *Observer* was not in the business of

[14] Ibid.
[15] Ibid.

recommending its readers to vote for one party or another. True, it was seen as a paper of the Left or, by those with nicer perceptions, of the revisionist Left, and had been so regarded since the Suez operation in 1956, if not before. As Anthony Crosland had said to Terence Kilmartin in 1957: 'The *Observer* is our bible.'[16] But this did not mean it had to support Labour in all circumstances.

In 1978-9 the compact between the Labour government and the trade union movement broke down. Both the social contract of 1974 and the solemn-and-binding agreement of 1969 were no more. At the same time the beetle of Scottish devolution was burrowing in the floorboards. In November 1978 George Cunningham, the Labour Member for Islington South and Finsbury, successfully proposed an amendment to the devolution Bill whereby a hurdle would have to be jumped: a simple majority would not suffice. On 1 March 1979, St David's Day, the Welsh voters comprehensively rejected devolution while the Scottish voters accepted it, but not by the majority required by the legislation.

The government did not know what, if anything, to do next; there was a motion of no confidence; the Scottish (though not the Welsh) nationalists withdrew their support, as did a number of Irish MPs, one of whom, Frank Maguire, crossed the sea specially 'to abstain in person'; the government was defeated, and went to the country, where it was defeated likewise. Thus the proximate cause of the fall of the Callaghan government was the failure of the Scottish electorate to surmount the hurdle erected by George Cunningham in 1978, and the government's consequential paralysis, which led to a loss of support in the House of Commons. The events of the winter of 1978-9 – rubbish in the streets, unburied dead and so forth – obviously influenced the result of the election of May 1979. But they did not bring about the fall of James Callaghan's government.

Some but by no means all of these events were in the future when the higher command at the *Observer* were enjoying, or enduring, their seemingly endless conferences. At one of them John Cole pleaded that, if they could not bring themselves to support Jim, they could at least thank him; whereupon Terry Kilmartin exploded, a rare noise, and a rare spectacle. Why, he demanded, should we thank Callaghan for anything? It was he who had wanted the job, where he had made a mess of things.

[16] Cockett, *Astor*, 139.

Callaghan, however, received not only thanks but support as well. Cole and O'Brien met, perhaps oddly, in a church across the Thames from the latter's houseboat. After admiring the church's architecture, O'Brien told Cole that, unless he disagreed violently, 'he would be disposed to support Callaghan'.[17] As O'Brien knew perfectly well, none better, this was what Cole had wanted all along. So O'Brien's qualification was by way of being a gentle joke. Accordingly O'Brien wrote to Thornton Bradshaw, the president of Atlantic Richfield, telling him that the *Observer* would give its support to Labour. Bradshaw replied, pleading with him not to act in this way. He implied that Robert Anderson, the chairman and the head of the company, would be 'very annoyed indeed' if this happened and would speedily find a way of manifesting his displeasure. 'The *Observer*'s advice had no impact on the election but it did have considerable impact on the *Observer* itself.'[18]

XI

Events now began to move quite slowly, more slowly than is normal in newspapers. In January 1980, Anderson bought the entire Astor family interest in the *Observer*. In February 1980, Anderson telephoned Goodman at University College, Oxford (where he was Master), and informed him, much to his surprise, that he was selling 60 per cent of his interest in the *Observer* to Outram's, the newspaper arm of the Lonrho leviathan.

In February 1981 the *Observer* board rejected Anderson's candidate for the vice-chairmanship, Kenneth Harris. Later, Harris wrote that Anderson had not consulted his fellow directors beforehand or taken them into his confidence because 'he remembered how hard Lord Goodman and David Astor had tried to keep secret their original negotiations with Rupert Murdoch in 1976'.[19] However, Goodman's biographer tells us that, before the meeting, Anderson invited Goodman to breakfast at Claridge's, where he proposed that Harris should become his deputy. Goodman said that if this happened he would resign as a director and he thought Astor would do the same.[20]

---

[17] Cole, *Memoirs*, 198.
[18] O'Brien, *Memoir*, pb edn, 376.
[19] Kenneth Harris, *The Wildcatter* (1987), quot. Cockett, *Astor*, 286.
[20] Brivati, *Goodman*, 226.

According to O'Brien, the proposal would have meant in practice that Harris would have control of editorial policy and that he, rather than O'Brien, would be editor-in-chief. O'Brien, Astor and Goodman combined to defeat the proposal.[21] Anderson had not suffered such an indignity before. With company boards and the like, he was used to having his own way. Together with the paper's support for Labour at the 1979 election, it was too much to bear. As part of a deal involving oil interests in South America and South Africa, he determined to sell the paper to Lonrho.

There are questions which puzzled me then, puzzle me still and are unresolved in the studies of Goodman and Astor by, respectively, Brian Brivati and Richard Cockett. Why did they object to Kenneth Harris as strenuously as they did? And, in any event, why were they still throwing their considerable weight about at the *Observer* at this stage of the paper's history?

In 1976 they had both wanted to sell the paper to Murdoch and had been forestalled by Harris's *deus ex machina*, Anderson. They had remained on the board partly to preserve continuity, partly to provide a fig leaf for Atlantic Richfield, for they both aroused awe, even inspired fear, in the higher journalism. But by 1 February 1980 Astor's function was honorary merely. By then Anderson had bought out his family's interest in the paper, no doubt with the intention of selling it to 'Tiny' Rowland of Lonrho, as he did partially in 1980 and fully in 1981. Astor should have departed early in 1980. Goodman, as his Pooh-bah, should have accompanied him.

In the event they stayed in office and tried to prevent the sale to Lonrho. The sale might still have occurred, even if Harris had been given the position which Anderson wanted him to have. Whether O'Brien, Goodman and Astor expected him to sell the paper if his wishes in regard to Harris were flouted is a matter for speculation. If they honestly believed that he would be disastrous for the *Observer*, it was of course their duty to oppose his appointment. O'Brien thought that, as Anderson's deputy, Harris would be in charge of the paper's policy: the chairman understandably spent most of his time in the United States. He inferred this from something Anderson said to him. But it is inconceivable that Harris, in his new role, would have occupied the chair at the *Observer*'s principal editorial conference, as O'Brien did, or taken any hand in the practical business of bringing the paper out, as Trelford did.

[21] O'Brien, *Memoir*, pb edn, 377.

Admittedly he could be pompous, and over-admiring of persons of wealth, power or both. But there had been a previous Harris-figure – or, rather, the figure Harris would have become if Anderson had had his way – in Lord Barnetson, the chairman and managing director of United Newspapers (which then published *Punch*), who was chairman of the *Observer* from 1976 to 1980. He was a Scotsman and, at the start of his career, a journalist. His chief recreation was playing the drums to 'big band' swing records in the basement of his house. He intrigued against Trelford by importing another engaging Scotsman, Iain Lindsay-Smith, into the paper with the intention of providing a rival, a possible successor.

Trelford – the Rocky Marciano of newspaper politics – saw the punch coming and defended himself by giving Lindsay-Smith a commodious office, a full set of daily newspapers, which remained neatly displayed on a side table, and nothing to do all day long. He became O'Brien's regular drinking companion, so filling an ancient office in Old Fleet Street. But even the genuine delights of O'Brien's conversation did not prove sufficient to keep him in St Andrew's Hill. Eventually he left to edit *Lloyd's List*. Barnetson likewise had departed by then. But if O'Brien, Goodman, Astor and Trelford too had been prepared to swallow a Barnetson, why should they strain at a Harris who was later to publish the standard Life of C.R. Attlee? I have worked for or with far more objectionable people. O'Brien wrote that Harris:

> ... loved the *Observer*. And I must admit that he was poorly rewarded for so signal a service.[22]

XII

The sale to Tiny Rowland was opposed not only by Lord Goodman and David Astor but also by Conor Cruise O'Brien, Donald Trelford, John Cole and Adam Raphael. They had the opportunity to make their submissions to the Monopolies and Mergers Commission, to which the Secretary of State for Trade and Industry, John Biffen, now referred the attempted transfer. Only weeks before he had nodded through Rupert Murdoch's bid to buy *The Times* on the spurious ground that the *Sunday Times* was losing money. As Woodrow Wyatt informed us:

[22] Ibid., 369.

I reminded Rupert [Murdoch] during the evening how at his request and at my instigation she [Margaret Thatcher] had stopped the *Times* acquisition being referred to the Monopolies Commission though the *Sunday Times* was not really losing money and the pair together were not.[23]

In Britain, Lonrho owned only George Outram, publishers of the *Glasgow Herald*. In reality and equity alike, there was no case for referring the *Observer* acquisition to the MMC. It was so referred because Rowland was hated in both political parties; MPs were asking questions in the House; figures such as Goodman and Astor were kicking up a fuss outside Parliament; not least, the Conservative government wished to demonstrate that it could, after all, be tough over newspaper acquisitions. No political risks were involved. It was a gesture which Margaret Thatcher's government could afford to make. In fact Biffen's apparent decisiveness over Rowland served only to remind those people who took an interest in these things of his pusillanimity over Murdoch.

The powers of the Secretary of State for Trade and Industry in these and similar matters are among the scandals of our constitution. They would remain scandalous even if the minister donned a metaphorical wig and red gown when he or she was taking the decisions – even if he or she behaved in what is, or used to be, called a quasi-judicial manner. They would still be decisions which the State should not properly take. As it is, unashamedly political decisions are taken all the time. The one in *The Times* and *Sunday Times* case was manifestly political. It was also corrupt, in that Murdoch was being indulged, the rules were being bent in his favour, to ensure the support of his papers up to and including the 1983 election, a support which was generously forthcoming.

The members of the commission found that 'on the available evidence' they could not conclude that Lonrho had 'interfered with the accurate presentation of news or the free expressions of opinion in its African newspapers'. On the contrary: the evidence suggested that 'as a newspaper group Lonrho respected editorial independence'. On 28 June 1981 they reported, Dr J.S. Marshall dissenting, that the acquisition of the *Observer* by Lonrho might not

---

[23] Wyatt Journal, 14 June 1987: *The Journals of Woodrow Wyatt*, ed. Sarah Curtis (3 vols, 1998-2000), I, 372.

be 'expected to operate against the public interest'. However, the commission recommended that the sale should not be allowed to proceed without the appointment of 'not less [sic] than six independent directors', who were duly appointed. In July 1981 John Biffen gave his consent. The *Observer* became part of George Outram and Co. of Glasgow. Atlantic Richfield received 20 per cent of Outrams and four-and-a-half million dollars in cash; Robert Anderson remained chairman for a further three years; while Lord Goodman and David Astor resigned from the board. I took no part in the endeavours to prevent Lonrho from taking over the *Observer*. I had had some role in securing a say by the staff in the appointment of R.H.S. Crossman's successor at the *New Statesman* in 1972. I had vociferously opposed (though not as loudly as Clive James) the acquisition of the *Observer* by Rupert Murdoch in 1976. But by 1981 I had had enough of newspaper politics:

> Let them have it how they will!
> Thou art tired; best be still![24]

Besides, I thought that, in two ways, Astor, Cole, Goodman, O'Brien and Trelford had brought their troubles on themselves. O'Brien and Trelford had allowed themselves to be browbeaten by Cole – no mean browbeater – into supporting Callaghan in 1979. Trelford's instinct, the correct one, had been to proffer no advice at all; O'Brien warmed to Thatcher, as Anderson did. There was no reason to support her; every reason to avoid slapping Anderson (an excellent proprietor) in the face. This was also what the board had done over Kenneth Harris. It was the second way in which Astor and the rest had brought their troubles on themselves. As a general rule I do not favour sucking up to proprietors. In this case, the two saviours of the *Observer* – Anderson and Harris – deserved better treatment from the people they had saved. Throughout this period, however, I had the distinct feeling that Astor and Goodman did not sincerely welcome Anderson as proprietor, and would have preferred the paper to go to Murdoch, as they had originally planned in 1976.

---

[24] Matthew Arnold, 'The Last Word' (1867).

XIII

John Cole did not think his relationship with Tiny Rowland 'would be of long duration'.[25] The day after the Lonrho takeover the BBC, 'totally unaware' of his 'personal drama', telephoned to ask whether he would be interested in becoming the corporation's political correspondent.[26] He had always wanted to work in the Westminster lobby, but told the BBC that he had a pronounced Belfast accent which might put off the viewers. The BBC said this was of no account. As things turned out, Cole's accent was his strongest suit. He became the most famous political correspondent in the history of the BBC.

Of those who had publicly opposed the Lonrho acquisition, Cole was the only one to leave the paper. O'Brien ceased being editor-in-chief but continued to write his column – like John Wesley, taking the world as his parish – in the top right-hand corner of the first leader-page. Raphael carried on as political correspondent. Trelford remained editor, without any editor-in-chief above him. Harris stayed an associate editor until 1984 but did not do very much and devoted most of his attention to George Outram and Co. Goodman and Astor were no more.

XIV

In the meantime Michael Foot had become leader of the Labour Party. He was the last to be elected under the old – and better – system of the exhaustive ballot restricted to Labour Members of Parliament, under which they voted with the bottom candidate or candidates dropping out until one of them secured an absolute majority. After James Callaghan resigned as leader it was thought by almost everybody that the candidates to replace him would be Denis Healey, Peter Shore and John Silkin. They represented respectively the Right; the Left with red, white and blue edges; and the old soft Left.

I had known Foot reasonably well since the mid-1960s. More to the point, I knew his wife Jill, and her ambitions on his behalf. I also knew the Labour Party, and its wish at that stage for some kind of unifying candidate which Healey could never be – though in

[25] Cole, *Memoirs*, 200.
[26] Ibid.

retrospect it might have been better if the party had fought its civil war under him rather than under Foot, for it was waged as ferociously under the latter as it would have been under the former.

In the autumn of 1980 I did not believe, as others did, that Foot would stand idly by, confining his activities to the support of Shore. On the morning of 18 October 1980, a Saturday, my column safely in bed, I sent him a telegram at his house in Pilgrims Lane, Hampstead, London N.W.3. In those days it was still possible to send telegrams. This one asked whether it would be possible to talk on the telephone. Foot obliged within half an hour and indicated clearly – though without committing himself precisely – that he intended to stand for the leadership owing to the pressure under which he had been placed by his numerous friends and admirers. He then, on the Saturday, flew to Dublin to deliver a lecture commemorating the death of one of his several unlikely heroes, Jonathan Swift. On Sunday 19 October 1980 I reported exclusively on the front page of the *Observer* that Foot intended to contest the leadership. This came as a surprise to many people, not least to Peter Shore.

I thought then, and for some time afterwards, that Michael Foot, whom I christened 'The Old Bibliophile' in the column, would unite the Labour Party and that his virtues, including decency, kindness and tolerance, would communicate themselves to the voters, not least because they did not really like Margaret Thatcher, if the opinion polls of the pre-Falklands period of 1979-82 were anything to go by. On both counts I was wrong, both about the party and about the people. The old party comrades (a favourite phrase of Conor Cruise O'Brien) scrapped away as vigorously as they had in the great days of Bevanism, if not more so. And the people resolutely refused to be susceptible to Foot's undoubted charm.

Particular exception was taken to the manner of his laying a wreath at the Cenotaph, in the company of the other party leaders of the time. He was wearing what was described as 'an old duffel coat', though his wife later protested to me that it was a loden coat, expensive, of excellent material. Whatever the truth about Foot's overcoat on this occasion, he did not appear to be wearing a formal, dark suit beneath it; he placed the wreath as if putting out the rubbish. Altogether John Cole was right when, shortly after Foot's accession to the leadership, he pronounced him to be 'unelectable', the first time I had heard the word used.

9

Living with Lonrho

Africa was always going to be a problem for the *Observer* under Lonrho's ownership because of the company's exterior interests there and Tiny Rowland's personal friendship with many leaders ... At the same time, it should be said that Rowland did give the paper some good story leads on Africa and some high-level introductions. One introduction was to a man called Mohamed al-Fayed ...

Donald Trelford, Observer, 12 March 2000

I

John Cole's departure for the BBC meant that Trelford had to appoint a new deputy. On the day Charles Windsor married Diana Spencer, 29 July 1981, he telephoned to ask my advice. On the same morning he telephoned Terence Kilmartin for the same purpose. He chose us, he told me subsequently, because he was fairly sure we would be the only people connected with the *Observer* who would not be watching the proceedings on television. About me, at any rate, he was correct, for royal weddings I can take or leave, and this one I chose to leave.

Trelford's inquiry was specific. Should he appoint as his deputy Anthony Howard, then editor of the *Listener*? This seemed to be a question expecting the answer Yes, the answer I should have given in any event. Nevertheless I thought, as Trelford had taken the trouble to consult me, that I ought to go through the pros and cons with a measure of gravity. The cons, I said, were chiefly Howard's aversion to talking about or commissioning articles on abstract ideas and his tendency to panic in a newspaper crisis. But these were far outweighed by Howard's pros: his sharp journalistic sense, his talent for gossip, his industry and (what is not quite the same thing, on papers anyway) his conscientiousness. If he said he would do something, he would do it – not qualities invariably displayed by Trelford himself, though I did not say this.

What I did say was that Howard, despite his many good qualities, would at some stage try to take Trelford's job. Trelford said he did not mind this at all: he was confident he could look after himself where editorial colleagues were concerned. Indeed, he gave the impression of thoroughly approving Howard's ambitions. It was, he seemed to be saying, exactly what he was looking for in a deputy. He was seeking someone who could take over if 'anything happened' to him – if Lonrho dismissed him – and who would maintain the historic traditions of the *Observer*. For this task Howard was admirably fitted. I duly concurred with these sentiments, and Howard accepted the deputy editorship on condition that Michael Davie did not want the job himself, as he did not.

Anthony Howard's achievement at the *Observer* was to create the best page on Sunday in perhaps any broadsheet journalism at that period, the 1980s. I write this without, I hope, giving undue offence to modesty, for my own column, 1,200 words or so, was spread across the bottom of the page. Conor Cruise O'Brien's slightly longer column was placed above it on the right. The rest of the page would be taken up with the 'profile', often written by that most underestimated of journalists, Laurence Marks, and illustrated with a caricature by Mark Boxer, 'Marc'. It was the cartoon that made the page; after Boxer went – he died of a brain tumour in 1988 aged 57 – no replacement was found because he was unique, which is not to depreciate another fine cartoonist, Wally Fawkes, 'Trog', who illustrated many profiles at the time.

II

This happy conjunction – Marc, O'Brien and myself – did not last for ever. In their evidence to the Monopolies Commission and on other occasions, Cole, O'Brien, Raphael and Trelford had all said harsh things about Tiny Rowland and Lonrho: but O'Brien had been the harshest. He was no longer editor-in-chief but he was the paper's leading columnist. Lonrho determined to get rid of him. To this end the company bombarded Trelford with memoranda, beautifully typed and enclosed in transparent plastic covers of the kind used by assiduous literary agents to try to make manuscripts appear more impressive.

This bombardment did not begin immediately after the acquisition; Rowland bided his time. The attack was directed towards O'Brien's journalistic ability or, as Lonrho preferred to believe, his lack of it as a columnist. But the plastic folders did not attack him for being, say, an apologist for the State of Israel, as they could well have done with some justice. They accused him of being repetitious, of writing too often about that country, about Northern Ireland and, to a lesser extent, about Africa. I told Trelford, who showed me the detailed dossiers (there were several) enclosed in their transparent plastic, that all columnists were entitled to their hobbyhorses, and Conor had his.

He did not, however, help the cause of the columnists' union by taking himself off to Dartmouth College in Connecticut as a visiting professor. I said to the editor that, with all the aids of modern technology, O'Brien could dilate on Israel, Northern Ireland and Africa just as well from across the Atlantic as he could here; perhaps better. He might even, in his new though temporary abode, add the United States to his repertoire. Though his absence was known about beforehand and had been approved, I knew he had made a mistake. He had provided Lonrho or Trelford with an excuse. He was in the position of the corrupt policeman who is dismissed from the force, not for corruption, but for overstating his petrol mileage.

So it proved. It was O'Brien's imminent absence in the United States which served as the excuse for getting rid of him. I do not think he minded greatly. He had written the column to much *réclame*; could write anywhere else he chose; had books to complete; could move to other pastures where he would be welcomed. It was not a tragedy. Nevertheless when I learnt of the end of Conor's column, I walked into the editor's office and said:

'This is a black day for the *Observer*, Donald.'

Trelford did not respond angrily – he was the most equable editor I have known – but proceeded to make a spirited defence of his own position. It was all very well, he said, for me to talk of black days. But what did I do? I showed up at the office when I felt like it, always in the mornings, attended the odd editorial conference, did my expenses, cracked a few jokes and went off with Terry Kilmartin, Bill Keegan or Tony Howard for a drink in the New El Vino's (a recently opened branch of the more venerable Fleet Street establishment) in New Bridge Street. He, by contrast, had to sit in his office for most of the day, dealing with Lonrho or even with Tiny Rowland himself. It was only because of his negotiating skills that I was able to enjoy the freedom I did in writing the political column.

There was a good deal of truth in this. I could see Trelford's point of view. He was justifiably cross, no more than slightly cross, at my barging into his office, talking about black days. O'Brien himself remained friends with him, taking the view that if it was to be a choice between Trelford's job as editor and his own as a columnist, the editor would naturally sacrifice the columnist.[1] When Trelford finally left the editorship nearly a decade later, O'Brien predicted to me that history would judge him kindly for having maintained the standards of the *Observer* in the most difficult circumstances.

III

From whatever cause, Lonrho and Rowland left me alone. Indeed, my only communication with the latter took place after my turn had come round to win the British Press 'Columnist of the Year' award in 1982. Signing himself 'R.W. Rowland', he wrote a short letter of congratulation which was civil but hardly effusive. I did not feel that, in the circumstances, any reply was required. I did not need any encouragement to write critically of Margaret Thatcher's government. I did not join in campaigns against individual ministers such as Norman Tebbit, for whom I had a soft spot, but who had offended Rowland over his failure, as Secretary for Trade and Industry, to support Lonrho in its increasingly tedious battle with Mohamed Fayed over his acquisition of Harrods. Nor was I asked to join in.

Likewise, I was not consulted about the attacks on the Prime Minister's son Mark and his business deals, which were alleged to have been secured through favouritism and summarised by the headline: 'The Son Also Rises.' I was uneasy about these stories but, as no one asked my opinion, did not make my doubts known. I had never met Mark Thatcher but, from what I had read, had formed no very favourable opinion of him. Few had: for once, I found myself with the majority.

---

[1] See O'Brien, *Memoir*, pb edn, 378.

But I was influenced by something Alistair McAlpine said to me at the time. McAlpine was then the Conservative Party's Treasurer and a friend and admirer of Margaret Thatcher but not a devotee of Mark. He said, however, that the boy had had a rough time, having been forced into what amounted to exile because at home he had become an embarrassment. This put a slightly different complexion on the matter, for it was always somehow implied that Mark Thatcher had gone abroad because the opportunities for lucrative deals were more promising than they were at home. It was, on the face of it, inconceivable that his doting mother should have expelled him from the country. Yet who else could have ordered him out? The Tory High Command would not have. But they could have persuaded the Prime Minister to exercise her maternal authority. The question remains interesting, unanswered and, probably, unanswerable.

IV

Among the Lonrho *apparatchiks* I would see wandering about the place from time to time was Sir Edward du Cann, joint deputy chairman of the company from 1982 to 1984 and chairman from 1984 to 1992. I had known him a long time, which was not surprising. He had been in politics since the 1950s: a Conservative MP since 1956, a junior minister and chairman of the Conservative Party in the 1960s, chairman of the Public Accounts Committee and the Expenditure Committee in the 1970s, and chairman of the 1922 Committee from 1972 to 1984. In 1975 he was the favourite to stand against Edward Heath for the leadership of the Conservative Party after the initial favourite, Sir Keith Joseph, had said he would not contest the election.

Such Conservatives as Peter Tapsell, a friend of both Anthony Howard and myself, assured me he would stand. It was, in Howard's phrase – he was then editor of the *New Statesman* – 'a bum steer'. Du Cann did not stand but Margaret Thatcher did. His prospective candidature was, however, serious, as both its prediction and its espousal by people like Tapsell demonstrated. Yet even then he was not wholly trusted in his own party. Du Cann, it was felt, was not quite 16 annas to the rupee. This was before the time when, it seemed, he was getting into trouble virtually monthly for non-payment of debts of one kind and another, chiefly rates.

At the *Observer* he tried, unsuccessfully, to get rid of Anthony Howard: according to du Cann, a dangerous Socialist who was having a deleterious influence on the paper. Trelford said at a board meeting that there would be nothing easier than to sack Howard but that, if that happened, the board would have to find a replacement for Trelford as well. After that, du Cann's campaign, such as it was, collapsed. Talking to du Cann was rather like walking downstairs and somehow missing the last step. You were uninjured but remained disconcerted.

In one respect he remained unhelpful, owing to an untypical excess of scrupulosity. Among the tasks of political writers of all kinds is attending the party conferences by the seaside in the autumn. Blackpool has many hotels but few that are any good. Laypersons seem to think that, on these occasions, journalists are chiefly interested in luxurious accommodation and in food and drink. Not at all, or, at any rate, not primarily. What journalists want is a bath or shower, a television set (preferably one showing satellite channels as well) and, most of all, despite the advances of modern technology, a telephone in the room. It is over the last in particular that Blackpool hotels are unsatisfactory. There was, however, one hotel which, so to speak, worked: the Pembroke. It was a modern, unbeautiful establishment that had been acquired by Lonrho as part of the company's hotels empire (later to be ended), together with the Metropole in Brighton. But whereas Brighton had numerous hotels with the requisite amenities, Blackpool had few, including the Pembroke. Du Cann gave his opinion that Lonrho's ownership of both the newspaper and the hotel did not give the newspaper's journalists any entitlement to preferential treatment when it came to reserving rooms for the party conference. Luckily, however, we discovered that the paper's managing director, Nick Morrell, did not share du Cann's somewhat priggish view.

V

Trelford had got rid of O'Brien after about a year's pressure from Lonrho to take this course. He had no clear successor in mind. For a time he tried the venerable woman columnist Katharine Whitehorn. She had not wanted her new position in the paper and was not happy in it. In 1985 Neal Ascherson suggested to Anthony Howard that he might fill the space.

It was surprising, in retrospect, that no one had thought of this before. Ascherson had been born in 1932 and educated at Eton – in his generation, Etonians were thinner on the ground in journalism, apart from City and racing journalism, than they were later to become – and at King's College, Cambridge, where he had won a starred first in History. I knew him not through Cambridge, where we did not meet, but through his first marriage to Corinna Adam, who had been my colleague at the *New Statesman*. He had, with her, spent much of his early journalistic life in Bonn, though never as West German correspondent but instead, in the period 1963-83, as Central Europe correspondent, Eastern Europe correspondent and foreign writer, all for the *Observer*.

He was instantly attractive to women. His first wife told me that this was because he talked very softly and listened very carefully: both characteristics the consequence of defective hearing brought about by an explosion when he was doing his uncomfortable national service with the Royal Marines in Malaya. Naturally a polite and pleasant man, Ascherson nevertheless found it necessary to walk through the office unsmiling and looking neither to the right nor to the left, lest a carelessly bestowed 'good morning' arouse hopes which could not be fulfilled.

Politically he was a romantic, combining a broadly Marxist analysis of events with a devotion to oppressed nationalities and small countries. Of these his favourite was Poland. Indeed, what Ireland and Israel were to O'Brien, Scotland and Poland were to Ascherson. He proved a worthy successor to the great Irish all-rounder. However, he left in 1990 to go to the newly founded *Independent on Sunday* not because he had a quarrel with the *Observer* but because he shared what were then the ideals of the original *Independent* of 1986: of a paper without a proprietor but of shareholders merely, none of them possessing a controlling interest.[2]

VI

In the 1980s I wrote frequently for the *Spectator*, chiefly book reviews and diaries (also called notebooks), when it was edited by Charles Moore. The *Spectator* diary is one of the most widely read

---

[2] For Neal Ascherson's departure from the *Independent on Sunday*, see p. 252 below.

features in journalism, in that it is read by somebody in every newspaper office on Thursdays as light relief from the rigours of the afternoon. Any interesting items are referred to news editors, features editors, even editors. On 19 May 1984 I wrote such an item, without realising it at the time:

> This is the end of my stint on the Diary. It is always agreeable to write for the *Spectator*, turn up at its offices or meet its contributors or staff on licensed premises. But it does tend to attract a class of person that can be called the Young Fogey. I owe the term to Mr Terence Kilmartin, though he may not be its inventor. I have nothing against the Young Fogey. He is libertarian but not liberal. He is conservative but has no time for Mrs Margaret Thatcher and considers Mr Neil Kinnock the most personally attractive of the present party leaders. He is a scholar of Evelyn Waugh. He tends to be coolly religious, either RC or C of E. He dislikes modern architecture. He makes a great fuss about the old Prayer Book, grammar, syntax and punctuation. He laments the difficulty of purchasing good bread, Cheddar cheese, kippers and sausages – though not beer, because the cause of good beer has been taken over by boring men with beards from the Campaign for Real Ale. He enjoys walking and travelling by train. He thinks *The Times* is not what it was and prefers the *Daily Telegraph*. He likes the *Observer* (particularly Dr C.C. O'Brien) more than the *Sunday Times*, which stands for most things the young Fogey detests. Mr A.N. Wilson is a Young Fogey. So is Dr John Casey [Fellow of Gonville and Caius College, Cambridge, and a prolific freelance journalist]. So, now I come to count them, are most of my friends. I am something of a Middle-aged Fogey myself. I shall have to watch it. The causes are mostly good but can become tedious to others if pressed too often and too hard.

Everyone went mad. The fierce Veronica Wadley, even then a power in middle-market journalism, declared that for the moment she was interested only in articles about Young Fogeys. I was asked to write a book about them, to be called *The Official Young Fogey Handbook*. Naturally I declined, though those who claimed to have my best interests at heart told me I was mistaken: 'You'd make far more money that way than by writing a lot of boring old stuff about boring politics.' At least three other journalists were reported to be writing books along these lines; one of them, by the engaging Suzanne Lowry, actually saw the light of day. Numerous articles appeared. The phrase was bandied about on the feature pages of newspapers and in the glossy magazines. My daughter, who was then 20, thought it monstrous that I was not drawing some substantial royalty. I told her that we lived in an unjust world and that there was no copyright in phrases or patent on ideas. I may have been wrong about this, but I made no approach to the lawyers who specialised in such matters, nor did they approach me.

The publisher, André Deutsch, said to his staff that he had read about Young Fogeys somewhere. Where was it? There might be a quick book there. The 'Pendennis' column in the *Observer*, came the reply. 'Pendennis' had indeed written about them, giving me due credit, as was only to be expected from a colleague. Let 'Pendennis' be summoned to lunch, Deutsch instructed. The regular author of the column, Peter Hillmore, accordingly had lunch with the publisher. Contracts were discussed. Returned to his office, Deutsch discovered that the 'Pendennis' item had not been written by Hillmore, who had been on holiday at the time, but by Simon Hoggart, who had been deputising for Hillmore. Whereupon the diminutive publisher fell into a rage, claiming he had been deceived, though the fault had been entirely his. Hillmore proceeded to tell his readers that he was not, after all, writing a book about Young Fogeys.

Several people thought it would discompose me to learn that the phrase had first been used by Dornford Yates in 1928. To me this did not matter in the least. If I had stolen the phrase from anyone, it was from Terry Kilmartin, who had used it of John Casey. It stuck, for a time – roughly, the 1980s – because, by chance, I had lighted upon a small social phenomenon. The more important phenomenon of the time was the urge by journalists to make lists and invent social categories, preferably those that could be expressed by acronyms. This derived partly from the terms employed by market researchers in the United States, partly from the tendency of all newspapers to turn themselves increasingly into magazines, which, well before the 1980s, had published regular articles on bogus social groups and endless lists of what was supposedly in and what was out.

At about the same time I started to use another phrase which caught on and enjoyed a longer life than Young Fogeys. Indeed, it is still used today (I am writing in April 2000). As *Brewer's Politics* puts it:

CHATTERING CLASSES: A UK, and specifically London, term for the intermeshing community of left-of-centre and middle-class intellectuals, especially writers, dramatists and political pundits, who believe their views should carry enormous weight and have considerable access to the BBC and much of the media. Originally this term was coined in the first years of Margaret Thatcher's ascendancy to disparage the liberal intelligentsia who raged impotently about Thatcherism around the dinner tables of North London. It was popularised by Alan Watkins, the *Observer*'s political correspondent [sic] ...[3]

I can remember exactly where the phrase was first used and who used it. It was in the study of my flat at 12 Battishill Street, London N.1, and the speaker was Frank Johnson. About the date I can be less precise: it was in the early years of the Thatcher administration. It was certainly before 1984, when I moved from Battishill Street to Barnsbury Street, not far away in what was then the People's Republic of Islington. What neither Johnson nor I can remember is whether he went on to use the phrase in print. I think he probably did, but neither of us has been able to track down the reference. During the relevant period he was political columnist of the short-lived *Now!* magazine and then parliamentary sketch-writer of *The Times*. I think the latter the more likely source. But whereas Johnson may have used the phrase in print once or, at most, twice, I certainly used it on numerous occasions; and it stuck.

VII

Johnson and I would make a roughly annual pilgrimage to Malcolm Muggeridge and his wife Kitty at their house outside Robertsbridge in Sussex. We would drive down in time for lunch in his stylish though distinctly uncomfortable Alfa Romeo two-seater. Though at that stage Johnson could have been a teetotaller without any inconvenience to himself, Muggeridge or, more likely, Kitty would have got in a few bottles of lager and some Rhône wine from Sainsbury's, for at that stage neither of them drank. Likewise, ham and salad would be provided for Johnson and myself, while our hosts consumed, not a strictly vegetarian meal, but smoked haddock, eggs or both. Muggeridge also had a liking for nuts and dried

---

[3] Nicholas Comfort, *Brewer's Politics* (1993, rev. edn 1995), 88.

fruit. Judged by the standards of, say, my parents, his diet was by no means that of an ascetic or of someone intent on mortifying the flesh. He claimed to live like a retired schoolmaster, which was reasonably accurate. Kitty's teas, which he enjoyed while I contented myself with a cup of tea and a biscuit, were likewise varied and sustaining: two sorts of cake, bread and butter, jam, scones, perhaps a boiled egg for Muggeridge as well.

We did not discuss sex, which he claimed to have relinquished once he was passed 60. He told me he had given up drink because he wanted to be able to carry on writing. He predicted, incorrectly as it turned out, that I would do likewise at the same age:

'You will find, dear boy, that one of the greatest luxuries in life is a clear head.'

Smoking, he said, he gave up from disgust. He was once in a hotel room in the United States, in the middle of an article, and interrupted his writing to go out for the Sunday papers. Returning to his room with his heavy load, he was nauseated by the smell and shocked by the overflowing and smouldering ashtray. After he had made his decision he experienced no further difficulties; or so he claimed.

We were once discussing Aneurin Bevan. I said he appeared to have been a very well-read man.

'Don't you believe it, dear boy,' Muggeridge said. 'He liked to give the impression he was well-read. Nye was an extremely agreeable but rather idle Welshman who asked for little more of life than a glass of whisky and a game of snooker. Grasp that,' Muggeridge added, in one of his favourite formulations, 'and you grasp all.'

He had once, he said, been taking part in a discussion with Bevan on the old Third Programme about *The Pilgrim's Progress*, which he claimed was one of his favourite books. Concealed in the weekly journal he held before him – it could have been *Tribune*, or the *New Statesman* – was a guide to the work in question designed for School Certificate students.

'It was obvious to me,' Muggeridge said, 'that old Nye had never read a line of Bunyan in his life. Or, if he had, it was a very long time ago.'

In the greatest good humour by this stage of the afternoon, he went on to discuss the literary pretensions of Sir William Haley. From modest beginnings, Haley had become Director-General of the BBC and editor of *The Times* and had, towards the end of his

life, written a weekly column in that paper of a distinctly, it may be
a deliberately, old-fashioned, man-of-letters kind under the name
'Oliver Edwards'. This had influenced Frank Johnson in his youth.

'He had read a lot of books,' Johnson said to Muggeridge.

'Of course he had, dear boy, but they were the *wrong* books. You
see,' Muggeridge went on, 'he had these library steps, and he would
use these steps to clamber about on the shelves, like a little mon-
key. You see, he was searching for Wisdom.'

Muggeridge had no library steps of his own conveniently to hand,
but proceeded to give an active demonstration among his own books
of Sir William's search. Taking one randomly from the shelves and
furiously turning the pages, he said:

'Ah, Aristotle. Must be Wisdom there. No, no Wisdom. Try Plato
instead.'

Muggeridge would seize another volume.

'No good. No Wisdom in Plato. Try someone else.'

Tiring of Sir William Haley, he turned to Germaine Greer and
Clive James.

'These Australians who come over here,' he said, 'are engaged in
a similar search. Only with them it is Culture they are after.'

To demonstrate their search Muggeridge turned from books to
curtains.

'Culture here?' he said, poking around between one of them and
the windows. 'No Culture there, I'm afraid. Try somewhere else,'
and he moved towards a cupboard.

As I grew older I came to realise that I got on better with people
who were considered to be on the right politically, such as Malcolm
Muggeridge, Michael Oakeshott and Anthony Powell, than with
those who were thought of as representatives of liberal enlighten-
ment, such as Noel Annan, A.J. Ayer and A.J.P. Taylor; though
there were obvious exceptions such as Tony Crosland in one direction and, say, Alfred Sherman in the other. For sheer entertainment value there was no one to beat Muggeridge. In the palace of
varieties outside which I had queued in the 1950s and entered some
time – it was difficult to say precisely when – in the 1960s, he was
without question top of the bill. However, he was not entirely
truthful. Great entertainers are rarely so.

I asked him why he was no longer friendly with Anthony Powell.
After Muggeridge had returned to London from his stint as Washington correspondent of the *Daily Telegraph* to rejoin and, later,

become deputy editor of that paper, they and their wives, Violet and Kitty, had rarely been out of one another's company. And Powell had been Muggeridge's literary editor when he was editor of *Punch*. What had happened? What was the cause of the *froideur*, if such it was?

Muggeridge said it was nothing at all. I would discover, he said, as I went through life, that friends simply dropped by the wayside, or went off in other directions, as one tottered down the road. Life changed. So it was with Powell and him. Powell's version of events was different, quite the opposite in fact. There was indeed a cause for the rift. He had published *The Valley of Bones* (1964) halfway through *A Dance to the Music of Time*. Muggeridge had written about it in the *Evening Standard*, where he was a regular reviewer, and asked: Why does Mr Powell bother with such decadent, useless people? Surely there are more important things to write about while civilisation is collapsing all around us? And so forth. That, Powell said, was not the most helpful contribution an old friend could make at that stage. Oddly enough, the novel in question was about war-time life in The Welch Regiment, with South Wales miners being officered by South Wales bank managers.

It was Muggeridge that was the cause of my knowing Powell at all. I wrote to him saying I was writing a longish piece about Muggeridge and that I should be grateful for his help. Could I come and see him? Powell replied immediately. He would, he wrote, be delighted to meet me – had long wanted to do so. But the one subject he could not discuss was Malcolm Muggeridge. He was about to write something about Muggeridge himself. This turned out to be one of the best sections in his memoirs.[4] This seemed to me less the behaviour of a distinguished novelist in his mid-seventies than of a young, ambitious feature-writer on, say, the *Daily Mail* who, having thought of an 'idea', wanted to keep it to himself for further use in the paper or in some other publication. Nevertheless I visited Powell in his house outside Frome in Somerset where I had a most enjoyable time, partly because he liked to regard himself as a fellow Welshman (Powell, of course, being derived from *ap Hywel*) and partly because he was informative on a period I have always found fascinating: the 1950s London of Foot's *Tribune*, Gilmour's *Spectator*, Martin's *New Statesman* and Muggeridge's *Punch*.[5] His wife

---

[4] Anthony Powell, *To Keep the Ball Rolling: Memoirs* (4 vols, 1976-82), III, 81-6, IV, ch. 3.
[5] See Malcolm Muggeridge, *Like It Was: Diaries*, ed. John Bright-Holmes (1981), *passim*. Powell's Welsh ancestry is dealt with extensively – perhaps exhaustingly – in his *Memoirs*, I, chs 1, 2.

Violet did not take second place to him. We talked about, among other things, Llandeilo and Dynevor Castle.

VIII

In the 1980s I saw more of Powell and Muggeridge severally than I did of Margaret Thatcher. I first had an interview with her on the suggestion of her press secretary, Bernard Ingham, with whom I have always been able to conduct a relationship both distant and cordial at the same time. We would meet in the press gallery of the Commons, he going about his tasks, I about mine.

'Good afternoon, Bernard,' I would say.

'Good afternoon, Alan,' he would reply, and we would go on our respective ways with further expressions of regard for each other.

On this occasion he ushered me into a sitting-room in No 10 where Mrs Thatcher, as she then was, was already waiting for me. It was 1981. The SDP had recently been launched. And there was trouble with the printers at the *Observer*, where the spirit of the 1970s lived on. Issues of the paper had been 'lost' by industrial action – chiefly by means of the mandatory chapel (that is, union branch) meeting held at 4.30 on a Saturday afternoon. The Prime Minister expressed her sympathy and hoped that we would, as she put it, 'stand firm'.

'Of course,' I said, 'they're all criminals. Chiefly from South London. Either that, or they're taxi drivers who turn up at the *Observer* in their spare time. They tend to live in Ilford, or Romford, or Woodford.'

Mrs Thatcher's eyes became more protruberant than usual and more open. I warmed to my theme of the iniquitous nature of the printing trade. Gratifyingly, I had succeeded in engaging her full attention.

'Of course,' I went on, 'they wouldn't do you any harm. Not physically I mean. They're not what I believe are called "hard men" but go in more for receiving stolen goods, or so I've been told. In fact some of them are friends of mine.'

'But this is terrible news. I never knew it was like this in Fleet Street.'

'Nothing new. Been like this for years. The big proprietors such as Beaverbroook and Rothermere would give in to their every demand to try to drive their poorer competitors out of business.'

'The Government must do something.'

'But what?'

'You must stand firm.'

As the interview proceeded, I could not hope to equal such an impression. Like the London greengrocer (also associated tradition-ally with the criminal classes), I had put my best strawberries at the front of the pile. Or, as the skilful barrister is supposed to do, I had made my best point first. I asked her about Roy Jenkins, then much in the news on account of the SDP. She said he had been the best Chancellor since the war. This seemed to me less than gener-ous to her own Chancellor, Geoffrey Howe. In his book on the post-war Chancellors, Edmund Dell was to rate Howe as the best of all.[6] Despite her admiration for Jenkins, she reprehended his departure from the Labour Party.

'You stay and fight,' she said.

She criticised David Owen for the same reason. She held a high opinion of him too, which was reciprocated. Indeed, if there was one feeling whose strength exceeded Mrs Thatcher's regard for Dr Owen, it was Dr Owen's regard for Mrs Thatcher. For some reason I turned to Lord Hailsham's phrase about 'elective dictatorship' as a description of our constitutional arrangements. I asked her whether we should enact a Bill of Rights. Why I asked about this I have no idea. I was either babbling or trying to provoke the Prime Minister. If there was one subject she was uninterested in, it was the constitution.

'Oh but we already have a Bill of Rights.'

'It isn't quite the same thing.'

'Oh yes it is. Exactly the same thing. It was in 1689. You go and look it up.'

Having no wish to prolong our discussion of the Bill of Rights 1689, I glanced at my watch instead, found I had already spent half-an-hour with the Prime Minister, thanked her and announced I would now have to depart.

'Oh no you don't. I'll tell you when to go. There are several other things I want to say to you.'

Say them she did. I have now forgotten what they were. But after

---

[6] Edmund Dell, *The Chancellors* (1996, pb edn 1997), ch. 15.

an additional ten minutes or so I emerged unsteadily into Downing Street, escorted by Ingham.

IX

This happened before the *Observer*'s attacks on Mark Thatcher had begun. Here the paper and Tiny Rowland were at one as they were not, or not entirely, over Africa, where Lonrho retained substantial business interests. Donald Trelford was an old Africa hand. He had been editor of the *Times of Malawi* in 1963-6 and an African correspondent for the *Observer*, *The Times* of London and the BBC during the same period, before his return to England as deputy news editor of the *Observer*.

Something under 20 years later, he returned to Zimbabwe primarily to interview the dictator Robert Mugabe, with whom Rowland maintained amicable relations. In his travels Trelford found evidence of the murder, torture and imprisonment of members of the Ndebele tribe which had been inspired by Mugabe. In particular he discovered mass graves in Matabeleland. On his return to London, he had to decide whether to 'publish an anodyne interview with Mugabe or tell the truth about Matabeleland, thereby damaging the interests of my proprietor'.[7]

Trelford chose the latter, and telephoned Rowland at five on the Saturday afternoon, which was too late for him to try to stop publication but before he could hear the news from anyone else. He 'slammed the telephone down after threatening the direst revenge'. On the next morning, the Sunday, Trelford turned on the BBC's eight o'clock news to hear his story condemned as 'lies' in an official statement by Mugabe. This was supported by a letter of apology to Mugabe from Rowland: 'I take full responsibility for what in my view was discourteous, disingenuous and wrong in the editor of a serious newspaper widely read in Africa.'

Rowland described Trelford as an 'incompetent reporter', announced that he would be dismissed and proceeded to write him an open letter – a form of literary composition to which Tiny was greatly attached and which he distributed to all the papers. This said that Lonrho would not go on supporting a 'failing editor' who 'showed no concern' for the company's commercial interests. Trel-

---

[7] Donald Trelford, *Observer*, 12 March 2000. This long article forms the basis for this section.

ford replied with an open letter of his own, saying that the circulation had gone up by 22 per cent in the eight years since he had been editor. Ever anxious to grovel, the Foreign Office briefed against Trelford. Prince Charles said to him: 'The Foreign Office tells me you were wrong about Matabeleland.'

Nor did Trelford receive the support he might have expected from other newspapers or from journalists outside the *Observer*. Paul Johnson wrote that editors had no business to be reporters. With one of his usual questions, John Junor asked: 'If Mr Trelford truly feels that way about Mr Rowland' – in fact Trelford's views had concerned Mugabe rather than Rowland, a typical Junor distortion – 'wouldn't it be more honourable for him to stop accepting Mr Rowland's money?' *The Times* suggested that Trelford had forced a *demarche*. The *Daily Telegraph* said: 'Those who pay the piper must be expected to demand some influence over the choice of tunes he plays.' While the *Guardian*, recalling the leaders before 1939 ('It is greatly to be hoped that men of moderation will come together, and wiser counsels prevail'), trusted that the *Observer* would 'find its salvation where the people who write the cheques and the people who write the words can work together'.

Alas, this proved difficult. Lonrho now put a stop on the cheques by sending in an accountant to prevent Trelford from spending any more money. This followed a ruling by the independent directors that Rowland had 'interfered improperly', which greatly displeased him. He then said he was going to sell the paper to Robert Maxwell. Trelford knew that, for various reasons, he had no intention of doing any such thing. Accordingly he wrote to Rowland offering his resignation: 'I could not allow the paper's future and the prospects of its staff to be jeopardised by my personal position, which sadly seems to be all that stand in the way of the paper's development.'

Just as Trelford knew that Rowland did not want to sell to Maxwell, so also he knew, though with less certainty, that Rowland did not want to find another editor. That is my guess anyway. They kissed and made up (Rowland was later to call the episode a lover's tiff) over lunch at one of Lonrho's London casinos and 'concocted a priceless statement that we shared an affection for three things – Africa, the *Observer* and each other'. It is worth setting down in full Donald Trelford's own view of the Lonrho proprietorship in relation to Africa:

Africa was always going to be a problem for the *Observer* under Lonrho's ownership because of the company's extensive interests there and Tiny Rowland's personal friendship with many leaders, notably President Moi of Kenya and Kaunda of Zambia, and his support for rebels in the Angola civil war. I was one of several witnesses opposed to the takeover, including the former editor David Astor and the paper's long-serving Africa correspondent, Colin Legum, who warned the Monopolies and Mergers Commission in 1981 that these conflicts of interest were likely to damage the newspaper's high reputation for coverage of Africa. In approving the sale, the MMC recognised this danger and placed its trust in Lonrho's assurances and in the appointment of independent directors to hold the ring. The independent directors were crucial in protecting my position over Matabeleland, but any hopes that this experience would set the ground rules were disappointed. Although there were no comparable public disagreements, there were internal tensions in the following years over several stories, particularly about Kenya, Angola and Malawi, where the paper apologised for a story after Dr Banda had warned Lonrho that he would seize all its assets unless we did so. We also fell out with Godwin Matatu, whom Rowland wanted to appoint as the paper's Africa correspondent. At the same time, it should be said that Rowland did give the paper some good story leads on Africa and some high-level introductions. One introduction was to a man called Mohamed al-Fayed, but that's another story.[8]

X

In the years when Lonrho owned the paper, 1981-93, there was a house rule that he should be referred to as 'Mr Fayed' without any 'al', whether capitalised or hyphenated. I shall follow the old *Observer* usage. After all, in his evidence in the libel action which Neil Hamilton brought unsuccessfully against him, he said he did not mind whether the 'al' was used or not: 'You can call me Al Capone if you like.' Luckily, I had no reason to call him anything, because I did not write about him. If both Rowland and I had hung on to the *Observer* after 1993 I should have had little choice in the matter. Fayed was to become an omnipresent figure in the last phase of the Major administration. One of the disadvantages of working for a proprietor who bears grudges or pursues vendettas such as Row-

[8] *Observer*, 12 March 2000.

land (or, before him, Beaverbrook) is that the lightest mention of the subject is assumed to have been inspired from on high. This is so even of a friendly reference. If I had attempted a defence of Fayed – something I had not the slightest desire to undertake – others would have asked: 'What's old Tiny up to, eh?'

The origins of the feud lay in Fayed's ownership of Harrods, in Rowland's wish that he owned Harrods instead and in Rowland's conviction that, had he not been cheated by Fayed – or so he alleged – he would indeed be the owner. The Tory MP John Stokes remarked in puzzlement that was only half-simulated: 'After all, it's only a shop.' Others were seemingly puzzled about the fuss made by Rowland about whether, in acquiring the shop, Fayed had misrepresented his origins, the source of his riches or both. If the bank did not bounce Fayed's cheques, what did it matter where the money had come from? Such was their robust point of view. It was not shared by Rowland. His more critical approach found frequent expression in the *Observer* from a variety of pens. With some skill, Trelford guided most of them towards the City and business sections of the paper.

He then made a mistake which adversely affected both his own reputation and that of the *Observer*. In March 1989 he brought out a 'special issue' of the paper, consisting entirely of the hostile report of Department of Trade and Industry inspectors on Fayed's affairs. It was previously unpublished; Rowland had obtained it through bribery. This special issue appeared in midweek and was got up to look like a normal edition of the *Observer*. Indeed, on an afternoon walk round the back streets of Barnsbury I called at a newsagent's to buy an *Evening Standard* and noticed a large pile of *Observers* stacked on an adjacent shelf. I did not buy one or, indeed, ask why they were there. I assumed that, on the previous Sunday, Mr Patel had ordered too many *Observers*, or they had sold particularly badly, and he had been neglectful about returning the unsold copies to the wholesaler. It was only when I reached home with my *Standard* and switched on the television news that I realised there had been a special edition that day.

It was a seven days' wonder which nevertheless did lasting damage. No doubt Tiny Rowland was entitled to his scoop, in however nefarious a manner it had been obtained. Trelford could have published it as a supplement to the normal Sunday edition or, preferably, given it away with the *Observer* in the typographical form of a Blue Book or White Paper; much as the comics of my childhood would occasionally dispense free gifts of cheap whistles or plastic combs, or as the papers of today stick compact discs on to their weekend magazines. I was glad that my opinion had not been sought and that I had been kept in ignorance of the operation; as, indeed, was everyone, except the secretaries who, under oath of secrecy, were given the task of typing the report for inclusion in the special issue.

XI

By 1989 the paper had already been occupying its new premises in Battersea for a year. They were in a large, new building into which varied classical influences had gone and which looked somehow not real, like a film set. When we arrived our co-tenant, occupying a separate part of the building, was the television company British Satellite Broadcasting which was later taken over by Sky and had square aerials – one of the most Beachcomber-like ideas in the history of British broadcasting. It soon departed. Friends and acquaintances who had been left stranded at Wapping or Canary Wharf after the great Fleet Street diaspora said they envied us our position on the map: with a bracing walk over Chelsea Bridge, you could be in that centre of civilisation Sloane Square in 10 minutes. William Keegan discovered a pleasant, small pub, the Fox and Hounds, south-east of the square, which I had last visited in my Cambridge days and to which I now returned over 30 years later. But it was too far away for a casual drink with a colleague.

It was in Battersea that I realised the magnitude of the change that had overtaken journalism. People would spend hours, seven, eight, often more, sitting in front of their computer screens, tapping energetically away, gazing lugubriously at them or, occasionally, making a telephone call. Some would create little shrines around them: photographs of nearest and dearest, potted plants, flowers in jars, some mugs containing pencils and ball-point pens, others containing instant coffee. You asked someone out for a drink.

'Nothing I'd like better, but there's something I've got to finish first.'

Or, alternatively:

'Yes, but where?'

That was indeed the question. The adjacent pubs were hellholes, even though there was hardly anybody in them: loud music, over-flowing ashtrays, spilled beer, an eccentric selection of drink ('sorry, mate, we don't do Guinness'). As a political columnist, I had always been able to go to Westminster in the afternoons. Others – Adam Raphael, Nicholas Wapshott, Simon Hoggart – had been able to use the same escape route. But for most of the journalists there was no alternative to spending the day in front of a screen in Battersea.

XII

One of those who was likewise a free man in the afternoon was Robert Harris. He came to St Andrew's Hill in 1987 as successor as political editor to Adam Raphael, who went to the BBC's *Newsnight* (and was to return next year, ransomed, healed, restored, forgiven, as an assistant editor). For once, I was asked my advice, this time by Tony Howard, who tended to consult me more than Trelford did. This was natural enough. We had worked together for a long time at the *New Statesman*. And we laboured in the same political vineyard.

I said the interesting appointment would be of a good, young political writer who need not necessarily have served his time in the hulks of the parliamentary lobby. I suggested Robert Harris and Michael Crick. Both were then primarily television journalists, but both had also written notable books and interesting articles in glossy magazines. Howard did not approach Crick – who told me later that he regarded himself less as a writing journalist than as an author and a maker of television films – but he did approach Harris, who responded encouragingly.

Howard then convened an interviewing panel in his room con-sisting of William Keegan, Adrian Hamilton and myself. I compli-mented Harris on his evident knowledge of the Labour Party and asked him what he knew of the Crossman-Padley compromise. This was an elaborate policy document of the early 1960s written by R.H.S. Crossman, Walter Padley putting his name to it, and de-signed as sticky tape for the gap between Hugh Gaitskell and the unilateralists. Only the closest students of the Movement, and not all of these, had even heard of it. Harris was not among them. He admitted it freely. I admired him for that, and apologised for asking a show-off question which was, in the circumstances, unnecessary. He responded gracefully. We have remained friends ever since.

Harris was tall, with bright brown eyes. His slight stoop, fresh complexion and habit of equipping himself with an umbrella on all possible occasions gave him the appearance of a clever Cambridge graduate (which he was, then aged 30) about to embark on the adventure of life. He was quite unaffected and, later, remained unspoiled by the success which deservedly came his way as a thriller-writer.

I do not think he was ever entirely happy at the *Observer*. He became more unhappy with the return of Adam Raphael from the BBC. Raphael thought his new job of assistant, later executive, editor involved some supervisory function in relation to Harris, who disagreed. Harris was good at writing feature articles, superb at long narrative pieces, which would appear on the third leader page. Indeed, in this field he was probably the best practitioner the paper had ever engaged. He was less comfortable in his primary task, which was to write a front-page political 'lead' story every Saturday.

All broadsheet Sundays judge themselves partly by whether they can secure a political scoop roughly every month. Inevitably this imposes some strain on those who are employed to produce such stories, the more so as they are given only one chance a week. Sir (as he became) Trevor Lloyd-Hughes used to be an auxiliary free-lance political correspondent of the *Sunday Express* before he became Harold Wilson's press officer at No 10. He had a tried and trusty story which he would write every so often, under the generic headline Government Has New Plan For Railways. As the Conservative governments of those days always did have a new plan for the railways, which would change every few months or so in accordance with fashion in transport and the results of by-elections, Lloyd-Hughes was betting on a certainty. The plan might not come to anything, but plan of some description there undoubtedly was, requiring for its delineation only a few telephone calls and, possibly, a quick leafing through the latest transport White Paper.

Other political correspondents (later misleadingly called political editors) were less scrupulous, then and subsequently. After a few months in his new job, Harris said to me:

'You know these political leads in the other Sundays? They're all made up.'

'Of course they're made up. How else d'you think they'd fill the papers every weekend?'

One of those who helped Harris was Peter Mandelson. At this period he was working for Neil Kinnock. On Thursdays he would lurk in Annie's Bar in the Commons to meet one or other of the Sunday political correspondents with whom he would have made a prior arrangement. He became particularly close to Harris, and they remained friends, Harris putting him up at his large former vicarage at Kintbury in Berkshire when Mandelson found himself in difficulties of one kind or another.

XIII

Peter Mandelson I had known for almost 10 years. We had first met in 1979, when he was chairman of the British Youth Council and I chairman of the Political Advisory Committee of the same body. It was not at all surprising that Mandelson should have occupied this post. It was just the sort of job he would have done at that stage of his career. My own position was, I think, more interesting. For the previous 17 years, since relinquishing my seat on the Fulham Borough Council, I had eschewed any form of public life or, indeed, public responsibility of any kind. I certainly did not belong to a political party, holding that anyone engaged in political journalism should not give his or her formal allegiance to one party. Perhaps this was, still is, priggish of me. Others – Ian Aitken, Anthony Howard, Peter Jenkins, Polly Toynbee – took a different view. There we are.

Anyway, I received a telephone call from somebody at the Department of Education and Science, as it was then called. Would I accept the post in question. Why me? I asked. Well, the reply came, the youth council represented several constituent elements. They ranged, as I was to discover, from the Conservative Party through the Communist Party to the Boy Scouts. John Bowis, later MP for Battersea, represented the Conservatives; Sue Slipman, later a leading figure in the SDP, represented the Communists; I cannot now remember who represented the Scouts. All their representatives – or other officials in the organisation on whose behalf they were nominated – had gone through a long list of suitable candidates for the post. I was the only one to whom no objection was taken by somebody or other.

I was not sure how flattering it was to be the highest common factor or the lowest common denominator, whichever it is. Nevertheless

I asked what the job entailed. Chairing a meeting once every three months, I was told. I accepted more out of curiosity or perhaps vanity than out of any desire for recognition or reward. Even so, at the back of my mind there was the thought that an MBE, perhaps an OBE, would be in the offing after my stint. Of course, I should have turned it down. There would have been no question about that. Alas, I never had the opportunity of turning anything down. Not a sausage, not a chipolata, came my way for my labours on behalf of the youth of Britain.

Mandelson took – still takes – a justifiable pride in his appearance. But the memory I retain is of a dark, tallish young man with very big feet which turned out an an angle of ten-to-two when he walked: that, and his left-wing opinions. They were not extreme exactly, more of the standard leftist variety: we lived in an unjust society, where the many were poor and the few rich. Though, later on, Robert Harris was his principal friend at the *Observer*, occasionally he used to talk to me.

'At this stage of your career,' he once said, 'your problem is ...'

At this point his attention was distracted, whether by somebody else that he wanted to talk to or by somebody who wanted to talk to him. He moved away effortlessly, as if he had castors, not big feet. So I never discovered what my problem was.

XIV

At this time it was certainly not any lack of publicity, even though I was appearing much less on radio and television than I had 20 years previously. In 1988, in the Queen's Bench Division of the High Court of Justice, before Mr Justice Hazan and a jury, there was contested the case of *Meacher* v. *Trelford and Others*, in which I was one of the others, together with The Observer Ltd. This was a libel action brought by Michael Meacher, a Labour MP, following a column I had written in the paper as long ago as 1984. I have written about the case at length and do not propose to go through it all again.[9] In the election for leader of the Labour Party in 1983 won by Neil Kinnock, Meacher had stood as the candidate of the Left. In the course of his campaign he had said several times,

---

[9] Alan Watkins, *A Slight Case of Libel* (1990). See also Adam Raphael, *My Learned Friends* (1989), 175-84; David Hooper, *Reputations Under Fire* (2000), 374-8.

almost always in response to interviewers' questions, that his father had been a farm labourer in Hertfordshire. I wrote:

> Mr Meacher likes to claim that he is the son of an agricultural labourer, though I understand that his father was an accountant who retired to work on the family farm because the life suited him better.[10]

The *apropos* for writing about Meacher at all that week, long after the Labour election in which he had been an unsuccessful candidate, was that Eric Moonman, a former Labour MP who was chairman of the Islington Health Authority, had resigned from his post. He had taken this course after Meacher, as shadow Minister of Health, had circulated a questionnaire to Labour members of health authorities throughout the country asking them to give the political affiliations of their fellow members. This I described as an 'admittedly shabby episode'. However, I did not wish to cast Moonman as the hero and Meacher as the villain:

> If it comes to a choice between Mr Meacher and Mr Moonman, I am tempted to recall the observation of Dr Johnson on the respective merits of the two poets: 'Sir, there is no settling the point of precedency between a louse and a flea.'[11]

This familiar quotation was to cause endless trouble. It formed the basis of Meacher's or, rather, his legal advisers' claim of 'malice': a legal term of art which, if accepted, destroys the defence of fair comment. Meacher's counsel, Gordon Bishop (who was not a QC), claimed in his opening address that, owing to the order of the words, Meacher was clearly meant to be the louse, Moonman the flea, which was not, in Bishop's opinion, so objectionable a form of insect life as the louse; whereas the entire point of the quotation was that they were interchangeable. This extravagance on the part of Meacher's counsel became embedded in the news agency reports. When the case was over, the BBC's nine o'clock news, trying none too skilfully to summarise what it had all been about, assured the viewers that I had 'called Mr Meacher a louse' which, of course, I never had done.

[10] *Observer*, 18 November 1984.
[11] Ibid.

England being England, the 'lowlier-than-thou' part of the case received much more publicity than the part concerned with the political composition of health authorities. No doubt it was interesting anyway, quite apart from the English obsession with class. In the course of the evidence it emerged, not only that Meacher senior had never been an accountant – he had unsuccessfully tried to become one – but also that he had hardly set foot in the family farm, living out the rest of his life as a *rentier* in a small house in Berkhamsted in which Meacher junior had grown up. On his death in 1969 he had left £40,000 which his son had inherited on the death of his mother. Like Michael Meacher, Meacher senior had attended Berkhamsted School. The case lasted three weeks, of which I spent three interrupted days in the witness box. Our counsel, Richard Hartley QC, thought I spent too much time trying to be funny – as Malcolm Muggeridge once wrote, one of the most damning phrases in the language – and so risked alienating judge and jury. I could see, from my position in the box rather better than Hartley could, that Mr Justice Hazan was thoroughly enjoying the proceedings; while the jury were looking more bemused than hostile. But then, it has long been a tradition of English law that only judges and, occasionally, counsel are allowed to make jokes. During the case I met Woodrow Wyatt, who recorded:

Went to Lord's to see if I could watch Middlesex playing Sussex. Met Alan Watkins. He told me he was waking up at four in the morning and lost half a stone in weight since the libel action brought against him by Michael Meacher had started. This was running week after week in the courts. I said:

'But I thought the *Observer* was backing you.'

'Oh, yes. But I don't want to make a fool of myself in the witness box. I don't think I did. I think I shall write a book about it.'

He said Meacher hadn't got a chance of winning which I didn't suppose he had ...

'But how much is this going to cost him?', and he said it couldn't cost him less than £150,000.

I asked:

'Has Meacher got that kind of money?'

'No, not a bit.'[12]

---

[12] Wyatt Journal, 30 May 1988: Woodrow Wyatt, *Journals*, ed. Sarah Curtis (3 vols, 1998-2000), I pb edn, 565-6.

In fact I was not feeling nearly so confident as my words to Wyatt suggested. Still, we won – the first libel case in over 40 to go the defendant's way. I think we may have turned the tide of: 'Give him the money, Barney', the catchphrase of the Wilfred Pickles radio show of the 1940s. Meacher made a contribution of over £80,000 towards the *Observer*'s costs. I went on to write the book I had promised Wyatt.

When it was published in 1990 I sent a copy to, among others, Graham Greene, whom I did not know. I thought he would be interested both because of the family connection with Berkhamsted School (which he and his brother had attended, and where his father had been headmaster) and also because of his own brush with the law of libel in the 1930s. As film critic of the newly established *Night and Day* magazine, which was intended as a London version of the *New Yorker*, he had written about the little-girl film star Shirley Temple, accusing her of a sexual pertness calculated to appeal to libidinous old men. The cost of the subsequent action caused the closure of the magazine. Greene replied:

> La Résidence des Fleurs
> Avenue Pasteur
> 06600 Antibes
>
> 10 August 1990
>
> Dear Mr Watkins,
> It's very kind of you to send me your book which I am certain I shall find interesting. I've naturally read a great deal about this case in the newspapers and it will be very interesting to read a complete record.
>   Yours sincerely,
>   Graham Greene

I was hoping for something, not so much more fulsome – though praise is always welcome – as more full: something about Berkhamsted, the place or the school, and about the Shirley Temple case. Anthony Powell, whom I did know, was more forthcoming:

> Alan Watkins sent *A Slight Case of Libel*, an account of an action brought against him by the Labour MP Michael Meacher ... Watkins (whom one suspects of being a frustrated novelist) is good on small points, clothes, etc. Both V [Lady Violet Powell] and I laughed a lot. Meacher must be a monumentally humourless ass. Watkins rightly won the case, tho' at moments thought he was not going to. I sent him

a postcard of *Rorke's Drift*, by Lady Butler, where 24th Regiment (later South Wales Borderers, now Royal Regiment of Wales) won five VCs. I suggested *Michael Meacher* would have been an excellent name for a Dickens novel, in which Alan Watkins would be the villain, oppressing the ill-used eponymous hero. The story full of Dickensian names, Moonman, Millinship, Mick Priggen, etc. Serjeant Buzfuz in fact quoted as an epigraph of one chapter.[13]

Eric Moonman has already been introduced. William Millinship was the managing editor of the *Observer*. Mick Priggen was Meacher's one regular daily supporter in the court, where he went under the name of Delaney. I discovered his name was Priggen when I met him at a subsequent Labour Party conference which he was attending in a somewhat uncertain capacity, long after the case was over. I am glad I experienced it – and I got a book, my own favourite, out of it – but, like my time in the RAF or on the *Sunday Express*, I would not want to experience it again.

XV

Tony Howard proceeded to fulfil my prophecy made on the day of the royal wedding in summer 1981 and to go after Donald Trelford's job. He had a certain justification because at this time, the late 1980s, the editor's chair was victim of lengthy absences, unexplained disappearances. Even so, I am fairly sure that Howard would at some stage have tried to become editor of the *Observer* however assiduous Trelford might have been in performing his daily tasks. He converted a majority of the board to his cause. He was often to be seen closeted with the managing director, Nick Morrell. But, as Randolph Churchill forgot Goschen, so Tony Howard forgot Tiny. This, at any rate, is Trelford's opinion.

Trelford was on holiday in Madeira with his wife Kate. Quite by chance, Rowland's yacht was anchored off the island. They made contact and Rowland dispatched a boat to convey the couple to the yacht for dinner.

'They tell me you're bored with editing the *Observer*.'

'Not bored at all, Tiny.'

'I'm very glad to hear it, because the moment you're bored with editing it, I'm bored with owning it.'

---

[13] Powell Journal, 5 August 1990: Anthony Powell, *Journals* (3 vols, 1995-7), III, 59-60.

This was Trelford's account. Shortly afterwards Howard and the *Observer* parted company, to general regret among the staff, and Adrian Hamilton replaced him as deputy editor.

XVI

Four years later Rowland did become bored with owning the *Observer*, even though Trelford was still editing it. Or, rather, Dieter Bock, the Frankfurt financier who was chief executive and managing director of Lonrho from 1993 to 1996 and vice-chairman of the company in 1997, became bored with owning it. Ever since Bock became connected with Lonrho, I thought – having no instinctive feel for the City or financial matters generally, if anything the reverse – that the company's connection with the paper would soon be severed. Independent Newspapers, then still under the sway of one of the three journalist-founders, Andreas Whittam Smith, made a bid with a view to amalgamating the *Observer* with the *Independent on Sunday*, which had been established in 1990, four years after the *Independent*. Indeed, so confident were Whittam Smith and his colleagues of completing the deal that, a week before it was due to be clinched, they inspected the paper's printing works.

At the *Observer* there was consternation. I did not altogether share it. I had been rugby columnist of the *Independent* since its foundation in 1986 and had always found the people there reasonable and civil – not attributes to be disregarded in newspapers.[14] I remember Roy Jenkins was specially vehement about the proposed arrangement, though it had nothing to do with him, except to the extent that he was a long-established contributor to, chiefly, the literary pages and a friend of David Astor. Whittam Smith, he prophesied, would simply absorb the title and kill the paper. These sentiments were shared by almost everyone but myself. The *Guardian* then entered the bidding. Accordingly Robert Low, a former sports editor (and biographer of W.G. Grace), now features editor, wrote a supplicatory letter to Rowland informing him, understandably but not wholly accurately, of the affection and esteem in which he was universally held at the *Observer* and urging him to sell the paper not to the *Independent* but to the *Guardian* instead. Though Low was a former father of the NUJ chapel, the letter was

---

[14] See below, Chapter 10.

entirely his own idea. He secured the signatures of most of the staff. It was taken round to Rowland's house in Belgravia by Jimmy Rennie, the editor's driver.

It did the trick. Rowland decided to sell to the *Guardian*. On his way to London airport, he telephoned Low and said: 'You know, Mr Low, it was your letter that did it.'[15] If Ken Harris had been the saviour of the *Observer* in 1976, Bob Low was its saviour in 1993. David Randall, a member of the staff, said on television that the takeover by the *Guardian* was 'a marriage made in heaven'.

It seemed to me more like a military occupation with Peter Preston, the editor of the *Guardian*, leading a triumphant army. Or, to alter the military simile slightly: a small, smart regiment, whose officers wore their hair long, was being amalgamated with the Royal Corps of Signals. Preston addressed a disconsolate gathering. What had happened, he told us, was largely though not entirely our own fault. We had become slack; were extravagant in our ways; would have to change. He and the *Guardian* would try to help us along the path of virtue to the best of their ability, but they could not work miracles or guarantee success. I, with many others (including Bob Low), was none too happy, but at that stage had not decided to leave the paper. Before I come to the circumstances in which I did depart, it is time for a short sporting interlude.

---

[15] Information from Robert Low, 3 May 2000.

10

This Sporting Life

Ymlaen Llanelli! ('On Llanelli!')
Traditional cry of encouragement at Stradey Park,
Llanelli, now rarely heard

I

For the England and Wales match, as for all internationals, my
father wore his best suit. He also wore a hat, a heavy overcoat,
leather gloves and, depending on the weather, a silk or woollen
scarf. Though he was by no means sympathetic to Communism –
quite the reverse – the general effect of his outfit was to make him
resemble a large but politically obscure member of the Politburo
who was about to take the salute at a parade of tanks, rockets and
so forth. While neither vain nor pushful, he felt he had standards
to maintain. He would no more have gone to the match with a leek
and a red-and-white scarf than appear in front of his class with a
false nose. I was expected to be correctly attired likewise, even if
less splendidly.

The first international match we saw together was not, strictly
speaking, an international. It was the 'victory international' of 1946
for which no full caps were awarded. We travelled from Tycroes to
Cardiff in a hired single-decker bus (there were few coaches then).
Also on the bus was another son of the village, Hugh Lloyd-Davies,
in his pilot officer's uniform, who was playing for Wales at full-back.

Lloyd-Davies was an exciting though unpredictable performer
who, next year, was to win the university match for Cambridge by
kicking two penalty goals. On this occasion he did not have the
happiest of afternoons. Two pre-war English players, Jack Heaton
and Dickie Guest, both of Waterloo (in fact the Bootle team),
effectively won the match for England, Heaton with his cross-

kicking and Guest with his elusiveness. Indeed, Guest was a wing in the class of Peter Jackson or Gerald Davies. But for the war, he would surely have won more than his 13 caps. He twice went round Lloyd-Davies to score.

We could see because we were standing by that right-hand corner flag. Despite my father's correctness of dress and demeanour, we never sat in the stand but always stood in the 'field' or the somewhat superior 'enclosure': partly because stand tickets were hard to come by, partly, I suspect, because my father did not believe in throwing his money around and partly, I suspect also, because he would have considered it 'spoiling' to show me relative luxury at too early an age. After the match we came on Lloyd-Davies, now back in his RAF uniform, behind the corrugated-iron stand. My father was stern with the young full-back.

'I could see,' he said, 'that you were looking at his face, not his legs. It was his legs that went round you, not his face,' my father added, to leave no misunderstanding about his views on correct play by a full-back.

At this and subsequent matches, we had a ritual. We did not eat before the match but had a substantial tea afterwards. The menu was unchanging and suited the tastes of both of us. We had fish and chips, cakes (or 'pastries' as my father called them) and a pot of tea. He was always emphatic with the waitress (invariably addressed as 'Miss') about the need for a pot: a cup each was not good enough. Thus fortified, we would walk to the headquarters hotel, in those days at Cardiff the Royal, not the Angel. This was certainly the most important segment of the day for my father and partly accounted for his best suit. He was able to enter the hotel with confidence not so much because of any renown as an old London Welsh forward (he was modest about his past playing abilities) as because of his friendship with Aneurin Jenkins, a Cardiff schoolmaster and a member of the Cardiff Rugby Club, who had been at the teachers' training department of Bristol University with him.

Jenkins ('Jenks', my father called him) was by now a widower with no immediate family who lived in lodgings: the Cardiff club was not only his home but virtually his life. Like many of his type, he took a keen, even obsessive interest in rugby politics. He was a great obtainer of tickets, forecaster of selections, nodder and winker and putter of fingers to the nose. He knew not only players, members of the great post-war Cardiff side, but also administrators, even the selectors, the most important people in Wales, 'the Big Five' themselves. Many years later, when we were both rugby writers, Bleddyn Williams, the Cardiff and Welsh centre three-quarter of that time, told me that Jenkins was the most boring man in the Cardiff clubhouse.

The year after the victory international was that of the first full post-war match between England and Wales. This was also a time of one of the great recurring Welsh outside-half controversies. It was not simple. Should the outside-half be Glyn Davies of Pontypridd, later of Cambridge University, one of the classic, darting Welsh outside-halves? Or should it be the more utilitarian W.B. Cleaver of Cardiff, 'Billy Kick' as he was called in West Wales?

But this choice did not exhaust the dispute. For there was also Bleddyn Williams to consider. He was acknowledged to be a great centre even then. But might he not turn out to be an even greater outside-half? In other words, was outside-half Bleddyn's true position? Or was it not? On this occasion, in 1947, the selectors decided it was. Bleddyn played outside the equally great Haydn Tanner at scrum-half, with Cleaver and Jack Matthews, also of Cardiff, in the centre. This combination was known in the public prints as 'the Cardiff triangle'. It was widely expected to beat England on its own. Alas, it failed; Bleddyn suffered a muscle strain in the first few minutes. Though Wales scored two tries to England's one, Wales lost because Nim Hall of St Mary's Hospital and Richmond dropped a goal. Hall was to die young but looked hardly strong enough to survive a match even in his playing days.

Afterward Jenkins, my father and I were sitting in the lounge of the hotel. Two Welsh forwards, Rees Stephens of Neath and George Parsons of Newport, had somehow attached themselves to our party – or we had attached ourselves to them. Quite what these young men made of having to converse with two middle-aged schoolmasters and a 13-year-old boy with a balaclava helmet was difficult to say, but they were civil enough. I remember Stephens drinking orange squash, wearing a navy-blue suit and purchasing a packet of Gillette gold, extra-sharp razor blades from an itinerant vendor who had insinuated himself into the premises. Then Jenkins espied one of the selectors, David Jones (Blaina), who was always called 'David Jones (Blaina)' owing to the number of David Joneses in circulation; Jenkins invited him to join us.

'So the mighty triangle didn't come off,' my father said to him, somewhat presumptuously, I thought, in all the circumstances.

He took it well.

'We live and learn,' said David Jones (Blaina).

II

On this occasion there was no Hugh Lloyd-Davies to accompany us on the bus home. He had been displaced in the Welsh side by Howard Davies of Llanelli. Lloyd-Davies made no complaint about this but did resent Howard Davies's successor, Frank Trott of Cardiff. He thought he was a better player than Trott, that he rather than Trott should have been the Welsh full-back. I do not want to go into rugby technicalities, but there was a good deal to be said for Lloyd-Davies's point of view.

As a player in his position, he was several decades ahead of his time. Though under 5ft 8ins and light even for those days, he was fast and elusive and liked nothing better than to join in an attack. He was a prodigious kicker, whether from the hand or when he was taking a shot at goal. He was certainly a better kicker than Trott. If Trott had been the traditional solid citizen in this position, with a mighty kick in both feet, Lloyd-Davies might perhaps have been less bitter. At all events, the preference of the selectors for Trott was widely held to explain, or partly to explain, the tragic history of Lloyd-Davies.

In 1926 he was christened Rheinallt Lloyd Hughes Davies. As a child he became known as Hugh Lloyd Davies. His father was a conductor on the local Rees and Williams buses. However, the Davies family had a substantial interest in the bus firm. In early adolescence he was refused a bicycle – one of the few things he was refused. What did he want a bicycle for when he could travel free on the buses at any time he liked? He was brought up by his grandparents, who had a house by the side of the Rees and Williams garage. His brother Heddwyn and his sister Mair were brought up by their parents on the other side of the garage. No satisfactory explanation for this arrangement was ever put forward: my own guess is that it made the best use of the two houses that were available.

Lloyd-Davies went to the Amman Valley County (later Grammar) School, Ammanford, where he showed early promise as a rugby footballer and played for the Welsh Schools. He also did his stint firewatching at the school, when members of the staff and of the sixth form would mingle on terms of greater familiarity than they could display during the day. He wooed and won the French mistress, Mary Michael, whom he later married, though the marriage proved to be of short duration. She was with him on the bus taking us to and from the victory international in Cardiff in 1946, an event I have already described.[1]

In the middle of the war Lloyd-Davies went straight from the sixth form into the RAF, as countless others did at the same time. But he was sent on a course at Trinity Hall, Cambridge. At that period the coalition government and the Oxford and Cambridge colleges had entered into an agreement whereby those servicemen of the appropriate age who had been sent to colleges for service purposes would be readmitted when the war was over. Lloyd-Davies might well have been able to get into Cambridge on his rugby-playing abilities alone, but that did not arise: he got in because he had been on a course. Trinity Hall was famous for legal studies, and it was Law that Lloyd-Davies read, intending to become a barrister.

He had two vices: sexual intercourse, to which he was inordinately attached, and snobbery, which was rarer in South-west Wales. He claimed to come from 'an old Carmarthenshire county family', which was true only in the sense that his family had, like mine, lived in the county for a long time; his uncle was the local MP, Jim Griffiths. He inserted a hyphen between the 'Lloyd' and the 'Davies'. When people asked him where he had been to school, he would reply 'Ammanford, actually,' placing the accent on the second syllable: so that in the team programme of the time and in subsequent record books he is described as coming from a non-existent, presumably public, school, 'Ammanford'.

Before he went up to Cambridge for his second spell, he had a brief liaison with a woman called Lydia Noel-Buxton, whom he took to a hotel. He went downstairs to buy an evening paper and read on the front page: 'The Hon. Lydia Noel-Buxton ... missing in the West End ... Last seen with an RAF officer.' Later, at Cambridge, he said to Grenville Jones, who will appear later in this chapter, that 'of course she wasn't a real aristocrat' but 'only the daughter of a Labour peer'. When Jones pointed out that he was currently

---

[1] See pp. 213-14 above.

involved with the niece of another Labour peer, Lord Listowel, he replied that the Listowels were of ancient lineage and that the then earl had taken the Labour whip in the Lords; whereas the Noel-Buxtons were a Labour creation only.

On the morning of the university match of 1947 Lloyd-Davies failed to arrive at the appointed meeting-place for the journey to Twickenham. Clem Thomas, who was travelling with the team even though he was not to gain a Blue till 1949, and who will also appear later in this chapter, went to Trinity Hall with another friend to search for the Cambridge full-back. They found him sound asleep as the result of his heavy drinking the night before; bathed and dressed him; and somehow conveyed him to the ground, where he proceeded to win the match for Cambridge 6-0.

Like most sexual adventurers, he was both bold and undiscriminating, with a particular and, to me, peculiar predilection for pregnant women. He was handsome, with pale, smooth skin, black curly hair that grew in a peak, very bright brown eyes and very white teeth. He possessed loads of charm. In drink, however, he could be verbally vicious. In October 1947 he returned to Cambridge as the first-choice full-back. But he refused to train and was dropped from the side, to be replaced by Barry Holmes, an Argentinian who was to be picked by England. One evening he was in a pub and was ordered to leave the premises by one of the proctors.

Pubs and their governance by the proctors played a disproportionate part in the life of the Cambridge of the 1940s and 1950s. The proctor involved on this occasion was Trevor Thomas, a law don from Trinity Hall who looked like a town clerk and was already known by Lloyd-Davies. He addressed Thomas in disrespectful and familiar terms, telling him not to be so silly and to go away. He said all this in Welsh, which Thomas could understand, even though he came from Swansea – a non-Welsh-speaking area, even in the late 1940s. Next day Lloyd-Davies was not rusticated but sent down completely: a severe punishment for cheeking a proctor in Welsh.

He joined Gray's Inn, the traditional Inn of Court for Welshmen, and played briefly for Swansea and London Welsh and then for the Harlequins, where, he said, you met a better class of girl. In Edinburgh with the Harlequins, he said he liked it there and thought he would stay for a bit. He then ran up bills which were paid by Sir Wavell Wakefield, the club's president, a Conservative MP and an England international of the 1920s.

Finding himself short of money, he turned up at the Barrow rugby league club wearing a bowler hat and striped trousers and carrying a rolled umbrella. As a demonstration, he kicked three practice-goals without changing his shoes. He was signed on for a fee of over £1,000, the first Cambridge Blue to become a professional. He also claimed to have seduced Miss Barrow 1951, slept with the chairman's wife and turned out for only one training session. He certainly played only one match for his new club, after which he decamped to Paris, so becoming the most expensive signing in the history of rugby league. He then joined a French rugby league club but again lasted for only one match.

Then he went to jail. I am giving the full report partly to demonstrate the high standard of court reporting in those days. Lloyd-Davies was never a full Welsh international, but he always said he was, and certainly felt he deserved to be one. So the error in the report is understandable:

Nine Months for Rugby Star

Rheinallt Hugh Lloyd-Davies, aged 26, Y Fron, Tycroes, Ammanford, the Cambridge Rugby 'Blue' and Welsh international, was yesterday sentenced to nine months' imprisonment at Liverpool City Quarter Sessions for obtaining a diamond ring and a pair of gold cuff links by false pretences from a Liverpool jewellery firm.

Lloyd-Davies had pleaded guilty and the Recorder (Mr H.I. Nelson, KC) told him, 'A man of your standing and education knew perfectly well that such an offence could not be passed over without some punishment.'

Lloyd-Davies was alleged to have told the Liverpool jeweller that he was a barrister. [He was never called to the Bar.] He made out a cheque for £94, the value of the ring and cuff links. The cheque was later returned marked 'RD'. Lloyd-Davies pawned the ring for £10 and the cuff links for £2 10s 0d [£2.50].

Mr J.D. Cunningham (defending) said that Lloyd-Davies was thoroughly ashamed of himself. Every penny had been repaid and Lloyd-Davies was having a course of treatment not unconnected with drink.

This savage sentence did not act as a deterrent. Lloyd-Davies went to prison again for stealing an overcoat from the library of Gray's Inn. He then returned to Tycroes, where he did odd labouring jobs. He went back to London. There were reports of sightings, on one occasion in the company of Jack Doyle, the former boxer. He was passing himself off as a colonel; had gone bald; was sleeping rough; was a gardener with the Islington council (if he was, I never came across him in the borough). In 1987 I learnt from the journalist David Jones, whose father had been at Cambridge with Lloyd-Davies, that he had died in the previous year, when he would have been around 60. There were no obituaries, which was a pity.

III

My period at the *Sunday Express* put an end to watching rugby or to playing it, should I have possessed the energy, which I doubt. That was because Saturdays were fully occupied. The *Spectator* was different. I started to watch London Welsh at Old Deer Park, the club for which my father had played some 45 years previously, though at Herne Hill in South London rather than at the splendid new ground at Kew. London Welsh were a more impressive outfit than they had been in his own playing days but not by very much: the great era was still to come. However, John Dawes and Roger Michaelson were already in the team. Michaelson was to create the side of the late 1960s and early 1970s through his ambition and organisational ability; while Dawes was to become the club's most famous and the British Isles' most successful captain. His later days as an administrator and coach were not so glorious. But then, why should a fine player make a good administrator or coach?

Neither at the *Spectator* nor, later, at the *New Statesman* was I encouraged to write about rugby. In Iain Macleod's period of editing the former, I contributed one or two items on the game to the column he wrote as 'Quoodle' (which derived from G.K. Chesterton's lines: 'And Quoodle here discloses, all things that Quoodle can.'). This was because Macleod had a genuine liking for and some knowledge of rugby, having joined Saracens – a little-known biographical fact – shortly after coming down from Cambridge, when they were a more modest, less successful club than they were to become in the 1990s. When I gave evidence for Auberon Waugh in his action for wrongful dismissal against the *Spectator* held at the Marylebone County Court, which surprisingly he won, counsel asked me to define or, at any rate, to encapsulate the paper. I replied:

'The *Spectator* is a weekly review of politics, literature and the arts.'

The learned judge was much taken with this formulation, asked me to repeat it, wrote it down and afterwards quoted it approvingly several times, as in:

'The *Spectator*, we have been told, and no one has contradicted the evidence, is a weekly review of ...' Whereupon he would flatteringly repeat my words.

Sport played no part in this summation. Nor were things very different at the *New Statesman*. In the previous couple of decades that excellent journalist, Oxford rugby Blue and Labour MP, J.P.W. ('Curly') Mallalieu, had contributed some notable sports articles to the paper, including a few on rugby. But in 1967-70 we were in a fallow period as far as sportswriting was concerned. Certainly the then managing director, Jeremy Potter, thought that sport had no place in the *NS*. This was odd in a way. Potter, who was very good at the commercial side of his job, was an accomplished club cricketer and hockey player. As often happens with this combination, he was adept also at racquets and real tennis. But he did not want sport in the paper.

The editor at that time, Paul Johnson, shared the same opinion, though he possessed a sentimental regard for cricket. Matters changed slightly when R.H.S. Crossman became editor. Crossman had played rugby at Oxford, though he had attended a soccer school, Winchester. Indeed, there were those who considered that, if he had not taken up the game relatively late in life, he would have been in contention for a place in the university side.[2] After taking his degree, he had also played in a team that included Patrick Gordon Walker and Frank Pakenham, later Lord Longford. Unlike these two, however, Crossman evinced little interest in the game during his mature years. The reason the *Statesman* of his day carried the odd article on rugby was that his part-time foreign and defence correspondent was Lord Chalfont, formerly Alun Gwynne Jones, a Welshman and a rugby enthusiast who had played a few times for Newport.

Crossman's successor, Anthony Howard, was not merely uninterested in sport but positively opposed to it, at any rate in its more aggressive or nationalistic manifestations. However, he had been known to play tennis, and always considered the captain of the England cricket team worthy *ex officio* of a 'profile'. The *NS* of his

[2] Anthony Howard, *Crossman: the Pursuit of Power* (1990), 27.

period carried several good articles on the business and politics of sport: by Clifford Makins, who had recently ceased being one of the best of the *Observer*'s sports editors, and by Geoffrey Wheatcroft, who had just left his job in publishing to try his hand at journalism.

Wheatcroft has already appeared in this narrative.[3] We became friends after I moved to Islington, where he also had a flat. In 1975 he joined the editorial staff of the *Spectator* and in 1977 became literary and arts editor. Unlike most literary editors, Wheatcroft believed in giving books to people who might write an interesting review rather than to those were were conventionally expert in the general area covered by the work in question. By now I was thoroughly sick of writing reviews of *Coketown: a Study of a Typical Midlands Seat* by R.J. Aaronovitch and Morton Bagel, both of the University of Michigan. Wheatcroft realised this and gave me books to review in which I was more interested. Several of them were on rugby. He also carried the occasional article by me on the game in his arts section.

IV

It was a change in the higher command of the *Spectator* which led to my second tour of duty as a rugby writer, with the *Field*. In 1984 Alexander Chancellor resigned as editor after a disagreement with the then proprietor, J.G. ('Algy') Cluff, and departed via *Time and Tide* to the *Sunday Telegraph*. Chancellor's deputy, Simon Courtauld, left simultaneously, as is often the way when editors change, and after a few months was appointed editor of the *Field*. Courtauld had, unlike me, briefly practised as a barrister. He had also held the position of managing director at the *Spectator* together with that of deputy editor. He was a good cricketer and looked like an army officer. He bore a striking resemblance to the Duke of Kent, was of the well-known Huguenot family and wrote an excellent history of the *Spectator* entitled *To Convey Intelligence*.

The *Field* had traditionally confined itself more to strictly rural pursuits, notably hunting, shooting and fishing, than had its rival, *Country Life*, which ranged more widely, particular attention being paid to domestic architecture. Its articles on the last were, indeed, often cited in biographies and works of scholarship. Its very full accounts of furniture, pictures and other *objets d'art* made it the

[3] See pp. 149, 153 above.

favourite reading matter in many of H.M. Prisons. Courtauld wanted to broaden the scope of the *Field* also, but in slightly different directions. He wanted to include articles of wider appeal by writers who were professional or well-known or, preferably, both. To this end he recruited Gillian Widdicombe to write on music, William Deedes on golf, Geoffrey Wheatcroft on racing, John McEwen on art, myself on rugby, and Jo Grimond, Peter Paterson and Alec Douglas-Home on whatever came into their heads. None of us was *outré*. Indeed, some of us would, I suspect, have appealed to the paper's old readers. But we were a mixed bunch all the same. What the readers made of us I do not know.

I dealt chiefly with Jeremy Alexander, who had come from the *Guardian*, knew a lot about soccer but was by no means ignorant of rugby, saving me from error on several occasions. There was also a talented young sub-editor called David Jones, who has already appeared in this chapter in connection with the death of Hugh Lloyd-Davies. Jones wrote occasionally in the *Spectator* under the name Lewis Jones because he thought that it sounded more impressive and that there were too many David Joneses in the world anyway. The secretaries looked as if they had enjoyed a morning's hacking and, the offices being near Blackfriars station, were conveniently placed to catch the District or Circle line to South Kensington or Sloane Square.

The *Observer* office, in which I then appeared four times a week, was placed, equally conveniently from my own point of view, a few hundred yards away on the City side of Blackfriars. Once a fortnight, at the beginning of the week, I would take my rugby copy across New Bridge Street to the *Field*'s offices in Carmelite Street, by what were then the premises of the *Daily Mail*. The *Field*'s offices were in a pre-1914 building, all encaustic tiles, shiny linoleum and polished brasswork, with one of those lifts with metal grilles in which I always fear I am going to catch my fingers. The uniformed commissionaires appeared to have come with the building, concealing beneath a forced deference an indolence and an inefficiency which were remarkable. Copy marked 'copy' would be delivered in three or four hours; whereas copy marked 'urgent copy' would be in the editor's hands next day. The best procedure was to say who you were, walk upstairs past their disapproving looks and deliver the column personally to Courtauld or one of his young assistants.

It was too good to last; nor did it. The magazine was owned by Associated Newspapers, which had – the word is like a knell to any journalist – 'plans' for it. First it was transformed into a monthly from having been a weekly (even though my rugby column had appeared only fortnightly). As an outsider I thought this was a sensible move which accorded with the character of the magazine. In the nature of things it worked to a monthly, even a seasonal view of the world. Simon Courtauld did not see matters in this light and was upset. So were his staff. They turned out to be right. The change was the beginning of the end for Courtauld's *Field*. Shortly afterwards it became a 'lifestyle' magazine based on the 'concept' of country living. Courtauld left eventually for another magazine. But well before then I had left the *Field* to start a rugby column in the *Independent*.

V

It came about in this way. In January 1986 Stephen Glover invited me to lunch with him at Sweetings in the City. He was one of the three journalists from the *Daily Telegraph* – Matthew Symonds and Andreas Whittam Smith were the others – who had left that paper to found the *Independent*. The new paper was now reasonably certain to be launched, though the probability did not become certainty until a few more months had passed. Glover wished to sound me out about the prospects of joining or, at least, contributing to the new enterprise.

I had met and liked Glover, who had that carefree, even indolent air which I find sympathetic. He was a *Telegraph* friend of Frank Johnson; we had met several times in Johnson's Islington flat. I now told him over our fish that I was perfectly happy writing my political column in the *Observer*. Nor could I write the odd piece about politics for his new paper, because my contract with the *Observer* prevented me from doing so. In any case, one's stock of ideas was limited, about politics or anything else. However, I went on, my opportunities for freelance work outside politics were wider than most people seemed to suppose. I wished the new paper well and was keen to help it in any way I could. Glover suggested: what about sport?

I distinctly remember him saying 'sport' rather than 'rugby'. I may have replied that, while I could make a reasonable stab at cricket, and knew something about boxing, rugby was the one game where I was surefooted. I did not add that tennis, athletics and golf bored me. At all events, we settled on rugby, and parted with mutual expressions of good will.

The next stage was for me to meet the sports editor. He was Charles Burgess, who had come from the *Guardian*: in his early thirties, large, curly-haired, with laughing yet simultaneously dangerous green-blue eyes. His father was a newspaper entrepreneur from Carlisle who had been knighted. Charlie was one of those journalists who did not draw any distinction between heavy and light newspapers or – to put it more precisely – did not claim any superiority for the former over the latter. His vision of my column was that it should be free of the imprimatur of 'the Wing-Commander'. The officer in question, though loosely modelled on that higher-ranking Air Force figure Bob Weighill, was fictitious, Burgess's hypostatisation of the Rugby Football Union, as the English Rugby Union perhaps somewhat conceitedly call themselves. He expected me to get around the clubhouses and talk to players and officials, he explained: but he did not want me to represent official views, as full-time rugby writers had to do quite properly from time to time. In practice I was reluctant to approach players unless they made it clear that they wished to speak to me. They were most of them very young. It was easy for someone of my age to be a bore, or a 'heavy', as some of them used to say. Young men preferred to talk to other young men – or to young women. Their most popular topic of conversation seemed to be curry and where best to obtain it.

Charlie Burgess's view was that I should represent, in his phrase, 'the intelligent punter', the man in the stand, on the touchline or sitting at home in front of the television set. Indeed, in journalism only television itself is approached in the same way. Admittedly some rugby journalists wrote about other things: for instance, that prince among phrasemakers, Christopher Wordsworth, sparkled with equal brightness in the literary pages of the *Guardian* and the *Observer*. But the *Independent* column was deliberately written from the standpoint of an enthusiastic amateur. I was sometimes mistaken or plain wrong: but I never, I think, pretended to a knowledge which I did not possess.

How should I have felt if a full-time rugby writer had been plonked down next to me in the press gallery of the House of Commons and I had been told: 'This is old so-and-so. He has always taken a close interest in politics and has read a few books on the subject. And he always watches the political programmes on television. He'll be writing a column every week when Parliament is sitting, giving his own impression of what's going on'? I like to think I should have welcomed the appointment and given the newcomer any help I could. But I cannot be sure; still less am I sure of the response which my colleagues in the press gallery would have made.

The rugby staff of the *Independent* when I started in October 1986 were, however, friendliness itself. They could not have been more helpful. This may have been because we all came from 10 miles or so of one another: Geoffrey Nicholson from Swansea, Tim Glover and Steve Bale from Neath, I from Ammanford. Even so, Welshmen are not famous for getting on well together. But Nicholson, the chief correspondent, I already knew, both from the *Observer*, where he had been number two to Clem Thomas, and from his membership of the *galère* who had originated in the Swansea of the 1950s, had moved to London and included Kingsley Amis, Nicholson's wife Mavis (the most sympathetic of all television interviewers), and John Morgan and his wife Mary.

VI

In rugby writing, my greatest debt was to someone also from Swansea, R.C.C. (Clem) Thomas. Perhaps I should not write 'Swansea' because, though born in Cardiff, Clem came from Brynamman, a village at the top of the Amman Valley, at the start of that magical road to Llangadog which you climb with the menacing Black Mountains of north-east Carmarthenshire on either side of you, until you surmount a brow and turn a corner and there, spread before you, is the whole Towy Valley, set out like an 18th-century landscape. Brynamman was one of that string of frontier villages – Tycroes was just within rather than on the frontier – dividing industrial from agricultural Carmarthenshire. Clem's father was a farmer who owned a small slaughterhouse. It was presumably his early experience of handling large animals that laid the foundations of his exceptional physical strength, which he was to retain until his death from a heart attack in September 1996.

Untypically Clem was sent away to school rather than to one of the local grammar schools. He explained this later by saying he was too unruly to control at home. It is, however, equally possible that his parents wanted to do the best they could for their child. He was sent not only to Blundell's School, Tiverton, but, before that, to Bryntirion, Bridgend, one of the very few Welsh preparatory schools, where his young companions included Huw Thomas, later a famous television newsreader, and Geoffrey Howe.

They remembered that in those days he had a club foot. At some stage there must have been an operation to correct the impediment. In 1953, when Clem was 24, Wales played New Zealand in Cardiff. He gathered the ball from a line-out and cross-kicked, Bleddyn Williams gathered and passed to Ken Jones, Jones scored and Wales won a famous victory. So the author of the most famous kick in Welsh rugby had begun life with a club foot! Clem later made no reference to it, though I noticed that his relatively small feet did not point straight ahead, as those of so many accomplished games-players do, but rather slightly inwards. His school friends also remembered that in those early days of the war they were never short of food, because Clem had extra supplies sent from the farm. Wanting pocket-money in the holidays, he and a few Brynamman boys would catch and kill scores of rabbits and transport them in a borrowed van to Swansea market, where they would sell them to the butchers' stalls. Clem was to remain an entrepreneur for the rest of his life. His journalistic career, chiefly with the *Observer*, was run in tandem with his livestock and butchery business. This he later sold, which left him comfortably off. But his urge to do a deal remained with him. Even at the end of his life he held the Audi car concessions for Swansea.

After going up to St John's College, Cambridge, he missed a Blue in his first two years. He blamed Hugh Lloyd-Davies for his failure to appear sooner in the university match.[4] Lloyd-Davies told the Cambridge captain, Eric Bole, that if Clem Thomas was good enough for Swansea he was good enough for 'this fucking lot' – an entirely just but perhaps less than tactful observation to which the university captain, an evangelical Christian from a school called Wycliffe, did not take at all kindly. The result was that Clem played for Wales against France in Paris before he played for Cambridge against Oxford or Twickenham. In those days he was slightly under 6ft 2ins and slightly over 14 stones. He was one of the biggest men

[4] For Hugh Lloyd-Davies, see pp. 216-20 above.

in the Swansea side that nearly beat the South Africans in 1951.
Today he would have been considered just about tall enough for an
open-side flanker but at least a stone too light.

He took as much pride in his connection with the *Observer* as
chief rugby correspondent for over 30 years as he did in his achievements on the field – perhaps more. He never claimed to be a fine
writer in the manner of his predecessor H.B. ('Bert') Toft. Indeed, I
once remarked that it was sometimes difficult to say whether Clem
was writing like a butcher or a wing-forward. But in his generation
his knowledge and understanding of the game were unrivalled. He
both spoke and wrote his mind, a completely honest witness, his
own man. Perhaps the outstanding example of his independence was
provided during the disappointing British Isles tour of New Zealand
in 1977, when he told the readers of the *Observer* in convincing detail
about how the management were not doing their job properly.

His dismissal from the paper in 1993, when the *Guardian* took
control of it, caused him distress and clouded his few remaining
years, even though he was to find an honoured place, covering
chiefly Welsh rugby, with the *Independent on Sunday*. There was
nothing personal in it, he was told: all sports writers who were
freelance (as he was) rather than employees were given their
notice. Clem remained resentful and unconsoled. But even before
his dismissal he had not been entirely happy at the *Observer*. It had
already been decided (before his first heart attack, suffered while
reporting the international from Paris) that the job was becoming too
much for him and that henceforth, while remaining with the paper,
he should be employed on lighter duties. His successor, Eddie Butler,
had nothing to do with this decision. But Clem – a generous, warm,
affectionate, lovable yet, often, unreasonably unforgiving man –
treated Butler with a suspicion which was unwarranted.

Next to his family and rugby, his greatest love was France. He
had a small, modern house in the Médoc which I visited several
times. It seemed he was more esteemed in French rugby circles
than in those of England and Wales.

VII

Another Swansea writer on rugby, and on much else besides, who
died too young – at 59 rather than at Clem's 67 – was W. John
Morgan, as he signed himself, presumably because there were so

many other John Morgans. He was many other things too: a television reporter, best known for his work on *Tonight*; both a lover of opera and an opera librettist; an entrepreneur of a sort, having been largely responsible for setting up the consortium which inaugurated Harlech television. He was a great Welsh rugby supporter and a pioneering writer on the game.

John Sparrow, the Warden of All Souls, once observed that someone could be a great racing driver but not a great taxi driver. Why ever not? In the cafés and little shelters scattered throughout London there are surely drivers who are acknowledged by their peers as great practitioners of their trade. Likewise, there can be great rugby supporters, just as there are great players. Though John relished gossip about the misdeeds of rugby's administrators in Wales – the more malicious it was, the better he was pleased – he was the most loyal and romantic of supporters. We were going to win; we always were. I remember, on the evening before the England match in February 1980, casting doubt on Wales's chances. It turned out to be a bad-tempered match. Paul Ringer was sent off in the first minutes and Wales went down 8-9. But as it was two tries to three penalties, this was a moral victory for Wales and for John.

'Alan has always been against the Welsh,' he complained shortly afterwards to Tony Howard, who admired him greatly.

He loved the trips, the travel, the whole atmosphere surrounding an international match. Here, from the book he wrote with his friend Gerald Davies, *Side-Steps*, a diary of 1984-5, is part of his account of a visit to the Paris match:

> A group from the Swansea Valley arrived in the hotel, having taken three hours to walk the one mile from the Pigalle. They thought they may have lost their way. A party from Aberavon, not feeling too well, were looking for the doctor who had come with them. They discovered he was ill in bed.[5]

This is not at all cruel but is close to the black humour of Carmarthenshire. John came from Morriston, West Glamorgan, to the east of Swansea, where his father was a builder, though the family had originally been Carmarthenshire farmers. He was educated at Swansea Grammar School and at University College,

---

[5] Gerald Davies and John Morgan, *Side-Steps: a Rugby Diary 1984-5* (1985), 122-3.

Swansea. At school he was a promising outside-half and centre, and later played for Morriston. He was close to six feet tall and powerfully built. But, with his sixth-form friend Geoffrey Nicholson, he would often on Saturday afternoons go to see the local soccer team, Swansea Town (before it became Swansea City), during the marvellous days of Ivor Allchurch.

With Nicholson he wrote *Report on Rugby*, which was published in 1959, and was an innovative work: for the first time the game was treated as a social phenomenon, particularly in relation to Wales. John possessed much historical imagination and could sympathetically recapture imperial South Wales, when its coal kept the Royal Navy afloat and Swansea was the metallurgical capital of the world. Likewise his rugby reports in the *Observer* in the late 1950s went beyond the game. His account of the train journey to Edinburgh is still remembered as a piece of writing. With H.B. Toft, he did much to raise the standard of rugby journalism. He also made several memorable television programmes with his friends of the great years, Gerald Davies, Carwyn James and Barry John. And he was responsible for the – sadly, mist-enshrouded – television film of Llanelli's win over New Zealand in 1972.

John was something of a romancer. He once claimed to me to have played for Swansea against South Africa in 1951.

'That's funny, John,' I said. 'I saw that match, and I can't remember you in the Swansea side.'

'I never said I actually played,' he interjected quickly. 'But I was asked to play.'

'Why didn't you, then?'

'Too scared.'

Almost 20 years after this match at St Helen's, he was to be found at the same ground, demonstrating against the same fixture together with Peter Hain, among others. The game was called off amid scenes of much ill-feeling and some disorder. He never thought that rugby could be separated from politics or from life. But he was equally clear that, though rugby could not be separated from life, it was not the whole of life either.

VIII

Another great supporter who shared the same view and was a friend of mine from the mid-1960s was Grenville Jones (1922-

2000). He was a political consultant from a bygone age, quite different in his nature and in the character of his firm from those fly-by-night figures who would flash across our television screens in the 1980s and 90s. He never paid an MP, rarely asked a favour of any journalist.

The exiled Nelson Mandela was once a client of the concern which he founded in 1960, External Development Services, and which at one time numbered a somewhat unsatisfactory Jeremy Thorpe among its directors. The Mandela connection resulted in three burglaries at its premises carried out by Boss, the South African security service. Other clients included the government of Biafra in the Nigerian civil war; the Banaban islanders in their claim over phosphate against the British government; and the Canadian Red Indians in the case of the repatriation of the Canadian constitution. But he did not take on exclusively leftist or progressive causes. One of his longest-standing clients was the Ruler of Dubai. He had other clients in the Gulf states as well. With all of them he regarded himself less as a lobbyist or PRO than as an ambassador or consul. He advised on legal representation in the UK courts, on nationality and immigration, on property and on schools.

He would, however, have preferred to be an MP In 1950, when he was still an undergraduate (though 27 because of war service), he contested the Isle of Ely and came third. In 1959 he stood for Leominster. With no Liberal organisation and acting as his own agent, he came second to the Conservative. With better organisation, he likewise came second at Tavistock in 1964. In the mid-1960s he joined the Labour Party and became chairman of the Richmond and Twickenham Fabian Society and a JP. He never stood for the party at an election but remained an intensely political person. Like many former Liberals, he was passionately opposed to Britain's membership of the European Union.

Grenville was small, dark, an Iberian Celt. His father and mother were both of Breconshire farming stock, his father a printer and a choirmaster who became mayor of Builth Wells. He was educated at Llandrindod Wells County School and at St Catharine's College, Cambridge, where he read History and Law, was on the Union committee and became chairman of the Liberal Club. At Cambridge he was the friend not only of rugby players such as Hugh Lloyd-Davies and Clem Thomas, who have already been commemorated in this chapter, but of those who were to make a mark in a wider world: Percy Cradock (later a neighbour in Twickenham), Geoffrey Howe and Ronald Waterhouse.

While no conversation with Grenville, as he as universally called, was complete without some reference to or anecdote from his Cambridge days, he rarely talked about the war service which had preceded them. He had been a wireless operator-air gunner in the RAF, a dangerous trade. The only story he ever told concerned his brief period as a navigator. The aircraft was supposed to drop leaflets over Paris but managed to drop them over Blackpool instead. It was never wholly clear whether Grenville had mistaken the Blackpool Tower for the Eiffel Tower or the Irish Sea for the English Channel or, perhaps, both.

He was a generous host at the dinner parties which his wife Jill gave at their house in Montpelier Row, Twickenham ('the workers' end', he would sometimes explain). He was one of those patriotic Welshmen who would do anything for their country except live there. He was always neatly, even carefully dressed. A sociable man, he nevertheless disliked clubs and rarely entertained in restaurants. For over 30 years his daily routine was to walk – he did not drive and whenever possible liked to walk – from his office near Pall Mall to El Vino's in Fleet Street, where he would pick up the gossip and lunch on one or two sausages, pickles, some French bread and butter, several glasses of red wine, a glass of Armagnac and a large cigar.

Though he was an accomplished pianist who had in his youth played the organ as a scholar at both Brecon and Hereford cathedrals, his chief recreation was watching rugby, almost always London Welsh at Old Deer Park. There, in his long overcoat of a peculiarly violent reddish brown, he was somehow a reassuring presence – a symbol of the continuity of civilised life – in his regular place behind the goalposts. One Saturday after the match, he and his friends went to the clubhouse for a drink and, inside, found their way barred by some thick, decorative red ropes. It was explained that the area so delineated was for players and members of the committee and their guests only.

'That,' Grenville said, 'is completely contrary to the spirit of rugby union football,' and led us away to have a drink somewhere else in Richmond, which remained our regular post-match meeting place until the end of his life.

IX

In the 1986-93 period I had been writing a political column in the *Observer* and a rugby column in the *Independent*. I had also published three books – *Sportswriter's Eye* (a collection), *A Slight Case of Libel* and *A Conservative Coup* – in addition to contributing book reviews and diaries to the *Spectator*. In 1993 I left the *Observer* to write a political column for the *Independent*'s younger sister, the *Independent on Sunday*. Particulars of how and why that move came to be made are to be found in the next chapter.

11

Boycott and Beyond

A man who has reached the age when all he wants is some good wine and some good cheese and a little work ...
Graham Greene, 'May We Borrow Your Husband?' 1967

I

Donald Trelford did not, I think, want to stay on as editor of the *Observer* after its acquisition by the *Guardian*; anyway, he was succeeded immediately by Jonathan Fenby. He was the *Guardian*'s joint deputy editor and, before taking over that position in 1988, had been a much admired home editor of the *Independent*. His background, however, was in foreign reporting, chiefly from France and Germany. His wife was a Frenchwoman. He spoke the language excellently. His father, Charles Fenby, had been editor of the *Birmingham Gazette* and a pillar of the Westminster Press. On the face of it, few could have been better qualified to edit the *Observer*.

Soon, however, I had my doubts. Though he was affability itself, he seemed, like the White Rabbit, to be always in a hurry and not quite certain of what it was that he was supposed to be doing. No doubt this was partly the consequence of his walking everywhere at a great rate. This healthy habit led him to arrive at appointments looking sweaty and discomposed. It was certainly the spectacle he presented when he entertained me to lunch at the Gay Hussar a few days after taking over the editorship. He asked me to continue as political columnist, to which I agreed. Neither of us made any mention of money.

At this time I was being paid an annual retainer of £45,000 to write 46 political columns a year, together with any political profiles, news stories or leading articles which I might feel inclined to undertake. I was asked to write few of these; in reality I was being paid for a weekly political column. My friend Simon Hoggart, then political editor, told me I was underpaid. He advised me to ask for more. I have no doubt that Hoggart had my best interests at heart. At the same time, I do not – and did not then – underestimate his liking for mischief. As an old *Guardian* hand who was shortly to rejoin the paper, Simon must have known of its reputation for parsimony. At all events, I wrote to Fenby asking for my retainer to be increased to £60,000 a year. He has described the episode in the following terms:

> Mr Watkins ... speedily voted with his wallet: demanding a 30 per cent pay increase at a time when colleagues of his were losing their jobs. Otherwise, he said, he would cross to a rival paper. I refused his demand. So Mr Watkins left ...[1]

This is not quite what happened. First, I made no threat of any kind to leave the *Observer*. And, secondly, Fenby did not exactly refuse my demand – or if he did, it was in a pusillanimous fashion. Eleven days passed without reply or even acknowledgment. Then, late one morning, Hoggart told me that Adrian Hamilton, who was at that stage still deputy editor, would 'like a word' with me. I duly approached Hamilton, who told me that 'Jonathan' was 'very worried' about my letter because 'Peter' – Peter Preston, the former editor of the *Guardian*, now editor-in-chief of the *Guardian-Observer* enterprise – 'doesn't like paying anyone a lot of money just for writing one column a week'.

'That's a pity,' I replied, 'because I happen to know someone who does,' and immediately departed to see Ian Jack, the editor of the *Independent on Sunday*, at his offices in City Road.

II

Since becoming editor in the previous year, Jack had asked me several times to join the paper. He was a large, bearded, gentle Scotsman, originally from Dunfermline. In newspapers he had the highest reputation, though more as a writer than as an editor. Indeed, I gained the impression over the next two years that he did not really like editing, at any rate a national Sunday broadsheet. He was then 48. He seemed pleased to see me and readily agreed

[1] Letter in *Independent*, 19 June 1998.

the terms which Fenby at that stage had not exactly rejected but which he had not been prepared to accept. Jack said he was no good at writing contract-letters and suggested I should go home and write my own; he would countersign it. This I proceeded to do.

In the meantime Fenby had heard the news of my departure and telephoned to ask me to reconsider my decision, promising to talk again to Preston about the money I was asking for. I said it was too late: the deed had been done. I had no wish to behave towards Ian Jack in 1993 as I had towards Alexander Chancellor in 1975. Later, Fenby telephoned me again to say that Preston had proved obdurate. It would not have made any difference even if he had proved more accommodating. The time was past.

For some reason, Fenby was annoyed. He talked of holding me to the six months notice period in my contract with the *Observer*, which would have taken us into 1994. I wanted to start for the *Independent on Sunday* with the 1993 party conference season, which would be more convenient not only for me but for everyone concerned. In Old Fleet Street, I should explain, custom and practice was that the notice period was regarded as a protective device for the journalist rather than for the newspaper. It went further. A journalist who resigned to pursue other interests or was made redundant – there were several emollient phrases – could expect a severance payment including salary or retainer for his or her notice period together with a month's wages for every year of service. Of course, someone going off to another paper could not expect such generous treatment. That was only to be expected.

At the same time there was a rough-and-ready convention that people could leave more or less when it suited them, provided the paper could find a replacement. The new regime at the *Observer* did not behave in such a comfortable way, partly because, in 1993, we were living in a less comfortable age. My friend Hugh McIlvanney, the sports columnist, decided to take himself off to the *Sunday Times* and was held to his six months notice. It appeared that I would be treated in the same way by the new management. But two or three journalists had been acquired by the *Observer* from the daily *Independent*. The *Observer* wanted them to start work as soon as possible. Accordingly a deal was struck, a swap-arrangement made, whereby the movement of bodies was facilitated; and I was among the bodies. Andrew Billen, Madeleine Lim and John Sweeney entertained me to dinner at the Gay Hussar, which was thoughtful of them, and for which I was grateful. Otherwise there was no public farewell of any kind, though I had worked for the paper for 17 years. I did not mind. I had always found these occasions painful. Some years previously, when Russell ('Dai') Davies had left the *Observer* for the *Sunday Times*, Donald Trelford had said to me at his leaving party:

'I don't quite know why we're giving Dai this party when he's going off to our chief rival.'

The answer was that Trelford would seize on any excuse for a party. In addition, he was properly proud of his speechmaking abilities on these occasions. Indeed, the more ignominious the circumstances of the departure, the more eloquent was Trelford's tribute to the irreplaceable qualities of the departing journalist. Fenby was no Trelford.

III

Though I did not realise it at the time, the failure of Andreas Whittam Smith to merge the *Independent on Sunday* with the *Observer* – or, according to some analysts, to kill off the *Observer*, leaving the *Independent on Sunday* in full command of a small field – was the beginning of the end of the original *Independent*, whose foundation stone had carried the message that no one individual or group should hold a controlling or even a dominating interest in the paper. The *Independent on Sunday* was founded partly as a response to the boom inaugurated by Nigel Lawson as Chancellor in Margaret Thatcher's last administration. Its first editor was Stephen Glover.[2] Andreas Whittam Smith was an editor-in-chief of an archiepiscopal character – hardly ever seen but an undoubted influence for good – from 1991 to 1994. Ian Jack was 'executive editor', in practice editor, from 1991 to 1992 and then a fully-fledged editor until 1995, when he left to become editor of *Granta*. Alas, to use the favourite phrase of Tony Blair's ministerial colleagues after 1997, the boom turned to bust. The *Independent* newspapers were among the victims.

'Do you think you've made the right decision?' a woman friend asked anxiously at intervals.

I said I had, because the *Observer*, first for a year under

---

[2] See Stephen Glover, *Paper Dreams* (1993), *passim*.

Jonathan Fenby, and then for two years under Andrew Jaspan, was not a very happy ship. Only recently has the paper settled down under Roger Alton. Ian Jack, by contrast, was running a ship which might need a lick of paint and some even more fundamental repairs, but whose numerically inadequate crew were a friendly lot, including such gifted practitioners as Paul Routledge, who had come with me from the *Observer*, Allison Pearson and Nick Cohen – all later lost, sadly, to other papers.

The prevailing atmosphere was lightened not only by the people but by the place, in the City Road, not far from the original Grub Street (which was so called and has now been renamed), next to Bunhill Fields burial ground, where lie William Blake, John Bunyan, Daniel Defoe, George Fox and Isaac Watts. Wesley's chapel and London house were opposite. There was a good Italian restaurant, the Alba, within walking distance.

Above all, there was the editor's secretary or personal assistant, Clare Bartley (later Mrs David Swift), in whom I was generously given a small share and who combined perpetual efficiency with unfailing good humour. Throughout my life in Sunday newspapers I have been undeservedly, inexplicably lucky with secretaries. At the *Observer* there had been, to begin with, Barbara Rieck, who went on to become Donald Trelford's secretary, and then Isabel Maycock (later Mrs Roger Boddy), who worked principally for Tony Howard but helped make my own life easier. At the *Independent on Sunday* my run of luck continued with Clare Bartley.

IV

In his column in the old *Reynolds News*, Tom Driberg used to insist that his own spelling preferences – for instance, 'tho', 'connexion' and 'enquire' – should supersede the paper's house style. I made no such demands, largely because the normal Fleet Street style (though there are variations from paper to paper) accords with my own usage. In one respect, however, I was at odds with the *Independent on Sunday*'s style, as I had been with the *Observer*'s. Their convention was to introduce a character by his or her Christian name and surname, and to append a title to the surname merely in any subsequent reference. Thus 'Tony Blair' later became 'Mr Blair'. I preferred 'Mr Blair' to be preceded, on his introduction, by 'Mr Tony Blair'.

A more intractable difficulty concerns politicians who become lords or ladies, as most of the chief ones do. The column tends to become cluttered up with 'as he then was' or 'as she was to become' or – my own invention – 'as he then wasn't'. What makes the problem more intractable still is that they will insist on changing their name, as Edward Short became Lord Glenamara of Glenridding, which sounds like a malt whisky. If I am writing about the 'Short Money' which went to the political parties in the House, as it still does, I tend to leave his future title out of the account. If I am writing about the devaluation of 1967, I tend to say that it was carried out by James Callaghan but to make any further reference to 'Lord Callaghan'. Books are easier than columns in this regard, because all names can be regarded as belonging to dead persons, who are not accorded the same courtesies as the living.

I did not write to my new editor about these difficult matters – he had enough worries as it was – but about the simpler 'Mr' point. He replied:

7 September 1993

Dear Alan

Thank you for your letter of 30 August. You must mister away to your heart's content. Barbara [Gunnell, the then chief sub-editor] has been made aware of your preference.

The column for September 26 and October 3 will be about 1,180 words in length. The new design should take effect on October 10, when the position and perhaps also the length will change. I favour about 1,250. It could be longer, if you wish it. Do say.

Best wishes.

Ian

Ian Jack

Editor

I did not ask for more, being perfectly happy with 1,250 words. After numerous relaunches, redesigns and what-have-you, the column is of 1,200 words, with which I am equally content. My principal object was, as it remains, to have control of my copy. My weekly dealings were almost entirely with the deputy editor, Peter Wilby. He was from Leicester, whose rugby team he supported, and was untidy, enthusiastic and partly deaf. He gave the appearance of being some small denizen of wood, field or hedgerow who was normally harmless but could turn nasty if provoked.

I am afraid I provoked him several times, sometimes intentionally, more often not. As an example of intentional provocation, I used the phrase 'dusky despot' in relation to some black African dictator. Wilby said (he was by this stage editor) that he could not possibly have such a phrase in the paper not so much because he objected to it himself as because the readers would object to it strenuously: using it would be more trouble than it was worth. I complied without demur. However, I managed to work the phrase in under Wilby's successor, Rosie Boycott. Unintentional provocation came about because Wilby sometimes had difficulty with my personal pronouns.

'Who's this "him"?' he would ask. 'Is it meant to be Major, or is it Blair?'

'I should have thought from the context it was pretty obviously Major.'

'Okay then, let's put "Major" in.'

And Wilby would tap purposefully at the keyboard.

'Make it "Mr Major" please, Peter. No, make it "the Prime Minister" because we've got quite enough "Mr Majors" cluttering up that par as it is.'

'Oh all right then,' Wilby would say.

In fact he had a high regard for clear and grammatical English. But he had little time for fantasy. He also knew a lot about politics, particularly about the politics of education. But he became irritated with me because he thought I had chosen the wrong subject for the week, or had gone about it in the wrong way. Part of the trouble may have been that he was a graduate of the *Sunday Times*. Products of that academy, which Wilby attended from 1977 to 1986, have, I have noticed, usually scant respect for what someone has actually written and want to shape it to their own preconceptions. Wilby, I should make clear, never altered a word of my copy without consulting me first. But it was equally evident to me that he would have liked greater freedom to do so. The relationship between an editor and a writer is something like a sexual relationship. Two people may hit it off where *prima facie* one would not expect them to; while another couple, superficially more suited to each other, fail to do anything of the kind.

And yet, I cannot have thought too badly of Wilby. When Ian Jack resigned in 1995, I recommended to Tony O'Reilly's group that he should be Jack's successor. I felt able to do this because I knew

O'Reilly slightly, having been introduced to him at the *Observer* by that other former great rugby player Clem Thomas, and because I knew Ted Smyth. With another diplomat, Richard Ryan, Smyth had been at the Irish embassy in London in the year immediately preceding the Anglo-Irish Agreement of 1985, on whose successful conclusion the Dublin government clearly set great store. Indeed, the plain people of Ireland had contributed substantial sums towards persuading the journalists of Westminster to look benevolently on the coming rapprochement. Smyth and Ryan dispensed the choicest burgundy, the finest claret, the most ancient armagnac in anticipation of the happy event. No wonder they became figures of the greatest popularity. Smyth – scholarly, moustached, bowtied, an expert on James Joyce who had something about him of a French intellectual – later became O'Reilly's man-of-business, in Philadelphia and in Dublin. I do not know whether my recommendation for Wilby helped him; Smyth later told me it did; who could tell?

'All Peter needs now,' I said, 'is a suit, a haircut and a hearing-aid.'

V

O'Reilly was involved in the choice of a new editor of the *Independent on Sunday* because in March 1994 his group and Mirror Newspapers had acquired equal shares in Independent Newspapers. In 1998 the group was to acquire outright control. The era of Whittam Smith was over. In 1994 O'Reilly and *Mirror* each possessed an equal holding of under 50 per cent, the balance being made up of various Spanish and Italian newspaper interests. Together they held a controlling interest. However, David Montgomery, the Chief Executive of Mirror Group Newspapers until 1999, secured a 'management contract' for the Mirror Group. Montgomery was an Ulsterman to whom, despite his propensity for serial matrimony, the adjective 'dour' attached itself with all the inevitability of eggs to bacon. He was short, slim, ascetic and ambitious. Our paths crossed only once: when we greeted each other warily at a *Mirror* party during a Labour conference. The *IoS*'s political writers at that time – Stephen Castle, Paul Routledge and myself – had not, as I remember, received invitations for the occasion. But we took the view that, as Montgomery was behaving as if he owned both *Independent* titles, the omission had been an unfortunate oversight. Not only did Montgomery demand redundancies. He also applied conditions of employment obtaining at the *Mirror* to staff at the *Independent*, even though those conditions had not been agreed. For instance, it was decreed that journalists should retire on attaining the age of 65.

It was also decreed that the *Independent* titles should move from City Road, London E.C.1, to that temple of contemporary capitalism, Canary Wharf, London E.14. It reminded me of my days working for the *Sunday Express* in New York, except that it lacked the human scale of the Rockefeller Center. Also present were the *Daily Telegraph*, the *Mirror*, the *People*, the *Sunday Mirror* and the *Sunday Telegraph*. This was a higher concentration of national newspapers than had been accommodated in Old Fleet Street, where only the *Express* and the *Telegraph* had possessed premises on the street itself.

But there was none of the fellowship of London E.C.4 before the diaspora. It was not that there was a shortage of licensed premises. On the contrary: this part of the new Docklands boasted numerous bars where young men in blue suits drank beer straight out of the bottle. But people did not want to go to them because the atmosphere was disagreeable; because they were wedded to their screens; most of all, because separation on a vertical pattern creates isolation, which the inhabitants of tower blocks have long known but their architects have yet to learn.

The move was accompanied by a change from one system of new technology to another. On 16 December 1994 Ian Jack, who was not to resign till the following year, dispatched a memorandum to his then columnists, Neal Ascherson, Geraldine Bedell, Blake Morrison and myself:

The new technology means that we shall have to abandon our previous courtesy of allowing writers to sub-edit their own copy to length, at least for the time being. In future their copy will be edited by [sub-]editors, who will of course consult (deadlines allowing) on any cuts or changes that may have to be made. The present system consumes too much personal and machine time, and causes delays which have repercussions for the paper as a whole. Printouts of subbed copy will not be faxed to writers for the same reasons.

We have good [sub-]editors and they should be trusted, just as

[sub-]editors were in a pre-electronic age when none of the opportunities afforded by our previous Atex system was available.
     Ian

This did not make sense to me. That we were moving from the
Atex to the Apple-Macintosh system did not seem to me to affect the
truth that writers such as Ascherson, Ms Bedell, Morrison and
myself were saving the sub-editors time which they could devote to
other tasks. Besides, I at any rate wanted to retain control of what
went into the paper under my name. I do not know what the others
did. I simply ignored the memorandum and carried on exactly as I
had before receiving it. No one objected or, indeed, commented in
any way.

This illustrates a wider axiom: that in newspapers, probably in
other forms of endeavour as well, it is sometimes more profitable to
ignore an instruction than to take a stand or make a fuss. There
was an example of this when I was at the *Observer*. It likewise
involved a memorandum from the editor, in this case Donald
Trelford. He asserted that copyright in any work done for the paper
by any *Observer* writer rested with the paper, irrespective of the
writer's contractual status. I said that this was a crude attempt to
override a recent Act which dealt with these matters. I said it to
Tony Howard, who had had nothing to do with this missive and had
also received a copy. The statute laid down that writers who were
not employees retained copyright in default of specific assignation
to the paper. I said to Tony that I intended to have a row about this.
Tony advised me not to be so silly, not to waste my time, and to
consign the memorandum to the wastepaper basket, as he had done
and as I duly did.

VI

At this stage I ought to make clear that I am not a complete enemy
of the new technology in printing. Nor is it simply that I accept it
in the spirit in which Thomas Carlyle advised the woman to accept
the universe. For a writer, it possesses several advantages. Though
I still write, as I have always, with pen and ink on lined foolscap
paper, copy that has been transferred to a screen is easier to deal
with than copy that has been punched out by a linotype operator
and set in metal lines. The old procedure meant that articles had to
be cut by removing lines rather than words. Thus in the 1970s,

when I came into the *Observer* on Saturday mornings, the printer would say to me:

'Right, Al, you're 12 lines over.'

It was only *Observer* printers who ever called me 'Al'. They called Adam Raphael 'Major Raphael' not on account of any military aspect to his demeanour (though he had done his national service in the army) but of his habit of using 'major' in the first or second paragraph of any story he wrote, as in: 'A major row broke out last night in the Labour Party over ...'

I would promise to cut the necessary lines.

'But it's got to be a nine and a three.'

I would scan the galley-proof.

'What about an eight and a four?'

'Can't manage that, Al, I'm sorry to say. But, tell you what, I can do you a 10 and a two, just about.'

'Thanks very much, that'll be marvellous.'

The new technology eliminated the need for such negotiations. It was not necessary to deal with printers or cut whole lines. The printers had gone, along with – a greater loss – the correctors of the press, known in newspapers as 'the readers'.

They tended to be middle-aged or elderly men with unbuttoned waistcoats and shirtsleeves hitched up with those expanding metal armbands. Some of them knew Latin or even Greek, maybe because they were disgraced schoolmasters or unfrocked clergymen. Evelyn Waugh used to maintain that the standards of accuracy in books had declined as schools and churches had become more tolerant of lapses, whether of a heterosexual or homosexual variety, in masters and incumbents. However, the invaluable readers I met challenged me on questions not so much of vocabulary, grammar and syntax as of fact, such as whether I was right in naming Istanbul as the capital of Turkey.

It was a relief that whole lines had no longer to be cut. Most writers overuse adjectives and adverbs. Superfluous adjectives can easily be got rid of: superfluous adverbs tend to stick unless they are watched closely. The new technology has made me more vigilant.

VII

In the 1990s the pattern of my life became more settled. Mondays, from the beginning of October to the end of April, would be devoted to my rugby column for the *Independent*.[3] It was of 800 words and would take two hours to write. I would then go over it carefully, dictate it to the copytakers who would put into the *Independent*'s system, and leave the rest to the sports desk's sub-editors. Any mistakes would usually derive from a mishearing by the copytaker which had not been spotted by a sub-editor.

In Old Fleet Street copytakers were exclusively male on the insistence of the print union, NATSOPA, to which they, in common with editorial secretaries (who were exclusively female), were compelled to belong. They were famous for surliness, as in:

'Jo Grimond, that's Jo without the *e* and one *m* in Grimond.'

'I can spell, thanks very much.'

Or, when a certain stage had been reached:

'Much more of this, is there?'

They were, however, often shrewder about a paper's requirements than the journalist dictating his copy. I was once dictating a political story to the *Sunday Express* at nine o'clock one Saturday evening. After 'much more of this?' the copytaker went on:

'Mind me saying something to you?'

'Not in the least. Fire away' (an expression of my father's).

'They're not going to use none of this, not at this time, they're not. So if I was you I'd stop.'

Stop I did. And none of what I had already dictated was used.

Philip Hope-Wallace (1911-79) was a particular victim of misprints, which, however, he took a melancholy delight in retailing at lunchtime in El Vino's. Owing to the nature of his work as, at various periods, theatre, music and opera critic of the *Guardian*, the bulk of his writing was dictated over the telephone. Once he intercepted a female sub-editor ('Why must they always employ young women from New Zealand?') sending down to the printers his review of *Doris Godunov*. On another occasion he finished dictating a notice: 'The programme had begun with an admirable performance of Elgar's overture "In the South". End [as in "end of story"].' This appeared as 'Elgar's overture "In Southend" '. Then there was his notice of *La Traviata*: 'The music-hall direction was in the capable hands of ...' And there was his account of *The Merchant of Venice* with Laurence Olivier as Skylark. But his own favourite, not from the *Guardian* but from the weekly *Time and Tide*, concerned

---

[3] See Chapter 10 above.

his description of a Tosca as being 'like a tigress robbed of her whelps'. The editor, possibly Lady Rhondda, who for a time owned and edited the paper and was an early feminist, changed 'tigress' to 'tiger' and 'her' to 'his'. The printer, on his own initiative, then changed, 'whelps' to 'whelks'. So Tosca appeared 'like a tiger robbed of his whelks'.

On Tuesday, Wednesday and Thursday mornings I would try to write 1,000 words (two sheets of A4 paper) of a book – *A Conservative Coup* appeared in 1991, *The Road to Number 10* in 1998 – or a book review for the *Spectator* or whatever it happened to be. In the afternoon I would go down to the House of Commons. At the beginning of the 1990s it would be for three afternoons and early evenings a week. At the end of the decade it would be on a Wednesday or a Thursday. Then I acquired a Sky digital television, which carried the BBC's parliamentary channel, and often found it more convenient to be Our Man in Islington With a Large Drink and a Colour Television.

The House remained necessary chiefly as a source of documents. Most journalists call it 'research' when they summon up the energy to open an old volume of *Hansard*. They are similarly wary of more contemporary records. Even 20 years ago, if there was to be a row on, say, the Committee of Privileges (now the Standards and Privileges Committee), *The Times*, the *Daily Telegraph* and the *Guardian* would publish the names of its chairman and members, even if in the smallest typeface available. Likewise, the broadsheets would publish a parliamentary page, a kind of mini-*Hansard*. I am not sure that the loss of this feature was altogether to be regretted. The speeches had of necessity to be cut drastically, and backbenchers did not get much of a showing. The *Independent* and other papers are now (in July 2000) making a brave attempt at running a parliamentary page of separate news stories. All round, however, there is a certain scarcity of raw political fact, which from time to time I try to remedy.

My writing rate is a fairly steady 400 words an hour. Preliminary notes are useful, sometimes, for making things clear in my head. But columns cannot be written to order, not even to the order of the person writing them. The practice recommended by my former English teachers – that an essay should be planned on the pattern of 1(a) (i) and so forth – does not work, for me at any rate. John (now Lord) Birt's idea when he was running *Weekend World* was that a journalist knew before he or she started writing how an article was to begin, continue and, above all, end. The conclusion was present from the start. Similarly, Birt reasoned, a television producer should know what the people on the programme would say.

Thus in June 1980, immediately after a gathering of Labour notables at Bishop's Stortford, I was visited at the *Observer* by Bruce Anderson, then a researcher on the programme, later a distinguished political columnist. He was typically and commendably frank. The programme's 'line', he said, was that the congress of Bishop's Stortford – which was concerned, among other matters, with a new method of choosing the Labour leader – was unimportant and a sham. I indicated dissent. In that case, Anderson continued, my contribution to the programme would not be broadcast, though I should be paid in full. I duly said a few words to the camera, they were not used and I was generously paid. Other political journalists proved more amenable to Birt's method of making programmes.

Having arrived at a conclusion that sometimes surprised myself, I would finish writing at about two, go through the column, telephone it to the copytakers who worked in Wetherby, Yorkshire – mainly women who were more efficient and more polite than their exclusively male predecessors had been in Old Fleet Street – and reach Canary Wharf at half-past three or four via the Bank underground station and the Docklands light railway. I would then buy a smoked-salmon sandwich at the Canary Wharf Tesco's and eat it while cutting and correcting my column, which would have been transmitted to London E.14 from Wetherby.

Peter Wilby had the habit, at once flattering and irritating, of reading the column before I had been able to correct it for literals, of which, despite the charm and diligence of the copytakers, there were always a few. More: he would come up with suggestions of his own for improving the product. He knew a good deal about politics, more than most editors. He also knew about column-writing: for instance, that a columnist will, like a comedian, maintain a stock of catchphrases, not because of any lack of invention, but because readers like to recognise familiar landmarks. With me they include 'The People's Party', 'Estopped, as the lawyers say', 'Be it so, as the barristers say', and 'What the late George Brown used to call a complete ignoral'.

But I did not want niggling every Friday afternoon. I had, over almost 40 years, climbed into the ring with John Junor, Dick Crossman and, the most pugnacious of the three, John Cole. I was growing too old for that sort of thing. I had no wish to be the Archie Moore of political comment. When Wilby was dismissed in 1996, I wrote to him saying he had been a good editor and that I thought he had been shabbily treated by the management. Both of these I believed to be true. Nevertheless I was not sorry to see a change.

VIII

Montgomery had said that he wanted a more sophisticated and metropolitan paper and that he did not think Wilby was the editor to provide it. Wilby heartily concurred with this view, and went on to become books editor and, later, editor of the *New Statesman*, where he tried his best to arrest a decline that had been proceeding for 20 years. He was replaced by Rosie Boycott. She was already quite a famous woman journalist: not as well known, perhaps, as Julie Burchill or Germaine Greer, but a recognised name nonetheless, at any rate in metropolitan circles, which partly accounted for her attractions for the management, in view of the kind of paper they vaguely wanted to publish.

In 1996, the year in which she became editor of the *Independent on Sunday*, she was 45. She had been educated, unhappily, at Cheltenham Ladies' College – a leviathan invariably mentioned in accounts of her career – and at the University of Kent, where she had read pure mathematics. She went on to have difficulties with drugs and with alcohol. In 1971 she was the co-founder of the women's magazine *Spare Rib*. She travelled the world in search of adventure and wrote a book about it, *A Nice Girl Like Me*. She went on to have a more conventional journalistic career in various more or less exalted posts at *Honey*, the *Daily Mail*, the *Sunday Telegraph*, *Harpers & Queen* and *Esquire*, which she had edited. In 1983 she had married the journalist David Leitch.

I had known Leitch at the *New Statesman*, during Anthony Howard's period as editor. I admired him both as a journalist who had made his name on the *Sunday Times* in its great days and as the author of an early autobiography, *God Stand Up For Bastards*, which I thought a minor masterpiece. Besides being gifted, Leitch was volatile and could be aggressive. Though short, he was undoubtedly sturdy. In the period of which I speak, he was writing occasional articles for the *Statesman*. For some reason, probably to do with court or other legal orders, he wanted to be paid in cash on the Thursday of the week in which his article was to appear. From time to time on Thursday at Great Turnstile I would receive an internal telephone call from Ted Peacock, the company accountant.

'Mind stepping down here for a moment, Alan. Spot of bother you might help sort out.'

I would go to Peacock's office to find there an enraged David Leitch demanding his money.

'No way am I disbursing any of the company's money in cash unless I have authorisation in writing from Mr Morgan. And you can scream as long as you like. No way.'

Jack Morgan was the company secretary. Ted Peacock was a very big man, bigger than Leitch, bigger than I was. I was clearly being introduced into the dispute more for my peacemaking than for any pugilistic qualities.

'There, there, gentlemen,' I would say, or words to this effect, 'Please compose yourselves. I am sure a way can be found.'

I would then suggest – for this little drama would be re-enacted – that Tony Howard's signature would be as valid as Jack Morgan's. Peacock would agree dubiously. I would then go to Howard's office and secure his signature on a bit of paper, and Leitch would receive his cash.

I told this story to Ms Boycott, thinking she was divorced from Leitch by now, in 1996. In fact she was still married to though separated from him. They maintained amicable relations (they were to divorce in 1998 and she was to remarry in 1999). At all events, it was clear I had said the wrong thing. Ms Boycott's handsome countenance resembled even more that of a bird of prey that had come across a piece of carrion not to its taste. I had forgotten one of the rules about talking to metropolitan women: that, whatever their own relations with husbands or lovers, past or present, it is impermissible for third parties, especially other men, to cast aspersions of any kind on them.

However, Ms Boycott was not one to harbour grudges – one of her most engaging features – and the *froideur* was momentary. She started off by giving me a glass of white wine and a big hug in her office early every Friday evening after I had finished with the column. Soon the hug was replaced by a peck on the cheek but the wine remained. Then the kiss was dispensed with altogether.

Finally there was neither kiss nor wine, merely a friendly wave. I did not repine. I was not offended. There was, I thought, nothing personal in it. Ms Boycott's span of attention for people was evidently almost as brief as her span of attention for ideas.

She once suggested I should go to Venice on the Orient Express and write about my experience. I replied, churlishly perhaps, that I had not the slightest wish to travel on the Orient Express and that I preferred to reach the city by air and to stay at the Luna hotel. Others in the room joined in. It would be a splendid idea, they said – echoing the new editor, as people tend to do – for me to go to Venice in the manner specified. Very well, then, I said: I would go. Afterwards, to my relief, I heard nothing further of the proposal.

A few months later the rather better idea was conceived of having Paul Routledge write a political column of gossipy items (which he was later to continue in the *New Statesman* under Peter Wilby's editorship). The editor promised a bottle of champagne to the person who produced the best name for the new column. I came up with Thomas Creevey, the political diarist of the early 19th century. Creevey it duly was. I am still waiting for my bottle of champagne.

IX

From my point of view, Rosie Boycott's happiest move was to bring in Stephen Fay as her deputy editor. Fay had already held this position before I joined the paper; later, with his friend Henry Porter, he had tried to raise the finance to buy the *Independent on Sunday* outright. I had known him for well over 30 years. Besides being a civilised man, he was an accomplished journalist. He was particularly good at encouraging the young, a quality he shared with Anthony Howard. Fay should in justice have been made editor of the *Independent on Sunday* at some point in the 1990s. He nearly did become editor. For a period, after Ms Boycott's departure briefly to edit the *Independent*, he was acting editor. But partly for reasons of health, the job he should have had eluded him.

Philip Hope-Wallace used to relate the advice his father gave him:

'Never work for a liberal newspaper, dear boy. They always give you the sack on Christmas Eve.'

This was what Rosie Boycott did with Neal Ascherson late in

1997. Successive editors of the paper had, I thought, made a mistake in not emulating the *Observer*'s first leader-page of the mid-1980s consisting of a profile and columns by Ascherson and myself. Instead he occupied the main leader-page space, as Peregrine Worsthorne had done for years in the *Sunday Telegraph*. The disadvantages of this arrangement are that it renders inflexible what ought to be the most important space in the paper and, connectedly, that in a curious way it depreciates the columnist who is filling that space. Even so, Ascherson was regarded by most journalists as one of the principal assets of the paper. Moreover, he had joined it from the *Observer* three years before I had, not to earn more money but to satisfy his ideals. Over the Christmas holidays he telephoned me in a state of some shock.

'They'll be coming for you next,' he said.

I departed for my usual new-year holiday at Beaulieu near Nice. From there, on 9 January 1998, I wrote a postcard to my son David:

> As our paths did not cross on the Mon evening or the Tue morning, I was unable to tell you that Rosie Boycott had given N. Ascherson the heave-ho, ostensibly on the ground that he was over 65. She has asked him to leave by the end of Feb, with no mention of the 3 months' notice period which he has. I have 6 months because I insisted on it; and there is nothing in my contract about attaining 65. I await developments.
> Love
> Dad

The reason Ms Boycott gave for dismissing Ascherson resembled what the Eastern European nations used to call a 'pretext' when they were accusing the West of some piece of skulduggery or other during the Cold War. There was no reason why the *Independent*'s managers and editors should import the *Mirror*'s terms and conditions of employment into dealings with their own staff. Even if they did cave in to David Montgomery's demands, there was nothing to prevent them from re-engaging someone in Ascherson's position as a freelance – a regular contributor on an annual retainer, such as myself. But, after his departure, I heard that he was considered 'unhelpful' and 'remote'. I was informed also that he had told Ms Boycott that she was 'intellectually unfit' to edit the *Independent on Sunday*. I had known Ascherson for over 30 years. This did not sound at all like him. He was one of the most polite men I had ever met. Even if he had thought this about Ms Boycott, he would not have said it either to her or, probably, to anyone else. He certainly did not say anything of the kind to me.

In his place Rosie Boycott appointed Anne McElvoy (Mrs Martin Ivens). She was in her early thirties, attractive, clever, something of an expert on Germany, Russia and Eastern Europe. She differed from other ambitious young women journalists of that time in having been, in her youth, a gymnast of international standard. She had worked for *The Times*, written a column in the *Daily Telegraph* and, before she fell out with Frank Johnson, been deputy editor of the *Spectator*. I told her, before she joined the paper – it was at the Labour Party conference of 1997 – that she would have to choose between being a columnist and being an editor. She replied that she could be both. She added that there was no room for her on what she called the 'executive ladder' of the *Telegraph*. Would I mention her name to Rosie Boycott? This I duly did in autumn 1997. Ms McElvoy was now with us. Virtually her first words to me were:

'We must talk.'

We met for lunch on Tuesday 4 February 1998 at the Gay Hussar, more my sort of restaurant, I thought, than hers, but that could not be helped. She wanted to arrange a time for consultation between us. I used regularly to talk to the number two or number three on the paper (a shifting population) about my intentions for the coming Sunday. I would do so at 10.45 on Thursday morning, to get in before the conference started. But I had never consulted with Neal Ascherson about these matters. If his successor wished to change the practice, I was amenable but unenthusiastic. As the meal progressed, however, it became evident that Ms McElvoy was thinking about consultations not so much in her present role of columnist as in her future position of editor. Rosie Boycott, she said, would soon be departing to edit the daily *Independent*, and she would succeed her.

X

I was, I confess, surprised. I felt like a minor prophet who was told he would in future be required to submit his prognostications for approval by one of Lot's daughters. But throughout the 1990s the editorial floor of both *Independent* titles was as *mouvementé* as the property market in Islington. What was happening at the daily affected what was happening at the Sunday, and *vice versa*. Ian Hargreaves had edited the *Independent* from 1994 to 1996. He was succeeded by Andrew Marr, one of the best political columnists of his time. I was sorry when he left the *Observer* in 2000 to do a job which involved standing outside No 10 Downing Street in the pouring rain speaking the obvious for 30 seconds into a BBC microphone.

Marr was – is – a thoughtful man. One of his ideas was that people received their daily information from television the night before or from the wireless in the morning. The builder with his transistor was better informed about the news than the editor at his conference. Accordingly a newspaper should not merely reprocess the previous day's news but try to explain what it meant. Marr would often devote the whole front page to a single report on the lines of Hugh Cudlipp's 'shock issues' of the old *Daily Mirror*. But Cudlipp would bring out papers of this kind once every six months. Marr was doing likewise two or three times a week.

Besides, the *Mirror* was a tabloid. Marr's approach would have worked better, I think, if the *Independent* had been a tabloid too. Tabloid form does not entail any lowering of tone. *Le Monde* and the *Church Times* are both tabloids. Articles can be longer, as the *Guardian*'s *G2* and the *Sunday Times*'s books sections have both shown. It can only be a matter of time before one of the broadsheet papers becomes completely tabloid in form. Marr was ahead of his age. The general verdict was that he was an excellent writer, a nice man but a rotten editor.

Marr was succeeded briefly by Rosie Boycott, who rapidly left to edit the newly New Labour *Express*. She was succeeded by a true professional in Simon Kelner. His latest job had been as editor of the *Mail on Sunday* magazine. I knew him from his previous jobs as deputy sports editor of the *Independent*, sports editor of the *Observer* and editor of the *Observer* magazine where, under his editorship, I had between 1992 and 1993 written a column on drink. It was pleasant to see a familiar face about the place. Throughout the various changes that were being made, his former colleagues, the sports staff of the *Independent*, under their editor, Paul Newman, proved as solid and reassuring a presence as the Trumpton fire brigade: Jones, Rea, Simon O'Hay, Bateson, Glover, Tench (Ken Jones, Chris Rea, Simon O'Hagan, Hugh Bateson, Tim Glover, Matt Tench). At the *Independent on Sunday*, Keith Howitt,

Catherine Pepinster and Jo Pugh all helped to make my life easier.

XI

But, alas! the departure of Rosie Boycott from the *Independent on Sunday* did not lead to the elevation of Anne McElvoy. The job went instead to Kim Fletcher, deputy editor of the *Sunday Telegraph*, who wrote to me:

> The Independent on Sunday
> Canary Wharf
> London
> E.14

May 11 1998

Dear Alan

The music has stopped and I find myself sitting in the Editor's chair.

I hope to be able to take you out to lunch very soon in return for a tutorial. Before then I wanted to say how proud I am that the paper carries your column and how much I hope you will continue to write it.

I will get in touch this week to arrange a meeting, and look forward to seeing you then.

> Best wishes
> Kim Fletcher

Fletcher was good-looking, of medium height, athletically built. He described himself as a Yorkshireman but had been educated at Heversham Grammar School, Westmorland, and at Hertford College, Oxford, where, I later learnt – he did not tell me at the time, somewhat surprisingly, I thought, in view of my own interest in the subject – he had read Law. But his career had, like mine, been in journalism. We enjoyed the friendliest relations, but he always looked worried, as if the job was getting him down.

Nor did he endear himself to the staff by importing two colleagues from the *Sunday Telegraph*: Rebecca Nicolson as his deputy and Stuart Reid as number three. I had known Ms Nicolson at the *Observer* and thought her a pleasant, well-mannered woman who might be a good features editor (the position she attained at the *Observer*) but needed more experience before becoming deputy editor of a national Sunday paper. Reid I had never met but I had known his father, Charles Reid, biographer of Sir Thomas Beecham and music critic, who held that post at the *Spectator* when I joined the paper in 1964. He had white hair and a ruddy complexion, wore a black overcoat with a velvet collar and a Homburg hat, and seemed to come from an even older Fleet Street.

'Don't let the Whig dogs have the best of it,' he had said.

His son Stuart had the reputation of being the best sub-editor in Fleet Street. He certainly had the ability, equalled in my experience only by Terence Kilmartin, to pick out a passage about which the writer himself had worried at the time he was writing it. The passage was not wrong exactly but could have been expressed better. Stuart Reid possessed this gift.

Kim Fletcher's error was not so much to import Reid as to import both him and Rebecca Nicolson at the same time. It gave people the idea that they were being taken over by the *Sunday Telegraph*. Nor did it help matters that Reid tended to commission old *Telegraph* favourites such as Anthony Daniels ('Dr Theodore Dalrymple') and Peregrine Worsthorne. All new editors, admittedly, are like football managers: they bring their old friends into the team, whether as coaches or players, as 'executives' or writers. Fletcher's error was to bring in too many.

XII

He was allowed just about a year before being succeeded by Janet Street-Porter. She was my fifth editor in six years, the others having been, in reverse order, Kim Fletcher, Rosie Boycott, Peter Wilby and Ian Jack. In the same period the *Observer* had had Roger Alton, Will Hutton, Andrew Jaspan and Jonathan Fenby. I had met Ms Street-Porter at *Private Eye* lunches and found her an engaging character. She also had a serious interest in architecture. Some of the snobbish things that were written about her by papers such as the *Guardian* were not only unfair, in that she had had no opportunity to prove herself, but would have been a disgrace in any circumstances. I told her so. But she was a woman of some resilience and pressed on. We both press on.

Index

A6 murder, A.W. writes about, 141; *Standard* receives solicitor's letter, 142; settles, 143; C. Wintour ignorant of details but still annoyed, 143
Aberdeen W., constituency, 3
Abersychan County School, 15
Absent Friends (Wheatcroft), 31n, 83n
Adam Smith, Janet, 96
Adam, Corinna, 102, 111, 144, 150, 189
Adam, Ruth, 144
Aitken, Ian, 47, 53, 54, 76, 131, 136, 205
Aitken, Jonathan, 77
Aitken, Maxwell. *See* Beaverbrook
Aitken, Sir Max, 41, 114
A.J.P. Taylor (Sisman), 46n
Alastair Campbell (Oborne), 60, 74
Alba restaurant, London E.C.1, 239
Albany, Piccadilly, 87
Aldershot and N. Hants, constituency, 87
Aldershot, Hants, 77
Alexander Fleming House, 124
Alexander, Jeremy, 223
All Souls College, Oxford, 102, 229
Allchurch, Ivor, 230
Alton, Roger, 239, 256
Amis, Hilly, 63
Amis, Martin, 112
Amis, Sir Kingsley, 20, 27, 226

Amman Valley, Carmarthenshire, 8, 226
Amman Valley Grammar School, Ammanford, 15; motto, 23; 24, 216
Ammanford, Carmarthenshire, 3, 17, 20
Ammanford Public Library, 26
Amory, Mark, 31n
Anderson, Bruce, 248
Anderson, Robert O., 164, 165, 170; buys Astor family interest in *Observer*, 175; sells 80% of own interest to Outram's, 175; determines to sell to Lonrho after rejection of K. Harris, 176; remains chairman after acquisition, 179
Angel Hotel, Cardiff, 214
Anglo-Irish Agreement 1985, 242
Annan, Noël, Lord, 194
Anne, Princess, 94
Annie's Bar, House of Commons, 126, 128, 205
Any Questions?, 63
Apple-Macintosh system, 244
Arab-Israeli War 1967, 87
Arab-Israeli War 1973, 31
ARCO. *See* Atlantic Richfield
Ardwick, Lord. *See* Beavan
Arlington House, London W.1, 44, 57
Arsenal FC, 139, 147
Ascherson, Mrs Neal. *See* Adam
Ascherson, Neal, 30; known as

'supermarket trolley', 67; 144; succeeds C.C. O'Brien, 188; described, 188-9; leaves to go to *IoS*, 189; 243, 244; dismissed by R. Boycott, 251-2, 253
Ascot races, 49, 149
Asquith, H.H., 96
Associated Newspapers, 52, 163, 165, 224
Astor trustees, 161, 163, 164
Astor, David, 24, 112, 152, 156, 158-9, 160, 161, 163, 164; stays on *Observer* board, 170; and K. Harris, 176; opposes sale to Lonrho, 177, 178; resigns from board, 179, 206, 211
Astor, Michael, 33
Atex system, 244
Atkins, Judith, 51
Atlantic Richfield, 164, 165, 176, 179
'Atticus' (*Sunday Times*), 30
Attlee, C.R., Lord, 32, 107, 124, 177
Australian, 162
Aw Sian, Sally, 163
Ayer, Sir A.J., 27, 194
Aynsley, Cyril, 82n

Bacon, Francis, 113
Bailey, David, 119
Baistow, Tom, 102, 110
Bale, Steve, 226
Balogh, Thomas, Lord, 101
Balzac, H., 13
Banaban islanders, 231
Banbury, constituency, 106
Banda, Hastings, 200
Bank underground station, 248
Barber, Lynn, 139
Barbican, London E.C., 113
Barker, Howard, 33
Barnes, Julian, 112
Barnes, Susan, 139
Barnetson, William, Lord, 177
Baron's Court, London, 147
Barrow RLC, 219
Bartley, Clare, 239
Basingstoke, constituency, 93
Bateson, Hugh, 254

Battersea, constituency, 205
Battersea, London, 2, 147; and change in journalism, 202
Battle of Downing Street (Jenkins), 92
Battle, Sussex, 63
BBC 3, 72, 116
BBC, 72
Beaulieu, near Nice, S. of France, 252
Beavan, John, 3, 120, 122, 123
Beaverbrook, Lady. *See* Dunn
Beaverbrook, Lord, 2, 3, 4, 39, 41, 42 & n; dislikes bishops and Royal Family, 43; 44, 47, 48, 49; A.W.'s relations with him in New York, 49-55; dictates 'Crossbencher' column to A.W., 57-8; deplores use of telephone, 58-9; dies, 60; 117, 119, 120, 134, 137, 159, 197
Bedell, Geraldine, 243, 244
Bedford Assizes, 142
Beecham, Sir Thomas, 256
Beerbohm, Sir Max, 24
Beloff, Nora, 74, 152, 156; and D. Sandys, 157
Belsen, 5
Benn, Caroline, 108
Benn, Tony, 101, 107, 108, 140, 141
Berkeley, G., 23
Berkhamsted School, 31, 208, 209
Berkhamsted, Herts, 208
Bernard, Jeffrey, 117
Berry, Michael. *See* Hartwell
Bessell, Peter, 56, 57
Bethnal Green, London, 144
Bevan, Aneurin, 5, 27, 62, 63, 90, 91, 107
Beyfus, Drusilla, 137
Biafran War, 78, 231
Biffen, John, Lord, 28, 140; and *Observer*, 177, 178, 179
Bill of Rights, M. Thatcher and, 197
Billen, Andrew, 237
Bird, John, 72, 85, 116
Birmingham Gazette, 235
Birt, John, Lord, 247, 248
Bishop, Gordon, 207

Bishop's Stortford Labour gathering, 248

Bishops, disliked by Beaverbrook, 43; attend *Observer*-ARCO dinner, 170

Black Friars, Queen Victoria Street, London E.C.4, 152-3

Black Mountains, Carmarthenshire, 226

Blackburn, Raymond, 142

Blackfriars, London E.C.4, 155

Blackpool, Lancs, 33, 136, 159, 188

Blaenau School, Carmarthenshire, 12

Blair, Tony, 87, 90, 122, 238

Blake, William, 239

Blakiston, A.F., 12

Bloomsbury Group, 96

Blundell's School, Tiverton, 227

Bock, Dieter, 211

Boddy, Mrs Roger. *See* Maycock

Bodmin, constituency, 56

Bole, Eric, 227

Booker Brothers, 150

Boothby, Robert, Lord, 27

Boss, S. African security service, 231

Bovis, 116

Bow Group, 87

Bow Street court, 142

Bower, Frank, 93

Bowis, John, 205

Boxer, Mark, 30, 31, 32, 119, 184

Boy Scouts, 205

Boycott, Rosie, becomes editor of *IoS*, 249; begins by giving A.W. glass of wine and hug, 250; gradually dispenses with both, 251; suggests A.W. goes to Venice, 251; forgets, 251; promises A.W. bottle of champagne, 251; forgets, 251; edits *Independent*, 251; dismisses N. Ascherson, 251; 253; edits *Express*, 254; 256

Bradshaw, Thornton, 170; predicts R.O. Anderson's annoyance at *Observer*'s stance in 1979 election, 175

Bradwell, Lord. *See* Driberg

Breeding of Farm Animals (Pincher), 77n

Brenton, Howard, 33

Brewer's Politics (Comfort), 191-2

Brief Lives (Watkins), 4

Brighton Labour conference 1957, 27

Brighton, Sussex, 73, 159, 188

British Youth Council, A.W. and, 205-6

Brittan, Sir Samuel, 3, 30, 34, 79

Brittenden, Arthur, 44-5, 50, 57, 58

Brivati, Brian, 163 & n, 165n, 175n, 176

Brixton prison, receives H. Fairlie, 63

Broadcasting House, London W.1, 3

Brooklands, Surrey, 17

Brown, George, 72

Brown, Ivor, 24

Brown, Tina, 88, 112

Brussels, 108

Brynamman, Carmarthenshire, 226, 227

Bryntirion School, Bridgend, 227

Bryntirion, Tycroes, 5

Buchenwald, 5

Buckingham, constituency, 126

Bunhill Fields, London E.C.1, 239

Bunyan, John, 193, 239

Burchill, Julie, 249

Burgess, Charles, 225

Bury St Edmunds, Suffolk, 33

Bush House, London W.C.2, 96

Butler, Eddie, 228

Butler, R.A., Lord, 10, 45, 59, 60, 125

Callaghan, James, Lord, 72, 75, 92, 121, 123, 126, 136, 141, 155, 161, 166, 167, 169; fall of government, 174; resigns, 180

Cambridge U. Labour Club, 27

Cambridge U. Conservative Association, 28

Cambridge Union Society, 32, 40, 66, 133, 165, 231

Cambridge, A.W. at, 25-35, 39

Cameron, James, 102

Campaign for Nuclear
Disarmament, 27, 89
Campaign for Real Ale, 190
Campbell, Jock, Lord, 100, 109, 110,
111, 116, 117, 150
Campbell, Lady Jean, 54
Campbell's tomato soup, hoarded by
Beaverbrook, 52
Canadian Red Indians, 231
Canary Wharf, London E.14, 243,
248
Cap d'Ail, S. of France, 44
Cardiff University, 3
Cardiff, Glamorgan, 24, 213, 226
Cardington, Beds, RAF station, 35
Carlton, Ann, 141
Carlyle, T., 244
Carmarthen, 8, 21
Carmarthenshire County Council, 25
Carmelite Street, London E.C.4, 223
Carreg Cennen castle,
Carmarthenshire, 23
Carrington, Lord, 135
Carron, William, 118, 119, 165
Carvel, Robert, 82
Casey, John, 190, 191
'Cassandra' (*Daily Mirror*). See
Connor
Cassells, publishers, 149
Castle Diaries, 92n, 125n
Castle, Barbara, Lady, 89, 90;
decides to reform industrial
relations, and is given lunch by
A.W., 91; does not enjoy occasion,
92; 101, 121, 122, 123; on C.
Forte's yacht, 124; 141
Castle, Stephen, 242
Castle, Ted, Lord, 91, 124
Cater, Douglass, 164, 165
Central African Office, 60
Central Park, N.Y., 50
Chalfont, Lord, 101-2, 221
Chancellor, Alexander, 149, 150,
222, 237
Chancellors (Dell), 197n
Chancery Lane, London W.C.2, 118,
172
Charles, Prince of Wales, 183; FO

briefs him against D. Trelford, 199
Chattering classes, origins of phrase,
191
Chelsea, C.C. O'Brien's houseboat
in, 173
Cheltenham Ladies' College, 249
Chertsey, Surrey, 99, 127, 145
Chesterton Road, Cambridge, 34
Chesterton, G.K., 220
Chivers, Cambridge, 35
Christiansen, Arthur, 119
Christiansen, Michael, 115, 116,
119, 121, 122, 123
Christie, Agatha, 94
Church Times, 254
Churchill, Randolph, 66, 70, 93
Churchill, Sir Winston, 3, 10, 150,
169
City of London girls' school, 113
City Road, London E.C.1, 236, 239,
243
Clark, Douglas, 45, 60
Cleaver, W.B., 215
Cluff, J.G. ('Algy'), 222
Coach and Horses, London W.1, 113
Coady, Matthew, 86, 87
Cockett, Richard, 160n, 163 & n,
165n, 174n, 175n, 176
Cockpit, St Andrew's Hill, 171
Cohen, Nick, 239
Cole, G.D.H., 26
Cole, John, 152, 153; relations with
A.W., 165-8; 170, 171, 173; wants
to thank J. Callaghan, 174;
persuades C.C. O'Brien to support
him, 175 & n; opposes sale to
Lonrho, 177; offered job by BBC,
180; 249
Coleman Street, City of London, 34
Coleman, Terry, 139
Collected and Recollected Marc (ed.
Amory), 31n
Colonial Office, 73
Colony Room, Dean Street, London
W.1, 112
Columbia University, N.Y., 51
Combe Florey, Somerset, 88
Common Market, 56, 106, 108, 112,

145, 157
Communism, in miners' union, 23
Communist Party, 205
Compton, Denis, 55, 153
Conan Doyle, A., 27
Connolly, Cyril, 95, 113
Connor, William, 127
Conservative Central Office, 82, 83,
   106
Conservative Coup (Watkins), 233,
   247
Conservative Party, 70, 73
Constable, publishers, 23
Contempt of Parliament, 41
Cooper, Lady Diana, 96
Cornwell, John, 162
Cosgrave, Patrick, 150-1
Council of Europe, 157
Council of Legal Education, 36
Country Life, 222
County Hall, London S.E.1, 143
Courtauld, Simon, 66n, 149n, 222,
   223, 224
Cousins, Frank, 118, 119
Coventry E., constituency, 100
Cradock, Sir Percy, 232
Creevey, Thomas, 251
Creighton, Harry, 150, 151
Crewe, Quentin, 119
Crick, Bernard, 40
Crick, Michael, 203
Critchley, Sir Julian, 87
Crompton, Richmal, 27
Cropredy, nr Banbury, 109
Crosland, C.A.R., 22; at Cambridge
   U. Labour Club, 27; P. Jenkins
   bases play on, 33; 73; polite to
   waiters, 74; mistaken for Tory by
   E. Waugh, and unrequited love
   for the Labour Party, 75; 89, 98,
   124; interviewed by A.W., 139;
   asks to see copy, 140; D. Lipsey
   demands changes, 141; A.W.
   refuses, 141; 144, 156; says
   Observer is 'our bible', 174; 194
Crosland, Susan. *See* Barnes
'Crossbencher' column, 43, 45, 56-7,
   59

Crossman (Howard), 99n, 100n,
   110n, 221n
Crossman Diaries, published, 99n,
   124n; unpublished, 103n, 104n,
   105n
Crossman, Anne, 124
Crossman, R.H.S., ix, 3, 22, 26, 27;
   converts T. Dalyell to Socialism,
   28; 61, 71, 73, 89, 90, 91, 98; as
   editor of *NS*, 99-100; continues as
   MP, 100-1; predilection for
   conferences, 101; relations with
   A.W., 103-5; and Europe, 107-8;
   and Royal Family, 107; dismissal,
   109-10; boorish to *NS* staff,
   109-10; succession, 110-11; 120,
   123; on C. Forte's yacht, 124; 132,
   203, 221, 249
Crossman-Padley compromise, 203
Crowley, Aleister, 114
'Crust, Venetia', 144
Cudlipp, Hugh, Lord, 86, 87, 99, 115,
   120, 122, 127, 128, 254
Cuningham, George, and devolution
   amendment, 174
Cunningham, J.D., 219
Curzon, George, Lord, 47

D Notice Affair (Hedley and
   Aynsley), 82n
D Notice affair, ix, 77-82
Dacre, Paul, 46
Dacre, Peter, 46
Daily Express, 30, 42, 44, 51, 53, 54,
   59, 77, 80, 82, 97, 98, 114, 115,
   117, 118, 119, 134
Daily Herald, 23, 42, 86, 120, 128
Daily Mail, 2, 51, 56, 61, 95, 115,
   132, 133, 134, 161, 162, 163, 165
Daily Mirror Newspapers, 86, 127
Daily Mirror, 23, 42, 86, 87, 91, 99,
   117, 118, 120, 122, 128
Daily Sketch, 51, 115
Daily Telegraph, 1, 2, 86, 105-6, 135,
   149, 190
Daily Worker, 23
'Dalrymple, Dr Thomas', 256
Dalton, Hugh, Lord, 75

Dalyell, Tam, 28, 29
Daniels, Anthony, 256
Dartmouth College, Connecticut, 185
Davenport, John, 160
David Astor and The Observer
  (Cockett), 160n, 163n, 165n, 174n,
  175n
Davie, Michael, 168, 184
Davies, Gerald, 24, 214, 229, 230
Davies, Glyn, 215
Davies, Harold, Lord, 123
Davies, Heddwyn, 216
Davies, Howard, 216
Davies, John, 104
Davies, Mair, 216
Davies, Mrs Denzil. *See* Carlton
Davies, Russell, 238
Davy's wine bar, Hatton Garden, 121
Dawes, John, 220
Day, Sir Robin, 87, 169
de Gaulle, Charles, 157, 160
de Hoghton, Sir Anthony, 31, 32
de Montherlant, Henry, 160
de Quetteville, Hugh, 111
Deauville, Normandy, 146
Deedes, William, Lord, sayings of,
  135; 148, 223
Defeat in the West (Shulman), 137
Defoe, Daniel, 239
Delargy, Hugh, 123
Dell, Edmund, 197
Department of Education and
  Science, 205
Descartes, R., 23
Deterding, Olga, 163
Deutsch, André, 191
Devlin, Patrick, Lord, 37
Dew, Brenda, 59
Diana, Princess of Wales, 183
Dimbleby lecture by R. Jenkins, 108
Dimbleby, Jonathan, 144
Dinsdale, Dick, 117, 128
Docklands Light Railway, 248
Docklands, London, 243
Doge of Dover (Raymond), 93
Doughty Street, London W.C.1, 69,
  92
Douglas, Isle of Man, 165

Douglas-Home, Alec. *See* Home
Douglas-Home, Robin, 119
Dover, Kent, 10
Down and Out in Paris and London
  (Orwell), 26
Downing Street, 198
Doyle, Jack, 219
Driberg, Tom, 112-14, 239
du Cann, Sir Edward, 187-8; tries to
  get rid of A. Howard, 188
Dubai, Ruler of, 231
Dubious Codicil (Wharton), 147n
Dumas, A., 13
Duncan-Sandys, Lord. *See* Sandys
Dundee W., constituency, 3
Dunfermline, Scotland, 236
Dunn, Lady, 53
Dunn, Sir James, 53
Duxford, Cambs, RAF station, 36
Dwyfor. *See* Lord George
Dyfed County Council, 20
Dynevor, Lord, 7, 17, 18; and V.
  Powell, 196

East Bergholt, Suffolk, 66
East Lynne (Wood), 47, 48
Eaton Square, London S.W.1, 110,
  137, 138, 145, 146
Economist Intelligence Unit, 40
Economist, 138
Eddington, Paul, 33
Edelman, Maurice, 26, 89
Edinburgh E., constituency, 3
Editorial Board of *New Statesman*,
  non-existence of, 90
Edwards, Mike, 122
Edwards, Robert, 44 & n
El Vino's, Fleet Street, 2, 46, 85, 88,
  92-8, 109, 118, 121, 131, 134;
  referred to by Beaverbrook as 'El
  Vino's public house', 135; 152-3,
  232, 246
El Vino's, New Bridge Street,
  London E.C.4, 185
Elizabeth II, Queen, 43
Ely, Isle of, constituency, 231
Empire News, 115
Encounter, 122

Engel, Matthew, moves into flat
above A.W.'s, 147
England's on the Anvil (Raymond),
93
English Constitution (Bagehot), 61
English, Sir David, and giant
Peruvian earthworm, 51-2
'Establishment, The', 63
Eton College, 42, 102
Evans, Harold, 88, 104
Evans, Peter, 119
Evans, Trevor, 166
Evening Standard, 40, 42, 44, 65, 82,
132; A.W. writes column in, 138;
covers October 1974 election TV
for, 136; S. Jenkins edits, 138;
under C. Wintour, A.W.
relinquishes column, 143
Everyman's Library, 12, 23
Express Newspapers, 3, 132
External Development Services, 231

Fabian Society, 40
Fairlie, Henry, 25, 26, 36, 37;
described, 61-4; flees to
Washington, 63; and Lady
Antonia Fraser, 63-4; and Inland
Revenue, 64; 65, 74, 85, 93, 97, 98
Fairlie, Lisette, 63
Falkender, Lady. *See* Williams, M.
Farouk, King, 97
Fawkes, Wally, 184
Fay, Stephen, 149, 251
Fayed, Mohamed, 183, 186, 200
Fenby, Charles, 235
Fenby, Jonathan, becomes editor of
Observer, 235; refuses to pay
A.W. more, 236; A.W. leaves for
Independent on Sunday, 236; is
annoyed, 237; 238, 239, 256
Fenton, James, 112, 136, 144
Fetter Lane, London E.C.4, 2, 46, 93,
118
Field, A.W. rugby column in, 222-4
Fielding, Henry, 40n
Financial Times, 33, 34, 61, 65; A.W.
has brief flirtation with, 85
First World War, 7, 10

Fits and Starts (Richardson), 93
Flashman, in *Tom Brown's
Schooldays* and *Daily Mirror*,
112-18
Fleet Street, London E.C.4, 2, 4, 30,
42, 46, 48, 79, 93, 94, 95, 105,
118, 122, 131, 133, 134, 237
Fletcher, Kim, 255-6
Foley, Maurice, 91
Foot, Jill, 180
Foot, Michael, 44, 75, 89, 123, 157;
leader of Labour Party, 180; tells
A.W. he intends to contest but
neglects to inform P. Shore, 181;
criticised for laying of wreath at
Cenotaph, 181
Ford, Anna, 31
Foreign Office, briefs Prince Charles
against D. Trelford over Africa,
199
Forte, Charles, Lord, entertains
Castles and Crossmans on yacht,
124-5
Fortune, John, 85
Forum restaurant, Chancery Lane,
118
Fourteen-day rule, 25
Fox and Hounds, near Sloane
Square, 202
Fox, George, 239
Fraser, Lady Antonia, 63, 64
Frayn, Michael, 30
Freedom Under Foot (Beloff), 157
Freeman, John, 89
Frome, Somerset, A.W. visits A.
Powell in house near, 195
Frost, Sir David, 43
Fuller, J.F.C., 137
Future of Socialism (Crosland), 26,
74

Gaitskell, Hugh, 43, 62, 89, 203
Gale, George, 30, 63, 97, 150
Ganges restaurant, London W.1, 114
Gardner, Brian, 56
Gardner, Llew, 56
Garrick Club, 85, 120, 127
Gay Hussar restaurant, London

W.1, 44, 235, 237, 253
General Says No (Beloff), 157
George-Brown, Lord. *See* Brown
Geraldine House, off Fetter Lane (demolished), 118
Gibbon, Edward, 55
Gilmour, Ian, Lord, 3, 61; appoints I. Macleod editor of *Spectator*, 65; appoints N. Lawson, 73; relations with N. Lawson, 76; 145
Gino, from Café Royal, on C. Forte's yacht, 124
Girton College, Cambridge, 29
Glamorgan CCC, 13
Glasgow Herald, 82
Glaspant, Gorslas, 16
Glenamara. *See* Short
Glover, Stephen, 224, 238 & n
Glover, Stephen, 60n, 64
Glover, Tim, 226, 254
Glyn, Elinor, 47, 48
Goalen, Barbara, 87
God Stand Up For Bastards (Leitch), 249
Goldsmith, Sir James, and *Observer*, 163
Gonville and Caius College, Cambridge, 190
Goodbye Baby and Amen (Bailey and Evans), 119
Goodbye Fleet Street (Edwards), 44n
Goodlad, Lady. *See* Hurst
Goodman, Arnold, Lord, 106 & n, 161, 164, 165; stays on *Observer* board, 170; threatens to resign if K. Harris made vice-chairman, 175; votes against, 176; opposes sale to Lonrho, 177, 178; resigns from *Observer* board, 179
Goodman, Derrick, 106, 164
Gordon Walker, Patrick, 221
Gordon's gin, specified by T. Kilmartin, 160
Gorslas, Carmarthenshire, 6, 15, 17
Gower Street, London W.C.1, 69, 71, 92
Gowrie, Grey, Lord, 88
Gramophone Room, Cambridge

Union, 27
Granada television, 162
Grant, Donald, 169
Granta, Cambridge U. magazine, 31; and later version, 238
Gray's Inn Road, London W.C.1, 155
Gray's Inn, 3, 218, 219
Great and the Good (Heward), 82n
Great Turnstile, London W.C.2, 92, 96, 111, 116, 117, 250
Greene, Graham, 31n, 209, 235
Greene, Hugh, 31n, 72
Greer, Germaine, 194, 249
Gregsten, Michael, 142
Griffith, John, 40
Griffiths, Jim, 10, 35, 217
Griggs, Barbara, 134
Grimond, Grizelda, 88
Grimond, Jo, Lord, 223
Grizzard, Joe, 121-3
Grove, Valerie, 134
Grub Street, original, 239
Guardian, ix, 33, 42, 76, 97, 98, 112, 120, 147; takes over *Observer*, 211-12
Guest, R.H., 213, 214
Gunnell, Barbara, 240
Gwendraeth Grammar School, 15
Gwynne Jones, Alun. *See* Chalfont

Hailsham, Lord. *See* Hogg
Hain, Peter, 230
Haldane, R.B., Lord, 169
Haley, Sir William, 194
Hall, N.M., 215
Hall, Phillip, 107
Hall, Sir Peter, 30
Hamilton, Adrian, 203, 211, 236
Hamilton, Iain, 65
Hamilton, Neil, 201
Hammerskjold, Dag, 56
Hammond, Walter, 62
Hampshire N.W., constituency, 93
Handel, G.F., 98
Hanratty, James, 142
Hansard, 247
Hardy, Thomas, 13
Hare, David, 33

Hargreaves, Ian, 1, 2, 254
Harlech television, 229
Harlequin FC, 218
Harley Street, 3
Harmsworth family, 165
Harris, Bernard, 43, 56
Harris, Edwin John, grandfather of
   A.W., 6, 15
Harris, Kenneth, 164; R.O.
   Anderson determined to advance
   him in *Observer*, 165; organises
   Observer-ARCO dinner, 170;
   rejected for vice-chairmanship,
   175; 176; writes Life of C.R.
   Attlee, 177; should in A.W.'s view
   have accommodated; associate
   editor till 1984, 180; 212
Harris, Lily, aunt of A.W., 15
Harris, Robert, 203-5, 206
Harris, Rose, aunt of A.W., 15, 16
Harris, Violet. *See* Watkins, Violet
Harris, W.Ll., 6
Harris, William, uncle of A.W., 15
Harrison, Roger, 161, 164
Harrison, Walter, 126
Harrods, origins of dispute between
   T. Rowland and M. Fayed, 201
Hartley, Richard, 208
Hartwell, Lord, 86
Hatch, John, Lord, 90
Hattersley, Roy, Lord, 105
Haughey, Charles, 170
Have Pen: Will Travel (Pringle), 158
Hazan, Sir John, 206, 208
Healey, Denis, Lord, 75, 136, 141,
   166, 167, 180
Health, Ministry of, 72
Healy, Tim, 49
Heaton, Jack, 213
Heath, Sir Edward, 69, 70, 83n, 125,
   150
Hedley, Peter, 82n
Heffer, Doris, 132
Heffer, Eric, 133, 166
Herne Hill, London, 220
Herodotus, 55
Hertford College, Oxford, 255
Heseltine, Michael, 71n

Hetherington, Alastair, 2, 112, 166
Heversham Grammar School,
   Westmorland, 255
Heward, Edmund, 82n
Hewitt, C.R. *See* Rolph
Hibbert Journal, 12
'Hickey, William' (*Daily Express*), 30
Hillmore, Peter, 191
Hilton, Michael, 148
Hinden, Rita, 41
Hinds, Alfred, Beaverbrook and C.
   Wintour, 134-5
Hitchens, Christopher, 112
Hobbes, Thomas, 23
Hoey, Iris, 97
Hoffman, Jerome, 126, 127
Hogg, Quintin, 45, 125, 197
Hoggart, Simon, 191, 203; advises
   A.W. to ask for more, 236
Holborn Circus, London, 118, 120,
   121
Holborn, London W.C.2, 92, 96, 122
Holland Park, London W.11, 108
Holland, Mary, dismissed by C.C.
   O'Brien, 171; 172, 173
Hollingworth, Clare, 156
Holmes, Barry, 218
Home, Lord, 57, 58, 59, 69, 70, 73,
   125, 223
Hooper, David, 206n
Hope, Francis, 102, 111
Hope, Michael, 102
Hope-Wallace, Philip, 63, 88, 93, 96,
   97-8, 246, 251
Hopkirk, Peter, 51, 53
Horner, Arthur, 23
House of Lords, 49, 125
Howard, Anthony, ix; becomes
   political correspondent of *New
   Statesman*, 26, 60n, 63; brings
   news of H. Fairlie, 64; 64n, 74,
   93, 98, 99n, 102; and R.
   Crossman, 103ff; 108; editor of
   NS, 111-12; and T. Driberg,
   113-14; 117; jealous editor, 133;
   coins nickname 'Chilly Charlie'
   for C. Wintour, 134; A.W. asks for
   more money, 150; refuses, 150;

acts as A.W.'s agent with
Observer, 151-2; 153, 156, 169;
appointed deputy editor of
Observer, 183; achievement at
Observer, 184; 185, 187, 188, 203,
205; goes after D. Trelford's job,
210; leaves *Observer*, 211; 221 &
n, 229, 239, 244, 249, 250, 251
Howe, Geoffrey, Lord, 91, 197, 227,
232
Howitt, Keith, 254
Hugo, Victor, 13
Hurd, Douglas, Lord, 28, 71n, 125
Hurd, Sir Anthony, Lord, 28
Hurman, Roland, 118-19
Hurst, Cecilia, 83
Hutchinson, George, 82-3, 153
Hutchinson, Harold, 129
Hutton, Will, 256

'Ideas and Beliefs of the Victorians'
(Third Programme), 25
Illuminations (Jenkins), 33
IMF crisis 1976, 161
Imperial Hotel, Blackpool, 109, 133
'In London Last Night' (*Evening
Standard*), 144
In Place of Fear (Bevan), 3, 91
In Place of Strife, 91, 121
Independent directors of *Observer*,
conditions of MMC consent, 179;
uphold D. Trelford against T.
Rowland, 199
Independent Newspapers, 117; bid
for *Observer*, 211; 242
Independent on Sunday, 67, 132, 189
& n; A.W. joins, 235ff.
Independent, ix, 1, 33, 132, 189; A.W.
writes rugby column in, 224
Ingham, Sir Bernard, 28, 196, 198
Ingrams, Richard, 113
Inland Revenue, and H. Fairlie, 64;
and M. Richardson, 94
Innes, Judy, 33
Inquiring Eye (Watt ed. Mount), 65n
Institute of Journalists, 109
Intermediate Education Act 1889, 15
International Publishing

Corporation, 119, 120, 128, 161
IPC Newspaper Division, 127
Irish Republic, 3
Irvine, Alexander, Lord, 111-12
Islington Borough Council, 21, 150,
220
Islington Health Authority, 207
Islington S. and Finsbury,
constituency, 174
Islington, London, 21, 145, 147, 222,
224, 254
Ivens, Mrs Martin. *See* McElvoy

Jack, Ian, 67, 236-40; resigns, 241;
243, 256
Jackson, Len, 118, 119
Jackson, Peter, 214
Jacobson, Sydney, 128
James, Clive, on R. Murdoch as
gorilla, 162; 194
James, Carwyn, 230
James, Russell, 18
Jaspan, Andrew, 239, 256
Jay, Peter, 111
Jenkins, Aneurin, 214, 215
Jenkins, Dr, of Ammanford, 16
Jenkins, Peter, 30, 32, 33, 65, 205
Jenkins, Roy, Lord, 15, 72, 75, 107,
108, 123, 141; admired by M.
Thatcher, 197; and *Observer*, 211
Jenkins, Simon, gifted writer, 138; J.
Junor on, 138-9; edits *Evening
Standard* and *Times*, 138; 143
Jenkins, Valerie. *See* Grove
John O'London's, 95
John, Barry, 15, 230
Johnson, Frank, moves into floor
below A.W.'s, 147; career, 148;
162; uses 'chattering classes' in
conversation, 192; makes
pilgrimages to M. Muggeridge
with A.W., 192; 224, 253
Johnson, Paul, presides over largest
circulation of *New Statesman*, 26;
63, 86; asks A.W. to join *NS*, 87;
tolerant as editor, 89; liking for
political heroes, 90; supports B.
Castle on industrial relations, 91;

93, 97, 98, 99; note on editorship of *NS*, 100 & n, 102, 111, 116, 117, 132, 199, 221
Johnson, Samuel, 207
Jonathan Wild (Fielding), 40
Jones, David (Blaina), 215, 216
Jones, David, 220, 223
Jones, Grenville, 217, 230-2
Jones, Ken, journalist, 254
Jones, Ken, rugby player, 227
Jones, Lewis. *See* Jones, David
Joyce, James, 242
Junor, Sir John, elections fought, 3; A.W. meets, 41; 42, 43; bullies A. Brittenden, 44-5; maxims, 46; 47, 49, 55, 56; falls out with Beaverbrook, 57; falls out with A.W. over attack on A. Nutting, 60; generally, 41-9; discourages A.W. from joining *Spectator*, 66; 112, 127; on S. Jenkins, 138-9; 159, 199, 249
Jurby, Isle of Man, RAF station, 36
Justice and Administrative Law (Robson), 39
Jutland, Battle of, 7

Kagan, Joseph, Lord, 33
Kaufman, Gerald, 43, 74, 86
Kaunda, Kenneth, 200
Kavanagh, Pat, 88
Keats, J., 15
Keeble, Harold, 147
Keegan, Sir John, 83n
Keegan, William, 185, 202, 203
Keeler, Christine, 87
Kelner, Simon, 254
Kennedy, J.F., 53, 92; administration, 140
Kenny, Mary, 134, 143, 144, 145
Kernon, A.P., 104, 105
Keswick, Henry, 53
Keynes, J.M., Lord, 13
Khrushchev, N., 53
Kidwelly, Carmarthenshire, 24
Kilmartin, Joanna, 160-1
Kilmartin, Terence, 93, 94, 98; described, 159-61; 171, 173;

refuses to thank J. Callaghan, 174; 183, 185; and Young Fogeys, 190, 191; 256
King & Keys, Fleet Street, a hellhole, 147-8
King, Cecil H., 120, 122
King's College, Cambridge, 29, 31, 189
Kinnock, Neil, 190, 205, 206
Klemperer, Otto, 10
Knight, Victor, 59
Krug champagne, purchased for R. Crossman's convalescence by A.W. on behalf of NUJ at *NS*, 109

Labour Party, 40, 43
Labour, Ministry of, 73
Lamb, Sir Larry, 128
Lampeter, University of Wales, A.W. becomes Hon Fellow of, 23
Lancaster, Sir Osbert, 147
Laski, H.J., 26
'Last Word' (Arnold), 179n
Late Show, 72, 116
Law Society, 142
Law, A. Bonar, 53
Lawry, Bill, 66
Lawson, Nigel, Lord, 3; becomes editor of *Spectator*, 73; relations with I. Gilmour, and reinstates editorial conference, 76; inclined to dilatoriness, 77; accuses A.W. of misleading him over D Notices, 79; appears before Lord Radcliffe, 79-82; A.W. proud of his and N.L.'s part in D Notice affair; discourages A.W. from joining *NS*, 87; 238
Legge, Mrs Gerald. *See* Lewisham
Legum, Colin, 200
Leitch, David, 249-50
Lejeune, C.A., 24
Leominster, constituency, 231
L'Epicure restaurant, Frith Street, London W.1, 66, 91, 98, 99n, 118
Lever, Diane, 145
Lever, Harold, Lord, 145-6; advises A.W. on borrowing money, 146

Levin, Bernard, 26, 61, 65
Levy, Phillip, 127
Lewes, Sussex, 63
Lewis, Wyndham, 25
Lewisham, Lady, 143
'Liberace' libel case, 127
Liberal Dilemma (Watkins), 58n
Liberal Party, 58
Lib-Lab pact, 169
Liddell Hart, Sir B.H., 137
Life of Politics (Fairlie), 63
Lim, Madeleine, 237
Lime Grove television studios, 167
Lincoln's Inn Fields, London W.C.2, 92, 116
Lincoln's Inn, ix, 3, 36, 116, 169, 170
Lindsay-Smith, Iain, 177
Lipsey, David, Lord, 141
Listener, 24, 25
Little Nut-Brown Man (Vines), 57 & 58n
Little Pot of Money (Gillard), 127
Liverpool Street station, 39
Llandeilo County School, 15, 16
Llandeilo, Carmarthenshire, 7, 15, 17, 23; and V. Powell, 196
Llandrindod Wells County School, 231
Llandybie, Carmarthenshire, 17, 20
Llanedi School, Carmarthenshire, 12, 13
Llanelli County School for Boys, 7, 9
Llanelli RFC, 11
Llanelli, Carmarthenshire, 8
Llangadog, Carmarthenshire, 226
Lloyd George, David, 19, 53, 96
Lloyd, Selwyn, 78, 81
Lloyd's List, edited by I. Lindsay-Smith, 177
Lloyd-Davies, Hugh, victory international 1946, 213-14; dropped from Welsh side, 216; in RAF, 217; at Trinity Hall, Cambridge, 217; snobbery of, 217; wins 1947 university match, 218; cheeks proctor, 218; sent down, 218; joins Gray's Inn, 218; joins Rugby League, 219; goes to

prison, 219; dies, 220; 227, 231
Lloyd-Hughes, Sir Trevor, 204
Locke, J., 23
Lohan, L.G., 78, 80, 81
London College of Printing, 149
London Library, 95, 96
London School of Economics and Political Science, A.W. research assistant at, 39; 40, 42, 75
London Weekend Television, 161
London Welsh RFC, 11, 14, 218, 220, 232
Longford, Frank, Lord, 221
Loughor Valley, Carmarthenshire, 8
Lonrho, 175, 176; meagre newspaper ownership, 178; leaves A.W. alone, 186
Lord Goodman (Brivati), 106, 163n, 165n, 175n
Loren, Sophia, 87
Lorna Doone (Blackmore), 47
Low, Robert, ix, 211-12
Lowell, J.R., 15
Lowell, Robert, 150
Lowrie, Henry, 54, 55
Lowry, Suzanne, 190
Lucie, Doug, 131
Ludgate Circus, London E.C.4, 153
Ludlow, 'Lobby', 53
Lyceum, London W.C.2, 95
Lynd, Robert, 24
Lyric theatre, Hammersmith, 33
Luna Hotel, Venice, 251
Le Monde, 254

Macaulay, T., 15, 55
Mackintosh, John P., 74
Macleod, Iain, 2, 4, 46; feared by H. Wilson, 59; becomes editor of *Spectator*, 65; hires A.W., 66; avoids discussions, 68-9; his row with A.W. about dinner jackets, 69; and 1965 election for leader, 70-1; as writer, 72; coins 'nanny state', 73; threw away D Notices, 79; 125, 220
Macmillan, Harold, 53, 57, 59, 62, 83n, 125

Maguire, Frank, abstains in person, 174
Major, John, 28, 34, 122, 200
Makins, Clifford, 222
Mallalieu, J.P.W., 26, 48, 221
Malraux, André, 160
Manchester Grammar School, 123
Manchester Guardian. See Guardian
Mandela, Nelson, 231
Mandelson, Peter, 68, 205, 206
Mapp, Charles, 60n
'Marc'. *See* Boxer
Margach, James, 59, 61, 82
Margaret, Princess, 43
Maria Luigi II, C. Forte's yacht, 124
Marks, Derek, 57, 63, 98, 118
Marks, Laurence, 184
Marnham, Patrick, 113
Marquand, David, 65, 74
Marr, Andrew, 254
Marshall, Alfred, 13
Marshall, Arthur, 112
Marshall, J.S., 178
Marten, Neil, 106
Martin, Kingsley, 71, 89, 96, 97; memorandum to board of *NS* about R. Crossman, 99-100; 101, 132
Marylebone County Court, 220
Massingham, Hugh, 25, 61, 62, 156
Matabeleland, and D. Trelford, 198-9
Matatu, Godwin, 200
Matthews, Jack, 215
Maudling, Beryl, 126
Maudling, Reginald, 47, 70, 71; corruption of, 125; attacked in *Sunday Mirror* by A.W. for connection with J. Hoffman and Real Estate Fund of America, 126-7; sues A.W., 127; 128
Maupassant, G., 13
Maxwell, Robert, 126, 163, 199
'May We Borrow your Husband?' (Greene), 235
Maycock, Isabel, 239
McAlpine, Alistair, Lord, on Mark Thatcher, 187
McCarthy, Mary, 97

McCartney, Hugh, 82
McDowell, Keith, 166
McElvoy, Anne, 253; fails to succeed R. Boycott, 255
McEwen, John, 223
McIlvanney, Hugh, 237
Meacher v. *Trelford and Others*, 2, 143, 206-10
Meacher, Michael, 31n, 206-10
Médoc, S.W. France, 228
Mee, Bertie, 139
Melbourne Age, M. Davie edits, 168
Melchett, Lady, 164
Memoir (O'Brien), 170n, 171n, 172n, 175n, 176n, 177n, 186n
Men and Power (Beaverbrook), 55
Merlyn-Rees, Lord. *See* Rees
Metropole Hotel, Brighton, 188
Michael, Mary, 217
Michaelson, Roger, 220
Miller, Jonathan, 30, 89
Miller, Karl, 30, 111
Millinship, William, 210
Milton, J., 15
Mirror Magazine, 117
Mirror newspapers, 242
'Mirrorscope' (*Daily Mirror*), 86, 128
Mitchell, Christopher, 93, 121
Mitchell, Sir David, 93
Moby Dick (Melville), 23
Modern Records Centre, U. of Warwick, ix
Moi, Daniel, 200
Monckton, Lionel, 16
Moncrieff, Scott, 160
Monopolies and Mergers Commission, 177; qualified approval for *Observer* sale to Lonrho, 179; 200
Montego Bay, Jamaica, 44, 54
Montgomerie, John, 106
Montgomery, David, 242, 243, 249, 252
Montpelier Row, Twickenham, 232
Monty Python, 33, 121
Mooney, Bel, 144
Mooney's, Fleet Street, 46
Moonman, Eric, 207, 210

Moore, Charles, 135, 189
Moore, Dorothy, 34
Moore, G.E., 34, 35
Moore, T. Sturge, 35
Morgan, Jack, 104, 250
Morgan, Mary, 226
Morgan, W. John, 111, 226, 228-30
Morrell, Nick, 188, 210
Morris, John, 28
Morrison, Blake, 243, 244
Morrison, Herbert, Lord, 107
Morriston hospital, Swansea, 20
Morriston, Glamorgan, 229, 230
Mortimer, Sir John, 139
Mortimer, Sir Raymond, 95
Mount, Ferdinand, 65 & n
Mount, Julia, ix
Mugabe, Robert, and D. Trelford,
     198-9
Muggeridge, Kitty, 1, 63. 192, 193,
     195
Muggeridge, Malcolm, predicts
     extinction of A.W., 1; offered jobs
     despite drunkenness and lechery,
     2; charming Cold Warrior, 27;
     surprised A.W. never worked at
     Guardian, 42; 63; horror of
     abstract argument, 112;
     photographed by D. Bailey, 119;
     befriended by H. Cudlipp, 120;
     visited by F. Johnson and A.W.,
     192; substantial diet, 193; on A.
     Bevan, 193; imitates Sir W.
     Haley, G. Greer and C. James,
     194; falling out with A. Powell,
     194-5; 208
Mull, Isle of, 59
Murdoch, Rupert, 86, 117, 128; and
     Observer, 161, 162, 163, 164, 165;
     177
Muriel's. *See* Colony Room
Music of Time (Powell), 26, 195
My Learned Friends (Raphael), 206n

'Nanny state', origins of phrase, 73
Nap, A.W.'s dog, 18
National Coal Board, 166
National Executive Committee,

Labour Party, 166
National Union of Journalists, 42,
     109, 110n; *Observer*, and M.
     Holland, 172
*Nationalised Industries and Public
     Ownership* (Robson), 39
NATSOPA, 246
Ndebele tribe, D. Trelford reports
     ill-usage of, 198-9
Nelson, H.I., 219
Nener, Jack, 117, 128
New Bridge Street, London E.C.4,
     152-3, 155, 223
New College, Oxford, 94, 149
New Printing House Square, London
     E.C.4 and subsequently London
     W.C.1, 155
New Republic, 64
New Statesman, 3, 26, 36, 85, 86;
     A.W. joins, 87; 89, 93, 95, 96, 101,
     102, 105, 109, 110, 112, 115, 116,
     117, 121, 122, 123, 132, 133, 136;
     1950s profiles, 139; A.W. resigns
     from, 150
New York Review of Books, 109
New York, 42 & n; A.W. in, 49ff.
New Zealand *v.* Wales, Cardiff 1953,
     227; British Isles tour of 1977, 228
Newham S., constituency, 29
Newman, Paul, 254
News Chronicle, 23, 24, 102, 115
News International, 162
Newsnight, 203
Newton, Sir Gordon, 85, 86
Nice Girl Like Me (Boycott), 249
Nicholas Tomalin Reporting
     (Tomalin), 30n, 31n
Nicholson, Geoffrey, 226, 230
Nicholson, Mavis, 226
Nicolson, Rebecca, 255-6
Nicolson, Sir Harold, 95
Night and Day, 209
Nightingale, Benedict, 111
Nineteen Eighty-Four (Orwell), 26
Not So Much a Programme, 43
Nutting, Anthony, 60

O'Brien, Conor Cruise, 3; becomes

editor-in-chief, *Observer*, 170;
A.W. welcomes appointment but
has row over dismissal of Mary
Holland, 171; questioned by A.W.
before NUJ, 172; calls A.W.
'Vishinsky', 173; drinking habits,
173; would have voted for M.
Thatcher, 173; but agrees to
Observer's backing J. Callaghan,
175 & n, claims K. Harris as
vice-chairman would have
controlled editorial policy, 176;
sympathises with K. Harris, 177
& n; opposes sale to Lonrho, 177;
Lonrho attempts to get rid of,
184; Lonrho succeeds, 185; 186n,
190

O'Donovan, Patrick, 153, 160

O'Hagan, Simon, 254

O'Reilly, Tony, 241, 242

O'Sullivan, John, 148

Oakeshott, Michael, 194

Obank, K.P., explains mortgage to
D. Astor, 158; is mean over
expenses, 159

Oborne, Peter, 60n, 74n

Observer, ix, 2, 3, 24, 42, 61, 62, 85,
94, 95, 102, 104, 112, 114; easier
to write for Sunday paper, 136;
1940s profiles, 139; A.W. joins,
151-2; moves to St Andrew's Hill,
155; Foreign News Service, 160;
1975, decision to sell, 161; ARCO
dinner, 170; sold to Lonrho,
175-9, 190; bid for, by
Independent Newspapers, 211;
taken over by *Guardian*, 212;
A.W. leaves for *Independent on
Sunday*, 235ff.

Odhams Press, 128

Official Secrets Acts, 77, 79, 82

Old Bailey, London E.C., 82

Oldham, Lancs, 60

Opel cars, 18

Orpington by-election, 158

Orton, Joe, 117

Orwell, George, A.W. orders his
books from Ammanford library, 26

Oundle School, 133

Outram, George, print arm of
Lonrho, 175; owner of *Glasgow
Herald*, 178; acquires *Observer*,
179

Owen, David, Lord, 74; highly
regarded by M. Thatcher, 197

Oxford Union Society, 75, 165

Padley, Walter, 203

Page, Bruce, 111, 112

Pakenham. *See* Longford

Pall Mall Gazette, 139

Pall Mall, London S.W.1, 232

Pantyffynnon, Carmarthenshire, 7

Paper Dreams (Glover), 238n

Parcyrhun school, Ammanford, 10,
12

Parliamentary Labour Party, 101

Parnell, C.S., 49

Parson's Green Lane, London S.W.6,
50

Parsons, George, 215

Paterson, Peter, 90, 91, 122, 136,
144, 168, 223

Patrick, Victor, 55, 56

Paynter, Will, 23

Peacock, Ted, 250

Pearce, Joanna. *See* Kilmartin

Pearson, Allison, 239

Peart, Fred, Lord, 152

Peers, Donald, 15

Pembroke Hotel, Blackpool, 188

Pembrokeshire, 12

'Pendennis' (*Observer*), 164, 191

Penybanc, Carmarthenshire, 7

Penygarn Road, Tycroes, 5

People, 44

Pepinster, Catherine, 255

Pepsi-Cola, punitive drink of J.
Junor, 45

'Peterborough' (*Daily Telegraph*),
A.W. threatens to sue, 105-6

Peterhouse, Cambridge, 97, 133,
150, 151

Picasso, 94

Pickering, Sir Edward, 127, 147

Pillman, C.H., 12

Pincher, Chapman, 77
Pinter, Lady Antonia. *See* Fraser
Pitman, Robert, 44, 48, 55, 119
Political Quarterly, 122
Ponthenry, Carmarthenshire, 6
Pontyberem, Carmarthenshire, 6
Porter, Henry, 251
Portland Place, London W.1, 164
Potter, Jeremy, 221
Poulson, John, 126
Powell Journals, 210n
Powell, Anthony, 1; A.W. orders his
    books from Ammanford library,
    26; and A. Waugh, 88-9; 194;
    A.W. visits him, 195; gives
    different account from A.
    Muggeridge of falling out, 195;
    regarded himself as Welsh, 195;
    information on 1950s literary
    London, 195; on Meacher case,
    209-10
Powell, Dilys, 24
Powell, Enoch, 65, 70
Powell, Lady Violet, 195-6, 209
Praga, Anthony, 47
Prayer Book, 190
Press Complaints Commission, 76
Press Council. *See* Press Complaints
    Commission
Preston, Peter, 112, 166, 212, 236,
    237
Price, Christopher, 144
Priggen, Mick, 210
Pringle, J.D., 158n
Printing House Square, London
    E.C.4, 155
Prior, Jim, Lord, 92
Pritchett, Sir V.S., 95
Private Eye, 113, 144, 256
Privileges, Committee of, 41, 247
Profumo affair, 87
Proskairon, Tycroes, 5, 18
Proust, Marcel, 113, 160, 161
Public Record Office, Fetter Lane
    (defunct), 118
Pugh, Jo, 255
Punch, 2; under M. Muggeridge, 195
Pyrenees, 161

Queen Victoria Street, London
    E.C.4, 152, 224
Queens' College, Cambridge, A.W.
    gains admission to, 25
Quennell, Sir Peter, 31n
Question of Upbringing (Powell), 26
'Quoodle' (*Spectator*), 71, 73n, 220

RAB (Howard), 60n
Radcliffe, Cyril, Lord, ix, 78;
    questions N. Lawson and A.W.,
    79-82
Randall, David, 212
Rapallo, Italy, 24
Raphael, Adam, 156; opposes sale to
    Lonrho, 177, 203, 204, 206n, 245
Raven, Simon, 25
Raymond, Beaverbrook's brother, 53,
    54
Raymond, Cyril, 97
Raymond, John, 63, 85, 93, 95-7, 98
Rea, Chris, 254
Real Estate Fund of America, 126
Red Lion, Carter Lane, London
    E.C.4, 171
Redhead, Brian, 30
Rees, Merlyn, 166, 167
Reid, Charles, 256
Reid, Stuart, 255-6
Rennie, Jimmy, 212
Report of the Committee of Inquiry
    into D Notice Matters, 82n
Report on Rugby (Nicholson and
    Morgan), 230
Reputations Under Fire (Hooper),
    206n
Reynolds News, 42, 115, 239
Rhondda, Lady, 247
Rhôs colliery, Tycroes, 7
Rice-Davies, Mandy, 87
Richardson, John, 94 & n
Richardson, Maurice, 93-5, 98, 113
Richmond and Twickenham Fabian
    Society, 231
Richmond, Surrey, 232
Rieck, Barbara, 239
Ringer, Paul, 229
Rippon, Geoffrey, Lord, 104

Road to Number 10 (Watkins), 105n, 135n, 247

Robens, Alfred, Lord, J. Cole's scoop about, 166

Robertsbridge, Sussex, 1, 63, 192

Robson, W.A., 39, 42

Rochester and Chatham, constituency, 87

Rockefeller Center, N.Y., 51, 243

Rodger, Bill, 85

Rolph, C.H., 99

'Rorke's Drift' (Butler), 210

Rosé wine, and J. Junor, 45

Rothermere, 2nd Lord, 197

Rothwell, Bruce, 162

Routledge, Paul, 239, 242, 251

Rowland, R.W., ix, 163, 176, 177; hated in both parties, 178; 180; sole communication to A.W., 186; quarrel with D. Trelford over R. Mugabe, 198-9; makes up, 199; supports D. Trelford, 210; relinquishes *Observer*, 211; sells to *Guardian*, 212

Royal Air Force, A.W. does national service in, 35-6

Royal Courts of Justice, 2, 3

Royal Family, disliked by Beaverbrook, 43; and R. Crossman, 107

Royal Hotel, Cardiff, 214

Royal Linen Bank, Belfast, 94

Rugby Football Union, 225

Rule's restaurant, Maiden Lane, London W.C.2, 164

Rupert Murdoch (Shawcross), 163n

Rusk, Dean, 86

Russell, Bertrand, Lord, 27, 35

Ryan, Richard, 242

Salmon, Cyril, Lord, 32

Samuel, Jeffrey, 14

Sandys, Duncan, 60, 157

Saracens RFC, 220

Sayigh, Rosemary, 31n

Scarlet Letter (Hawthorne), 47

Scarsdale, N.Y., 51

Scilly, Isles of, 59

Scunthorpe, Lincs, 114

SDP, 196, 197, 205

Seagram drinks, 108

Sean, landlord of King & Keys, 147

Second World War, 10

Secrets of the Press (ed. Glover), 60n, 64

Selwyn-Lloyd, Lord. *See* Lloyd

Sendall, Wilfred, 43, 45, 82

Services Committee, Commons, 126

Shakespeare, W., 15

Shallow End (Lucie), 131

Sharpley, Anne, 134

Shaw, Bernard, 17, 23

Shawcross, William, 163 & n

Shell-Mex House, 78

Sherman, Sir Alfred, 194

Sherwood, Hugh, Lord, 58

Shinwell, Emanuel, Lord, 78

Shore, Peter, Lord, 180

Short, Edward, 240

Shortlands salt beef bar, Fetter Lane, 46

Shrimsley, Anthony, 162

Shulman, Milton, 134, 137-8; on sex and tennis, 138

Side-Steps (Davies and Morgan), 229 & n

Silkin, John, 180

Simenon, Georges, 93

Simmonds bookshop, Fleet Street, 2

'Simple, Peter' (*Daily Telegraph*), 93, 148

Simpson, Bobby, 66

Sisman, Adam, 46n

Skelton, Barbara, 97

Sky digital television, 247

Slight Case of Libel (Watkins), 3n, 206n, 209, 233

Slipman, Sue, 205

Sloane School, Chelsea, 44

Smith, Lorraine, 20

Smith, Stuart, 20

Smyth, Ted, 242

Snow, C.P., Lord, 26-7

Socialist Commentary, 41

Sorceror's Apprentice (Richardson), 94

'Souls, The', 96
South Kensington, London, 97
South Wales Borderers, 101, 210
South Wales Miners' Federation, 20
Spare Rib, 249
Sparrow, John, 229
Spearing, Nigel, 29
'Special issue' of *Observer* on
    Harrods, a mistake, 201
    Spectator, ix, 3, 25, 26, 33, 36, 42,
    60, 61, 62; A.W. joins, 64-7; 80,
    82, 85, 86, 95, 98, 112, 120, 135,
    149; A.W. offered political column
    by A. Chancellor, 151; A.W.
    diaries in, 189-90; defined by
    A.W. in A. Waugh action, 220-1
Spectrum: a Spectator Miscellany
    (ed. Gilmour and Hamilton), 62n
Spencer, Countess. *See* Lewisham
Spinoza, 23
Spitalgate, Lincs, RAF station, 36
Sportswriter's Eye (Watkins), 233
Spurling, Hilary, 76
St Andrew's Hill, Blackfriars,
    London E.C.4, 2, 155, 173, 177,
    203
St Andrew's-by-the-Wardrobe
    church, 155
St Catharine's College, Cambridge,
    231
St Clement Dane's church, 2
St Edmund's church, Tycroes, 14, 21
St Helen's Nursing Home, Swansea,
    17
St Helen's rugby ground, Swansea,
    13, 230
St John's College, Cambridge, 227
St Martin Ludgate church, 155
St Paul's Cathedral, 155
Star, 82
Statesman and Nation Publishing
    Co. Ltd, 116, 150
Stead, W.T., 139
Stephens, Rees, 215
Stevens, Jocelyn, 119
Stevens, Ron, 166
Stockton, Lord, *See* Macmillan
Stokes, John, 201

Stone, David, 144
Stop the Week, 137
Storie, Valerie, 142
Strachey, Charlotte, 33
Strachey, John, 32
Stradey Park, Llanelli, 11, 213
Strasbourg, 157
Stratford, E. London, 11
Street-Porter, Janet, becomes editor
    of *IoS*, 256
Streets Ahead (Waterhouse), 2, 116n
'Student of Politics' (*Sunday Times*),
    61
Study of Fishes (Pincher), 77
Summerskill, Edith, 14
Sun, 86, 115, 128
Sunday Dispatch, 51, 52, 115
Sunday Express, 2, 39, 41; A.W. at,
    42-60; 52, 56, 57, 66, 67, 82, 115,
    131
Sunday Graphic, 115
Sunday Mirror, 47, 59, 87; A.W.
    writes political column for, 115ff.,
    116, 119, 121, 122, 124, 126;
    settles with R. Maudling, 127;
    A.W. leaves, 129, 132
Sunday Pictorial, 120
Sunday Telegraph, 59, 68, 73, 77,
    83n, 122
Sunday Times Magazine, 30n, 32
Sunday Times, 2, 24, 30, 31n, 59, 61,
    82, 86, 95, 104, 177, 190
Surrey CCC, 65
Swansea Grammar School, 229
Swansea RFC, 218
Swansea Town (later City) AFC, 230
Swansea, Glamorgan, 8, 12, 24, 117,
    226, 227
Sweeney, John, 237
Sweetings restaurant, Queen
    Victoria Street, London E.C.4, 224
Swift, Mrs David. *See* Bartley
Symonds, Anne, 134
Symonds, Matthew, 224

Tacitus, 55
'Talking about Uganda'. *See* Uganda
Tanner, Haydn, 215

'Taper' (*Spectator*), 26
Tapsell, Sir Peter, 187
Taylor, A.J.P., 27, 46, 55, 63, 112, 194
Tebbit, Norman, Lord, 92, 186
Tell Them I'm On My Way (Goodman), 106n
Temple Bar, 2
Temple underground station, 34
Temple, London E.C.4, 3, 93, 155
Temple, Shirley, 209
Tench, Matt, 254
Terrace, Westminster, 101, 126
Thatcher, Margaret, Lady, 28, 90, 92, 122, 125, 150, 173; and MMC fix, 178; 190; interview with A.W., 196-7; 238
Thatcher, Mark, *Observer* campaign against, 186-7; 198
Third Avenue, N.Y., 51
Thomas, Catherine, grandmother of A.W., 6, 7
Thomas, Clem, 218, 226-8, 231, 242
Thomas, David, 6
Thomas, Gladstone, of Tycroes, 18
Thomas, Hugh, Lord, 30, 32
Thomas, Huw, 227
Thomas, Sarah Ann, 6
Thomas, Trevor, 218
Thomas, William, 7
Thompson, J.W.M., 68, 76
Thomson, G.P., 79
Thorpe, Jeremy, 57, 231
Three After Six, 64
Three Weeks (Glyn), 47
Thwaite, Anthony, 102
Times, 101, 148, 155, 177, 190
Tirydail, Ammanford, 20
To Convey Intelligence (Courtauld), 66n, 149n, 222
Toft, H.B., 228, 230
Tom Brown's Schooldays (Hughes), 117
Tomalin, Claire, 30, 95
Tomalin, Nicholas, 30, 32
Tonight, 229
Tonypandy riots, A.W. consults Home Office files and Blue Book on, 169
Toronto, Canada, 137
Torquay, constituency, 57
Towy Valley, Carmarthenshire, 226
Toynbee, Philip, 160
Toynbee, Polly, 33, 205
Trades Union Congress, 128, 159, 161, 165, 166, 168, 170
Trafalgar Square, 82
Transport House, London S.W.1, 111
Tregarn, Tycroes, 5, 20
Trelford, Donald, ix, 112; appoints A.W., 152-3, 155, 156, 157; denies 1976 leak to *Mail*, 162; 165; mollifies J. Cole about A.W. and A.W. about J. Cole, 167; persuades A.W. to write 'diary', 168; proposes ingenious solution to Home Office censorship demand, 169; tells C.C. O'Brien he regards himself as craftsman, 170; 171, 172; prefers paper to take no position in 1979 election, 173; 176; opposes sale to Lonrho, 177; appoints A. Howard as deputy, 183; bears burden of dealing with T. Rowland, 186; defends A. Howard from E. du Cann, 188; falls out with T. Rowland over atrocities in Matabeleland, 198-9; old Africa hand, 198; mistake in bringing out 'special issue' on Harrods, 201; A. Howard goes after his job, 210; leaves editorship, 235; 244
Trelford, Kate, 210
Tribune, 44, 89, 90
Tricks of Memory (Worsthorne), 85
Trinity Hall, Cambridge, 32, 217, 218
'Trimmer' (*Spectator*), 61
Tristram Shandy (Sterne), 23
'Trog'. *See* Fawkes
Trott, Frank, 216
Tudor Street, London E.C.4, 155
Turkish Airlines Paris crash, 102
Twickenham, Middlesex, 232
Tycroes Church of England School, 7
Tycroes, Carmarthenshire, 5, 6, 9,

12, 17, 18, 23, 213, 219, 226
Tynan, Kenneth, 24, 119
Tyrrell-Kenyon, Vanessa, ix

Uganda, talking about, origins of
    phrase, 144
United Newspapers, 177
University College, Dublin, 150
University College, Swansea, 229
University of Kent, 249
University of Wales, Lampeter, A.W.
    becomes Hon Fellow of, 23
Utley, T.E., 30, 148

Valley of Bones (Powell), 195
Vassall inquiry, 57
Vaughan, Mary, 6
Venice, 251
Verdi, G., 98
'Vicky', 102
Victoria station, 117
Vietnam War, 31, 121
Vile Bodies (Waugh), 144
Vincent, Neville, 116, 117
Vines, Colin, 57, 58
'Vishinsky', C.C. O'Brien calls A.W.,
    173
Voltaire, 32
Voyce, A.T., 6

Wadley, Veronica, 190
Wakefield, W.W., Lord, 12, 218
Walden, Brian, 74
Waldorf Towers, N.Y., 44, 52
Walking on the Water (Cudlipp), 127n
Waller, Ian, 59
Wapping, London, 155
Wapshott, Nicholas, 203
Warwick, University of, ix
Washington, D.C., 52, 53, 61, 63, 64,
    65, 85, 86, 162, 164
Waterhouse, Keith, 2
Waterhouse, Sir Ronald, 232
Waterloo RFC, 213
Waterloo station, 2, 77
Watkins, Daniel, great-grandfather
    of A.W., 6
Watkins, Daniel, uncle of A.W., 7

Watkins, David John, father of A.W.,
    birth, 5; ancestry, 6; education, 7;
    eating habits, 8; goes to teachers'
    training department, Bristol, 9;
    physical build, 9; war service, 10;
    nightmares, 11; plays for London
    Welsh, 11; dismissed from
    headmastership, 12; reading
    habits, 12-13; prostate operation,
    19; death, 14; opposes A.W.'s
    joining *Spectator*, 87; at rugby
    matches, 213-14
Watkins, David, son of A.W., 7, 147,
    252
Watkins, Jane, daughter of A.W., 21,
    191
Watkins, John, grandfather of A.W.,
    6, 7
Watkins, Ruth, wife of A.W., 34;
    supports A.W. over joining
    Spectator, 67; stoical in D Notice
    affair, 79; A.W. separates from,
    145 Watkins, Sarah Ann, aunt of
    A.W., 7
Watkins, Violet, mother of A.W.,
    ancestry, 6; marriage, 12; birth,
    15; education, 15; gives birth to
    A.W., 16-17; appearance, 17;
    political views, 17; Edwardian
    phrases, 18; mastery of English,
    19; death, 21
Watt, David, 64-5, 66, 85, 86
Watts, Isaac, 239
Waugh, Auberon, 87; and A.W., 88-9;
    feud with A. Powell, 88; 106, 112,
    120 & n, 144, 151; action against
    Spectator, 220-1
Waugh, Evelyn, 27; mistakes A.
    Crosland for Tory, 75; 88, 190, 245
Waugh, Lady Theresa, 88
Webb, Beatrice, 40
Webb, Sidney, 40
Weekend World, 247
Weidenfeld, George, Lord, 97
Weighill, Bob, 225
Welch Regiment, 195
Welch, Colin, 1, 30, 93, 148
Wellington, Duke of, 115

Wells, H.G., 17
Wells, John, 85
Wernos colliery, Tycroes, 9
Wesley's Chapel, City Road, London
    E.C.1, 239
West, Mrs Richard. *See* Kenny
West, Richard, 30
Westminster Press, 235
Wetherby, Yorks, 248
Wharton, Michael, 93, 147n, 148
What the Papers Say, 162
Wheatcroft, Geoffrey, compares Old
    Fleet Street to Byzantine Empire,
    2; on 1950s Cambridge, 29; 31n;
    brings news of H. Fairlie, 64;
    writes on G. Hutchinson, 83n;
    described, 149; part in departure
    of A.W. from *NS* to *Observer*, 153;
    as literary editor of *Spectator*,
    222; writes for *Field*, 223
Wheeler's restaurant, Old Compton
    Street, London W.1, 33
Wheen, Francis, 112
White, David, 6
White, Sam, 44, 45
White, Sarah, grandmother of A.W.,
    6
White's Club, 66, 70, 125
Whitehall, London S.W.1, 82
Whitehorn, Katharine, 188
Whitelaw, William, Lord, 69, 135,
    150
Whittam Smith, Andreas, 211, 238,
    242
Widdicombe, Gillian, 223
Wig and Pen Club, 2
Wigg, George, Lord, 149
Wigoder, Basil, Lord, 82
Wilby, Peter, 67
Wilby, Peter, deputy editor, *IoS*,
    A.W.'s relations with, 240-2,
    248-9; A.W. recommends him to
    T. Smyth as I. Jack's successor,
    241; becomes editor, 242;
    dismissed, 249; editor of *New
    Statesman*, 249; 256

Wildcatter (Harris), 175n
Williams, Amy, 6
Williams, Bleddyn, 215
Williams, Marcia, 59
Wilson, A.N., 190
Wilson, Harold, Lord, July
    measures, 1966, 26; 58-60, 72;
    believes N. Beloff has affairs with
    hostile Labour MPs, 74; 75, 78,
    86, 89, 90, 92, 103, 105, 107, 120,
    121, 122, 125, 135, 141, 149, 150,
    161, 204
Winchester College, 102, 221
Winn, Godfrey, 119
Winterson, Jeanette, 135
Wintour, Charles, 40, 41, 133-5; asks
    A.W. to write London column,
    138; advises A.W. to cultivate
    Lady Lewisham, 143; 144
Wisden, 147
Wodehouse, Sir P.G., 27
Woodland, Christine, ix
Woodrow Wyatt Journals, 178n, 208n
Worcester College, Oxford, 44
Wordsworth, Christopher, 225
Worsthorne, Claude ('Claudie'), 148
Worsthorne, Sir Peregrine, 30, 63,
    85, 95, 97, 98, 148, 252, 256
Wyatt, Woodrow, Lord, 177; reminds
    R. Murdoch of fix over
    Times–Sunday Times
    non-referral to MMC, 178; 208,
    209
Wycliffe College, 227
Wyndham, Francis, 119

Yes, Minister, 33
Yorkshire, 117
Young Fogeys, 190-1
Yvonne Arnaud Theatre, Guildford,
    126

Zimbabwe, D. Trelford makes a
    visit, so causing row with T.
    Rowland, 198-9